Physical education and sport

CHANGE AND CHALLENGE

Physical education and sport
CHANGE AND CHALLENGE

CHARLES A. BUCHER, A.B., M.A., Ed.D.

Professor, Department of Health, Physical Education
and Recreation, University of Nevada, Las Vegas;
Consultant to the President's Council on
Physical Fitness and Sports

NOLAN A. THAXTON, B.S., M.S., D.P.E.

with 59 illustrations

The C. V. Mosby Company

ST. LOUIS • TORONTO • LONDON   1981

Cover photo by Ron Edwards

The C. V. Mosby Company
11830 Westline Industrial Drive, St. Louis, Missouri 63141

Library of Congress Cataloging in Publication Data

Bucher, Charles Augustus, 1912-
   Physical education and sport.

   Bibliography: p.
   Includes index.
   1.   Physical education and training—United
States.   I.   Thaxton, Nolan A., joint author.
II.   Title.
GV223.B8   613.7′0973   80-25237
ISBN 0-8016-0876-7

GW/VH/VH 9 8 7 6 5 4 3 2 1   01/D/005

Preface

Students majoring in physical education and sport, as well as practitioners in the field, are interested in knowing more about the future of their chosen field of endeavor. They want answers to such questions as "What potential does physical education and sport have as a profession in the 1980s?" "What areas of specialization represent the best professional opportunities?" "How can one become a leader in his or her profession?" and "What do futurists predict for physical education and sport in the years ahead?"

In addition to knowing more about the future of their profession, students and practitioners also want to know how they can render the most valuable service to their clientele. They want to know how to develop a sound philosophy of physical education and sport, use a systems approach in program development, teach scientifically so that outcomes of learning can be predicted with more certainty, close the gap between research and practice, provide for the needs of handicapped persons, and conduct an educationally sound sports program.

This text provides students majoring in physical education and sport, as well as practitioners, with the answers to these questions. It is designed to challenge physical and sport educators to correct past professional weaknesses and to build a bright future for their field of endeavor. It indicates the steps that must be taken if physical education and sport is to achieve its destiny and become a more dynamic and respected profession. It represents a professional blueprint for the future.

Charles A. Bucher
Nolan A. Thaxton

Contents

Part one

PHYSICAL EDUCATION IN TODAY'S SOCIETY

1 □ Physical education and sport's potential

Courtesy Westchester Co., N.Y., Department of Parks, Recreation and Conservation.

Today, as never before, physical education is being challenged. Opportunities are presenting themselves that will enable it to become one of the truly great professions. The services it has potential for rendering are in great demand. The public is spending millions of dollars to achieve health goals, many of which are closely related to physical education. Men and women want to control their weight, understand scientific movement concepts, develop physical skills, flatten their stomachs, prevent heart attacks, understand their bodies, and stay healthy. Physical educators should play an active role in helping people to achieve such goals.

The public has never been more interested in health and fitness than it is today. Health care legislation is being proposed that could

3

cost as much as $80 billion a year. Federal and state governments are allocating millions of dollars for physical education for handicapped persons. Nearly 100 million adults in the United States, 18 years of age and older, are now actively engaged in physical fitness activities. Membership in health spas increased by 25% in 1 year. An estimated 1300 books on fitness are currently in print. At least 50,000 United States firms spend an estimated $2 billion on fitness and recreational programs for their employees. Millions of joggers are a common sight on the highways, streets, and sidewalks of the country. Athletic shoes are a big seller—$13 million worth sold in 1 year. The membership rolls of Weight Watchers and stop-smoking groups are growing.

Physical education is being challenged. It is being challenged to play a more active and dynamic role in furthering the health and fitness of the nation. It is being challenged to become all that it is capable of becoming. The question is, Will physical education accept the challenge? Will this field of endeavor take advantage of the public's interest in health and fitness? Will it be looked on as a profession that can provide some of the critical health services the public is seeking? Will it become known and respected for the leadership it can provide?

The term *physical education* means training the physical, and equally important, educating people about their body and its needs. In other words, to meet the challenge and provide the health services the nation needs, physical education must be concerned not only with physical activities—games, dance, sports, and other forms of physical activity— but also with communicating to the public the biological impact that physical activity has on the human body. Furthermore, physical education, as used in this text, incorporates the term *fitness*. The statement by a joint committee of the American Medical As-

sociation and the American Association for Health, Physical Education, and Recreation in the May, 1964 issue of the *Journal of the American Medical Association* elaborates on the term *fitness:* ". . . fitness for effective living implies freedom from disease; enough strength, agility, endurance and skill to meet the demands of daily living; sufficient reserves to withstand ordinary stresses without causing harmful strains; and mental development and emotional adjustment appropriate to the maturity of the individual." Thus in light of this statement, physical education is concerned with the country's fitness.

WHY IS THERE A NEED FOR PHYSICAL EDUCATION TODAY?

Why is it that so many people are jogging today? Why are new health clubs being opened at an increasing rate of speed? Why are so many companies developing corporate fitness programs for their employees? Why are aerobic dancing and yoga popular? Why is the public vitally interested in its health? Why are people becoming more involved in sports? Is it because clothes are more revealing today and exercise will help people to look halfway respectable? Is it because it is a passing fad? Is it because men and women are afraid of having a heart attack? Three reasons have been suggested.

The medical profession is giving support to physical education

One important reason for the need for physical education today is that the medical profession is giving active support to matters with which physical educators are concerned. Today, it is difficult to find a doctor like Peter Steinchron of Hartford, Connecticut, who more than 30 years ago wrote the books *You Don't Have To Exercise —Rest Begins at 40* and *How to Stop Killing Yourself* (through an absence of exercise), or to hear statements like those expressed by Dr. Hutchins, former president of the University of Chicago, who echoed the sentiments of many medical doctors when he pointed out that every time he had the urge to exercise he would lie down until the feeling passed.

Times have changed. The medical profession has spent considerable time over the years conquering communicable and other diseases. They have done an excellent job in eradicating pneumonia, tuberculosis, and scarlet fever. Now, however, they realize something else must be done if the health of the nation is to be improved. Some statements from eminent medical doctors support this premise. A doctor who was involved in the development of health policy of the Department of Health, Education and Welfare states, "Fitness can contribute as much to the nation's health (in the future) as immunization and sanitation advances have done in the past." Dr. Kenneth H. Cooper, who is well known for his work in the area of fitness, points out that such leading causes of death in Americans as heart disease, lung cancer, accidents, cirrhosis of the liver, and strokes are related to such things as lack of proper exercise, obesity, diet, and alcohol. He raises the question, "Are we actually killing ourselves?" Psychiatrists are emphasizing exercise and diet in treating such problems as chronic lethargy, mild depression, and frustration. Some state that they notice dramatic changes in their patients, including better health practices regarding eating, smoking, and drinking. They point out that people who are in good physical condition have a better self-image than persons who are in poor physical condition.

The medical profession today supports the professional goals that physical education is attempting to achieve. In many instances, physical educators are working side by side with medical doctors in schools, colleges, industry, sports medicine, and other programs that are actively involved in improving the health of Americans. The membership rolls of such organizations as the American College of Sports Medicine include medical doctors and physical educators.

Emphasis is on preventive self-help medicine

According to a representative of the American Medical Association, medical doctors can do something about 10% of the usual factors that determine a patient's state of health. However, it is pointed out that the remaining 90% are determined by factors over which doctors have little or no control. Such factors as exercise, smoking, drinking, and diet depend on the individual. This statement reinforces a premise that exists today, namely, that the best way to promote the health of the nation's population is to get Americans to do something for themselves. In the words of the United States Public Health Services Forward Plan for 1977-1981, "We believe it is more productive to focus our attention on the underlying conditions of preventable disease than to concentrate on the diseases themselves."

Seneca, a Roman senator and philosopher, said, "Man does not die, he kills himself." Today, a respected physician in the East states, "The automobile kills more people by depriving them of the opportunity to walk than it does by hitting them." Dr. Lawrence E. Lamb, who edits a health newsletter, states, "The leading causes of death and disability today are no longer infectious diseases caused by germs, but rather the products of our way of life." These statements indicate the need for preventive self-help medicine, of which physical education can play an important part.

For physical educators, preventive self-help medicine includes stressing the *education* in physical education. Many people who jog and engage in other forms of physical activity do so because they have been informed

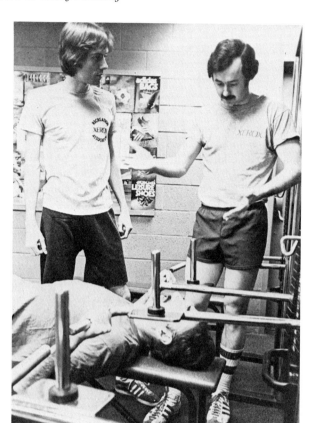

Courtesy Springfield College, Springfield, Mass.

about the importance of making physical activity a part of their life-style. Conversely, the reasons some people do not exercise is because they do not understand and appreciate the benefits of physical activity. As one uninformed person observed, "I look at joggers and see that pained expression on their faces and just know that such an activity has little value and can even be harmful to those who participate."

Physical education cannot be conducted in a vacuum. It cannot be limited to arms and legs and good intentions. There must be some understanding and appreciation for what muscular activity does for the human body, the contribution it makes to one's

physical, mental, and social welfare. Getting people to buy a pair of running shoes is not difficult. However, getting them to put the shoes on and jog regularly three times a week is another matter. There must be some inward motivation that gets them into action. *The catalyst is education.*

Physical *education* is essential. Usually, the reasons people do or do not exercise can be traced directly to a physical education program taught by instructors who failed to get at the *why* of the activity as well as the activity itself and who failed to emphasize and document the value of exercise as it relates to good health. The health of the nation depends on each individual's willingness to do

Courtesy Springfield College, Springfield, Mass.

something about his or her own health. As a result, the life each person saves may be his or her own.

Research findings support the need for physical education

Many surveys, experiments, and studies have shown that adults who regularly engage in sports and fitness activities do not become ill very often, have greater productivity, are at work every day, and have fewer accidents than adults who do not engage in sports and fitness activities. Other research indicates many other benefits from participating in physical education programs.

One research study conducted by medical people and reported in the *New York Times* involved a study of 17,000 Harvard University alumni. The study found that there were fewer heart attacks among those who engaged regularly in strenuous activities such as jogging, swimming, tennis, and mountain climbing than among those who were less active. This study suggested that strenuous, leisure time exercise has a definite protective effect even for the individual who has other characteristics such as high blood pressure or overweight that increase the risk of heart disease. This study also pointed out that the protective effect existed among those individuals who participated in intense physical activity for at least 3 hours a week. These people expended a total of 2000 or more calories each week through exercise.

Another study, also reported in the *New York Times*, involved 3600 longshoremen in San Francisco. This study, conducted over 22 years, found that longshoremen between 35 and 54 years of age who had very strenuous jobs had the lowest risk of fatal heart attacks of persons in the same occupation. Less active longshoremen had a three times greater risk of having a fatal heart attack.

The National Aeronautics and Space Administration conducted a study in cooperation with the Heart Disease and Stroke Control Program of the Public Health Service that involved a three-times a week exercise program for 259 men, 35 to 55 years of age. The findings showed better job performance, improved stamina, weight loss, more attention to diet, and other benefits.

Such research is not confined to the United States. In France, the May-June, 1976 issue of *La gymnastique volontaire* cited research studies that proved the worth of physical education in that country. One study, for example, showed that 76% of the persons involved had more endurance, 25% had to see a doctor less often, and 75% believed that their social relationships were improved. Another study of a group of elderly people who participated in a physical education program showed that 97% reported physical improvement, 98% indicated improvement in their morale, and 60% noted psychomotor improvement.

Research in the Soviet Union, a country deeply involved in sports medicine, showed that working people who engage regularly in physical education are more productive, see a doctor less often, are less prone to industrial accidents, and have a lower absenteeism rate.

Many other research studies could be cited, but it is not necessary since they add up to the same conclusion—physical education is essential to the nation's health. Studies reveal that it builds such things as strength, endurance, skill, and stronger organic systems of the body. It can also contribute to one's body image, mental and emotional health, and social relationships. Equally important, it contributes to the quality of life that each individual leads.

THE NEED FOR PHYSICAL EDUCATION IN TODAY'S MECHANIZED AND INDUSTRIAL SOCIETY

There is a great need for physical education in today's mechanized and industrial society. This need exists among children and youth in society who need to possess physical skills and health knowledge prior to entering adult life. This need exists for all children and youth, whether they are normal or handicapped, skilled or unskilled. The need also exists in the adult population. Assuming that employees in American industry represent a cross section of the American adult population, the need for physical education is great. Some interesting statistics include:

1. Each year premature deaths (many caused by poor fitness) cost American industry $25 billion and 132 million workdays of lost production.
2. Heart disease alone accounts for 52 million lost workdays each year.
3. Recruiting replacements for persons who suffer heart attacks alone costs industry $700 million each year.
4. According to a government report, General Motors spends more on its employee health plan than it spends on purchasing steel from U.S. Steel, its principal supplier. Also, in 1 recent year health benefits added $175 to the price of every car and truck manufactured by the company.
5. Backaches, often caused by muscular deficiencies, result in $1 billion in lost production and one quarter billion dollars in workmen's compensation claims.

6. The rate of disability retirements among federal employees has increased by 170% since 1955.
7. Absenteeism in the executive branch of the government costs an estimated $1.34 billion a year and 25 million lost workdays.
8. There are many hidden costs, for example, those persons who are ill do not recover as rapidly. Also, chronic fatigue results in an increase in the number of industrial accidents, inefficiency, and loss of production.

THE CHALLENGE

Physical education is being challenged to achieve its destiny. Opportunities exist today, more than at anytime in its history, for this profession to be recognized and respected as being vital to the health and well-being of America. Physical educators are the professionals who can render the services and achieve the objectives the public is seeking.

The public must realize that there is no shortcut to fitness. There is no machine, muscle builder, magic diet, slant board, or pill that will do the job by itself. Instead, the road to fitness involves sound health habits and cutting down on such risk factors as lack of exercise, smoking, drinking, and a fatty diet. It means possessing knowledge about one's body and what it needs to thrive and prosper. It means becoming *physically educated*.

This text provides the guidelines and modus operandi for meeting the challenge. It includes a discussion of past accomplishments, objectives, challenging opportunities for the future, and the path to leadership. It indicates the need for developing a sound philosophy for one's profession. It provides the know-how for developing an instructional program that follows a systems approach. It shows how each individual can be helped, whether young or old, handicapped or normal, weak or strong, male or female, dub or athlete. It tells how to make the teaching of physical education scientific rather than just an art. It stresses the need to close the gap between research and practice and how this can be done. It sets forth how sport can make its greatest contribution to the participant. This text provides a blueprint for the conscientious person who aspires to be a leader in the new physical education.

DISCUSSION QUESTIONS AND EXERCISES

1. List some services that physical educators render today that are in public demand.
2. Cite evidence that clearly shows that the public is health and fitness minded today.
3. How is physical education being challenged in today's world?
4. In 250 words or less define the meaning of the term *physical education*.
5. What evidence is there to show that the medical and physical education professions are more closely allied today than ever before in history?
6. Define the term *self-help medicine*. What are some implications of self-help medicine for physical education?
7. Cite three research studies that support the value of physical education as a contributing factor in improving the nation's health.
8. Some people indicate that most adults are not physically fit. Cite evidence that supports or rejects this statement.
9. Outline what you believe are the essentials to becoming physically educated.
10. Why do you believe that it is an opportune moment for becoming a member of the physical education profession?

SELECTED REFERENCES

Bucher, C. A.: Administration of physical education and athletic programs, ed. 7, St. Louis, 1979, The C. V. Mosby Co.
Bucher, C. A.: Foundations of physical education, ed. 8, St. Louis, 1979, The C. V. Mosby Co.
Bucher, C. A., and Koenig, C. R.: Methods and materials for secondary school physical education, ed. 5, St. Louis, 1978, The C. V. Mosby Co.

Bucher, C. A., and Thaxton, N. A.: Physical education for children: movement foundations and experiences, New York, 1979, Macmillan Inc.

Cornish, E. S.: Planting seeds for the future. Prepared for Champion International Corporation, Stamford, Conn., by the World Future Society, 1979.

Gerber, E. W., and Morgan, W. J.: Sport and the body: a philosophical symposium, Philadelphia, 1979, Lea & Febiger.

Kahn, H.: The next 200 years, New York, 1976, William Morrow & Co., Inc.

Kahn, H., and Wiener, A.: The year 2000, New York, 1967, Macmillan Inc.

Rosen, S.: Future facts, New York, 1976, Simon & Schuster, Inc.

Rostow, W. W.: Getting from here to there, New York, 1978, McGraw-Hill Book Co.

Spears, B., and Swanson, R. A.: History of sport and physical activity in the United States, Dubuque, Iowa, 1978, William C. Brown Co., Publishers.

Steincrohn, P. J.: How to stop killing yourself, New York, 1950, Wilfred Funk, Inc.

Toffler, A.: Future shock, New York, 1970, Random House, Inc.

Welsh, R., editor: Physical education—a view toward the future, St. Louis, 1977, The C. V. Mosby Co.

2 □ Physical education and sport: past and present

A, From Library of Congress photographic collection. **B,** Courtesy Woodlands High School, Hartsdale, N.Y.

Students in classes at an eastern university have frequently been asked to graphically analyze the historical progress and growth of physical education. The students were instructed to depict historical milestones in physical education together with the rationale for their selection. These milestones were to represent periods in history when physical education had its greatest respect, public recognition, and growth. Students pictured physical education historically as having various peaks of accomplishment and growth. There was no unanimous agreement as to when physical education had achieved its most prestige.

Some students pointed out that physical education has reached its highest point in present times. To support this belief, they listed such reasons as physical education has finally gained maturity, become more professional, developed into a discipline, and developed a solid scientific foundation to support its worth. The students also pointed out that today physical education provides programs for many segments of the population, including females, handicapped persons, employees in industry, and elderly persons. The students also believed that today there is considerably more public interest in physical fitness than at any other period in history.

One group of students believed that the establishment of the President's Council on Physical Fitness and Sports and its accomplishments have been the high point in the history of physical education. These students believed that the establishment of the Council resulted in a much greater emphasis on physical education programs in general and particularly in the schools. The Council gave and is giving support to many research projects, has created demonstration centers, has enlisted the help of corporations and other segments of society, has stimulated the interest of presidents of the United States, and has provided national exposure for this profession. These students also believed that the Council, through its many endeavors, set off a chain of events that led to the current fitness boom in the United States, from which physical education has received many benefits.

A few students cited the period from 1776 to 1839 as being the high point of physical education, primarily because of Per Henrik Ling and his work at the Central Institute of Gymnastics in Sweden. The part of Ling's philosophy that stressed that physical activity should be prescribed on the basis of individual differences particularly seemed to capture the admiration of these students. Indeed, they believed this philosophy helped to change the thinking of many educators and physical education leaders in the years following Ling's death.

A significant number of students selected the Renaissance period between the fourteenth and sixteenth centuries as the most notable time for physical education accomplishments. Many outstanding leaders, such as Rousseau, Locke, and Rabelais, gave support to physical education. The circulation of the blood, for example, was traced by Harvey (1578-1657), and Vesalius (1514-1564) founded the science of anatomy. At this period in history, society became interested in and wanted to know how the body could best be maintained. The emphasis was on living in the present rather than preparation for the hereafter, as had been the case in the years preceding the Renaissance. Scientists were interested in improving the quality as well as the length of life.

The period that received the most support from students as representing the pinnacle of physical education's respect and accomplishment was the time of the ancient Greeks. No country in history, these students pointed out, has held physical education in higher respect and contributed more to the growth of the profession than did ancient Greece, as depicted in Athenian culture. Physical education was a vital part of the educational process. The Greek philosophy was centered on the total person, with the perfection of the mind and body as its ideal. Physical education was not only necessary for preparing for military service, but equally, or more importantly, represented the means with which to attain a strong, healthy body, an appreciation of aesthetics, and a more vibrant mental capacity. The gymnasium was not only a place for physical activity but was also a place for intellectual stimulation. The Greeks engaged in physical activity to develop their bodies and live a fuller and more vigorous life. They believed that physical education contributed to courage, discipline, physical well-being, and a sense of fair play. The Greeks were also instrumental in laying the foundations for the modern Olympic Games.

One general conclusion that may be drawn from the students' analyses of the milestones in the history of physical education would be that many periods in history have represented times of growth for the profession. Much has been accomplished over the years, and many persons, countries, and organizations have contributed to this growth. The challenge for individuals preparing to be leaders of physical education is to be familiar with and recognize these accomplishments and then to use them as the foundation on which to build and achieve in behalf of their chosen field.

A LOOK BACK

Many changes have taken place in physical education since its beginning. Analyzing what has happened reveals several important changes.

Physical education has changed from an unscientific to a scientific field

During its early history, physical education was, to a great extent, at least compared with today's standards, very unscientific. The training of physical educators illustrates this change. Physical educators at first received little preparation to fulfill their duties. The Normal Institute of Physical Education in Boston in 1861, founded by Dio Lewis, provided only a 10-week course for teachers in this field. The North American Turnerbund opened its doors in 1866 in New York City and offered a 1-year-course. From these early beginnings, the length of preparation gradually increased as the need for training in the scientific foundations of physical education was recognized. More and more courses were gradually required in such areas as anatomy, physiology, tests and measurements, history and philosophy, administration, and methods. Today undergraduate programs also include courses in such areas as physical education for handicapped persons, motor learning, exercise physiology, and biomechanics. In addition to undergraduate training, graduate education has become common for physical educators so that they may specialize further in the various branches of physical education. Research has also become a very important function of physical education, providing more scientific foundations for this profession.

In the early years of the profession, exercise was, more often than not, prescribed on the basis of the physical educator's own experience and judgment rather than on an understanding of the human body and how it functions. Skills were also taught in this manner. Also, physical education programs did not provide for individual differences.

Today, physical education is much more scientific. In addition to the various courses that provide the practitioner with a sound scientific foundation in the field, there is usually a requirement for an internship in the area of one's professional specialization to provide the opportunity to apply in a practical situation the knowledge and skills

Courtesy Springfield College, Springfield, Mass.

learned. When a person graduates from the best professional institutions today, he or she is well-prepared to render the specialized services that characterize physical education as a profession.

Physical education has changed from an unorganized to an organized field

Physical education's early history shows a loosely knit professional organization. For example, early physical educators did not have many formal meetings to attend, a national organization that worked to improve professional standards, nor professional literature to keep them informed of changes in their field. It was not until 1885, when the American Association for the Advancement of Physical Education was formed, that the beginnings of a formal organization emerged. The leaders in this organization were 35 physicians, educators, and individuals called together by Dr. William G. Anderson of Adelphi Academy. The purpose of this organization was to bring about a closer relationship among physical educators, upgrade the standards of the profession, publish professional materials for the membership, and stimulate interest in and an understanding of the work being performed by physical educators.

Since 1885 other organizations have been

INSTITUTE
FOR
PHYSICAL EDUCATION.

Nº 159 Crosby, near Bleeker St. New York.
ESTABLISHED FOR THE PROMOTION OF HEALTH
BY MEANS OF SYSTEMATIC PHYSICAL TRAINING
JOHN B. RICH, M. D. PRINCIPAL.

Dr. Rich's Institute for Physical Education. From the J. Clarence Davies Collection, Museum of the City of New York.

formed, such as the National College Physical Education Association for Men (1897), Physical Education Society of the Young Men's Christian Association of North America (1903), Phi Epsilon Kappa (1913), Delta Psi Kappa (1916), Phi Delta Pi (1916), The National Association of Physical Education for College Women (1924), Society of State Directors of Health, Physical Education and Recreation (1926), Canadian Physical Education Association (1933), American College of Sports Medicine (1954), and National Association for Physical Education in Higher Education (1978). Some of these organizations have changed their names since the time they were initially formed to more accurately reflect the services they now render.

Today, physical education is a much more highly organized profession. The American Alliance for Health, Physical Education, Rec-

reation and Dance has approximately 40,000 members. Thousands of physical educators attend their annual meetings. There are six regional district meetings of the Alliance throughout the nation as well as many state and zone meetings. In addition to the meetings of these national organizations, other meetings relating to such areas as athletics, psychology of physical education, physical education for handicapped persons, and intramurals are held.

Physical education is changing from an unspecialized to a specialized field

Physical education was the forebearer of many other professional groups. Persons who were associated with physical education started to specialize in such areas as health, recreation, and dance. The AAHPERD, for example, was organized in 1885. It added the word "Health" to its title in 1937, "Recreation" in 1938, and "Dance" in 1978. The addition of these areas of concentration to the name of the national organization was the result of urging by significant groups of members who believed their particular areas of expertise needed added emphasis and exposure.

Today, there is further emphasis on specialization. It is easy to discern such specialties as exercise physiologists, motor learning experts, specialists in biomechanics, sport psychologists and sociologists, administrators, teachers of physical education for handicapped persons, dance educators, and historians and philosophers. Specialists in these areas have formed their own organizations, have their own meetings, and publish their own materials. The trend toward specialization in physical education is analogous to medicine and dentistry. Medicine started with the general practitioner, but today doctors specialize in such areas as orthopedics, psychiatry, geriatrics, cardiology, dermatology, endocrinology, neurology, and radiology. Dentistry includes such specialties as endodontics, pedodontics, orthodontics, periodontics, and prosthodontics.

This is an age of specialization. Such developments as the expansion of knowledge, the need for specialized health services, and employment possibilities in physical education have resulted in the creation of these specialized fields of study.

The emphasis is changing from physical training to physical education

Early physical education programs were primarily interested in training the body. This included developing strength, endurance, agility, speed, and the other characteristics that describe a physically trained person. In fact, some programs used the terms *physical training* and *physical culture* rather than *physical education*. Initially, programs

of physical education consisted mainly of activities designed to develop various physical qualities. Such activities as those involving gymnastic apparatus, marching, calisthenics, wand and dumbbell drills, running, and similar activities were popular. If the participant could develop some skill in these activities, in addition to such physical qualities as endurance and strength, the program was usually considered successful. The stress was on the *physical* in physical education—on bones, muscles, circulation, respiration, and the like.

Today, at the professional level, the emphasis is on education *through* the physical as well as education *of* the physical. The goal is not only to have people engage in purposeful activity but also to have them learn about the makeup of their bodies and how physical activity affects such organic systems as the muscular, skeletal, circulatory, nervous, digestive, endocrine, and integumentary. Programs are also designed to help people understand how and what means are available to assess their physical fitness and where and what type of program and activities will help them to develop an optimum level of fitness.

The teaching of physical education has changed, using a more informal and democratic approach, rather than a formal approach

The teaching of physical education in educational institutions has changed from an autocratic, formal type of instruction to a more informal, democratic style. The type of physical education, for example, that characterized German gymnastics under Jahn and other early leaders was formal. It was a command-response type of approach. The instructor gave the commands, and the participants responded as directed. The instructor was the person in charge as well as the authority figure. In a sense, it was a militaristic approach to teaching. Activities were also formal, such as exercises performed on various pieces of apparatus, calisthenics, and various types of activity drills.

Today, physical education endorses a more informal and democratic type of instruction. Games and such innovations as movement education stress the importance of meeting the needs of the participant, rather than the teacher. Games represent a microsociety in which rules exist and the participant plays within the framework of the rules. The rules reflect the democratic way of life and are designed to enable each person to achieve the goals for which the activity is scheduled. Each person is encouraged to express his or her own unique way of solving a problem or executing a skill. Each person strives to better understand his or her body, especially as it relates to movement. The teacher is not an autocratic leader but is a person who guides rather than directs.

Physical education is changing from an emphasis on males and a few skilled individuals to an emphasis on all individuals

In early times, males had priority over females in many respects. Males frequently received priority in the use of facilities, had better equipment and supplies, and were given larger budget allocations for their programs. Administrative positions were often filled with males. In a sense, it was a man's world. To a great degree, skilled individuals also were given preferred treatment. The star athlete, usually a male, had the best of everything. More often than not, he was not required to attend regular physical education classes in school, received most of the exposure in school and community publications, and was the beneficiary of scholarships. The poorly skilled individual was often found sitting on the sidelines. Handicapped students were segregated in special institutions. Girls and women were discriminated against.

Today, it is a different story. As a result of such legislation as Title IX and P.L. 94-142, many changes have occurred. The day of affirmative action and equal opportunity has arrived. Girls and women, poorly skilled persons, and handicapped persons are gradually being given the attention they justly deserve. Today, physical education renders services to all segments of the population.

Sport is changing from an unorganized to a highly organized activity

Sport in the American culture has undergone dramatic change. During colonial days, few people engaged in highly organized sports. Some immigrants from England engaged in horse racing and hunting, and the Dutch participated in bowling and skating. However, there was no large-scale, highly organized sports. As the nation became industrialized, sports played a more important part in the American society. During the last half of the nineteenth century, for the first time in the United States, there was a Kentucky Derby, National League in baseball, Amateur Athletic Union, sports page in a newspaper, and a Madison Square Garden. In the 1920s, the golden age of sports emerged. This was the time of Babe Ruth, Jack Dempsey, Bill Tilden, and Ken Strong. It was also the dawn of sports becoming highly organized as big business with millions of dollars filling the coffers. Today, sports play a very important role in the American culture. Professional and amateur sports abound in every part of the nation.

The growth of sports in educational institutions has also undergone change. During the period 1875 to 1900, the first Harvard-Yale football game was held, a Big Ten Conference was organized, and an All-American team was chosen. Organized sports started at the college level and were then adopted by high schools, junior high schools, and in some instances, elementary schools. Sports

Courtesy Springfield College, Springfield, Mass.

Courtesy Springfield College, Springfield, Mass.

are now highly organized in educational institutions with leagues, athletic associations, and conferences.

Sports were a concern of educators from the beginning. Dr. Hutchins, former President of the University of Chicago, who articulated the feelings of many educators, pointed out many years ago that it would be much better for each college to substitute a stable of horses for skilled athletes. As Dr. Hutchins pointed out, in this way the horses could race and represent their educational institutions. They wouldn't have to miss classes and would be satisfied with a bucket of oats rather than expensive scholarships. Another educator questioned the nation's values when the Walter Camp Gateway to the Yale Stadium was constructed at a cost of $180,000—money that was easily raised. However, at the same institution, it was very difficult to raise $12,000 to recognize the great scientist Josiah Gibbs with a more modest tribute.

HISTORICAL PHYSICAL EDUCATION DETERRENTS AND CATALYSTS

Interest in physical education has prevailed since the earliest of times. Physical education has been used to improve society, meet the needs of human beings, and prepare for enriched living. Its accomplishments in furthering the health of people are well-established. It has also served other useful purposes such as the following. It has been used as a means of arousing a communal feeling, a camaraderie, and a sense of belonging among various groups of people. Native tribal groups used dance to develop a feeling of unity, oneness, and togetherness. The sport dimension of physical education has been a force that has united many student bodies behind their school or college teams that were trying to gain recognition. Physical education provides a means of communication through the body. It has also been used since early times as a means of enter-tainment so that spectators could experience the competition, the struggle, and the contest.

Although interest in physical education has prevailed since early times, it has experienced periods when it was unable to make any professional progress and other periods when it made considerable progress. Several beliefs and events have played crucial roles in these declines and advances.

Deterrents

The doctrine of *asceticism* that prevailed during the early Christian era was a deterrent. Asceticism advocated the importance of the spirit and the mind and the subjugation of the body. The body was evil; it had uncontrolled appetites. If one desired to elevate the mind and the spirit, one should punish the body, not meet its needs. As a result, persons who subscribed to asceticism did not believe in taking baths, lived in filth, and lashed their bodies. They pictured the body as a lion chained to the spirit-mind and believed that a lashing was needed from time to time to keep it under control.

Puritanism was another doctrine that acted as a deterrent to physical education. This movement was brought to America from England during the colonial period. Its adherents believed that it was a sin to waste one's time in play. Indeed, the business of living was a serious matter. One was put on this earth to work, not to play. As the song goes:

> Work for the night is coming
> Work through the morning hours
>
> •   •   •
>
> Work for the night is coming
> When man's work is done
>
> •   •   •
>
> Work till the last beam fadeth
> Fadeth to shine no more
> Work while the night is darkening
> When man's work is o'er.

The *Victorian era* in England was also a period during which the human body received little attention. This was the era of hoop skirts for women, when it was considered suggestive for women to show their ankles, and when gymnastics were thought to oppose the righteous will of heaven.

Historically, the thinking regarding *mind-body relationships* was also a deterrent factor. Years ago the mind and body were thought to be separate entities having no relationship with one another. This line of thought suggested that one could train the mind without giving any attention to the body. As a result, the needs of the body were ignored in early educational institutions. Schools were primarily concerned with those subjects that trained the mind. Psychological research, however, has shown that the body and mind are closely related. One affects the other. Psychosomatic medicine is an important field. Today it is generally accepted that people can think themselves into illness and that illness can affect their thinking.

Mind-body relationships historically have also been affected by asceticism and puritanism. These doctrines supported the premise that the mind was *good* and the body was *evil*. Physical education became allied to the concept that the body enjoys its appetites, at times is undisciplined, and follows the law of the jungle. On the other hand, the so-called solid and cultural subjects—language, science, and mathematics—cater to the mind, the higher self.

As the years have passed, physical education has become respectable, and the body is regarded as something that has needs that must be met to have good mental and physical health. However, we still have not reached the point at which physical education is on an equal level with the subjects of mathematics, science, and language. Physical education is not a requirement for entrance to most colleges. There is no reference to physical education on college entrance examinations. It is not included as one of the Carnegie units in education. It is not regarded as one of the *basics*. Physical education has considerable distance to travel before it gains equal footing with the so-called cultural subjects. Progress, however, is being made. The challenge physical educators face is to see that it becomes one of the *basics*, both in educational circles as well as in life itself.

Catalysts

Although there have been deterrents to physical education's progress, there have also been some catalysts that have given it support and helped it to advance as an important profession. From earliest times people and nations have been interested in physical activity, health, their bodies, and leisure time activities. One can go back in history and note that in 2698 B.C. the Chinese used the Kung Fu gymnastics as a means of improving their health because they believed that certain diseases were caused by physical inactivity. One can read Homer's Odyssey and note that people came far and wide to see Odyssesus throw the discus and perform other feats of skill and strength. This interest in health and physical skill has been a catalyst and has helped to further the cause of physical education.

Probably one of the greatest catalysts that has promoted the cause of physical education is *warfare*. One has only to study the accomplishments of Alexander the Great, the military conquests of Caesar, or the training of the feudal knights to know that each placed great emphasis on physical conditioning and the development of physical skill. The purpose of such physical development was to be prepared in the event of warfare. A soldier had to be in excellent physical condition to defeat the enemy. Physically soft armies did not survive.

Physical education in the United States has benefited from the warfare catalyst. Because many of the men recruited during World War I could not pass the selective service's physical examination, many states passed legislation that upgraded physical education programs in the schools. The following states enacted laws between the years 1917 and 1919: Alabama, California, Delaware, Indiana, Maine, Maryland, Michigan, Nevada, New Jersey, Oregon, Pennsylvania, Rhode Island, Utah, and Washington. To provide supervision and leadership for the expanded programs, many state departments of public instruction also established administrative heads for physical education. An interesting sidelight of this development was that many of the physical defects found in these men who could not pass the physical examination were not strictly related to physical education. Persons were classified 4F for such reasons as poor eyesight and dental caries.

Another example of the importance of physical education to the nation was noted in the 1950s. As a result of the Kraus-Weber studies of the physical fitness status of American and European youth, the *President's Council on Youth Fitness* (present name— President's Council on Physical Fitness and Sports) was created by President Eisenhower. A nationwide program was established that emphasized cooperation between the federal government and state, city, and town officials to raise the nation's level of fitness. Presidents Eisenhower, Kennedy, Johnson, Nixon, Ford, and Carter have all supported the fitness movement and the work that the Council is doing. This Presidential support plus the cooperation of leaders in the public sector, including the mass media, have had an impact on physical education.

More recent significant catalysts include Title IX, which has furthered the cause of physical education and sport for girls and women, and P.L. 94-142, which specifically states that "physical education for the handicapped" must be provided.

PROFESSIONAL GOALS FOR PHYSICAL EDUCATION TODAY

Many physical education leaders have set forth today's goals for physical education. Four goals or objectives that are most usually cited are fitness, physical skill, an understanding of the human body motivating good health habits, and a meaningful social experience.

Courtesy Springfield College, Springfield, Mass.

Courtesy Springfield College, Springfield, Mass.

Courtesy Springfield College, Springfield, Mass.

Fitness, a goal of physical education, refers to the efficient development and functioning of the various organic systems of the human body, such as the nervous, circulatory, respiratory, muscular, and digestive systems. Proper development of the organic systems of the body can help to ensure adequate amounts of strength, stamina, flexibility, endurance, and agility. It will enable a person to carry out daily tasks, recover quickly from fatigue, enjoy leisure time activities, and have sufficient reserve energy for emergencies. The achievement of this objective means that the individual can work hard over an extended period or perform physically up to his or her capacity and have rapid recovery from fatigue.

The second objective is *physical skill,* which refers to the development of the ability or capacity to perform selected physical movements with an economic expenditure of energy. It involves such qualities as perception, coordination, balance, agility, speed, and accuracy that enable an individual to move in a well-coordinated and proficient manner. It refers to all types of skills, locomotor and nonlocomotor, including sport skills and recreational skills, as well as such motor factors as accuracy and speed.

A third objective is an understanding of the *importance of physical activity to the human body.* The end result of such knowledge is the formation of sound health habits. It involves the acquisition of knowledge about how the human body functions and the ability to interpret and utilize this knowledge in a meaningful manner. This objective also involves such mental characteristics as understanding, comprehending, analyzing, synthesizing, problem solving, and decision making. It gets at the how and why of the activity as well as the activity itself. It results in an appreciation of the human body and how its fitness can best be developed and maintained. It includes an understanding of con-

cepts relating to strategies, rules, history, importance of proper health practices, physiology, and biomechanics. It also provides a needed catharsis or emotional outlet for the release of tension as well as self-expression.

Providing for a *meaningful social experience* through physical education is the fourth objective. This objective stresses such qualities as sportsmanship, self-discipline, consideration of others, integrity, honesty, and loyalty. It emphasizes the importance of accepting responsibility and the need to adhere to rules and regulations, have good peer relationships, and have proper moral and social values. It involves living and working harmoniously with others. It teaches cooperation, sharing, loyalty, and learning to communicate with others. It is concerned with the development of a sense of belonging, positive personality traits, and the constructive use of leisure time. It concerns itself with the attitudes, values, mores, and appreciations that an individual needs to acquire to enable him or her to adjust and function effectively as a member of a group and of society.

PROFESSIONAL PROBLEMS AND STEPS THAT NEED TO BE TAKEN TO GAIN PROFESSIONAL RECOGNITION

Physical education as a profession is being challenged to solve several problems that affect its future. Part Two of this text discusses some of the most pressing of these problems such as the need for each practitioner to develop a sound philosophy of physical education, fill the gap between research and practice, develop a science for teaching this discipline, develop programs using a systematic approach, provide physical education for handicapped persons, and establish athletic programs that contribute to the welfare of all rather than only a few persons. This chapter focuses its attention on a much larger and more pressing problem—the need for greater national exposure for physical education, public recognition, and a better professional image.

Physical educators should be recognized as experts in such areas as physical fitness, programs concerned with physical education and sports, and the best procedures for developing physical skill. This profession should be recognized as a full-fledged profession that possesses the expertise and know-how to further the health of the nation by means of the various activities and experiences it provides in its programs. Physical educators should be considered the experts in the areas relating to physical education and sport, just as doctors are experts in the field of medicine, lawyers in the field of law, and clergy in the field of religion.

Unfortunately, many persons, whether qualified or not, consider themselves experts in the area of physical education. The public does also in too many cases. Professional baseball, basketball, or football players are often considered as experts who know the best way to teach their specialized skills. Many health spa managers and instructors, although possessing little training, prescribe exercises and health routines for their members. Coaches of Little League teams expound on how they know what is best in the way of sports for their charges. Yoga experts say they have the answers to the nation's physical ills. Many coaches of sports teams have little or no training in physical education but are coaching and, in some cases, teaching physical education in schools and colleges. Physical educators too often are not considered by the public in general as the persons to consult and the ones who know most about physical activity, skill, and fitness matters. Unless physical educators become recognized as possessing expertise in these matters, physical education will never have the professional recognition that it deserves. Therefore, something must be done to bring about this recognition. Two suggestions follow.

Physical education must be recognized as offering a unique public service

Physical education programs must be organized and conducted in a way that unqualified persons cannot duplicate. To accomplish this, special training and expertise is needed to conduct these programs. When this happens, public recognition will follow. Some of the professional dividends accruing from such a move would be that the layperson who is seeking to improve his or her physical fitness will look to physical education for the answers. Those persons who want to understand the best procedures for developing physical skills will seek out physical educators for help. Owners and managers of professional sports teams will hire physical educators as consultants since, in their business, skill and fitness are important and they want the best advice possible. Physical education in schools and colleges will be considered one of the basic subjects that every student needs to experience.

Physical education must be very selective about who joins its ranks

It is not difficult at the present time to join the ranks of professional physical educators. If a person can pay the tuition, meet minimal academic standards, and is willing to spend 4 years getting a college education, there is some professional preparation program where he or she will be accepted and graduate with a degree. Then if a position can be found, this person will join the ranks of professional physical educators regardless of the degree of expertise he or she possesses. A frequent result—a poor image for the field of physical education. Furthermore, these persons compete with qualified persons in getting the diminishing number of positions that are available.

This problem is not easily solved. Colleges and universities, where physical educators are trained, have their own standards. They vary among educational institutions. Somehow there must be more uniformity in the application of high standards for all professional preparation institutions. There should also be some kind of comprehensive examination that physical educators must take prior to being permitted to practice, as is the case for doctors and lawyers. To pass such comprehensive examinations, practitioners would need to have a strong background in the scientific foundations, that is, the biological and other sciences, on which physical education rests, as well as other competencies that are needed to be successful in their chosen field. After they have graduated from college, passed comprehensive examinations, and acquired a position, they should not be licensed until they have proven themselves on the job. The first year would be a probationary period to determine if the individual could perform in accordance with set professional standards.

DISCUSSION QUESTIONS AND EXERCISES

1. Identify what you consider to be two of the most important milestones in the history of physical education. Document your answer.
2. Explain how physical education has changed from an unscientific to a scientific profession.
3. List some of the most important professional associations that include physical educators on their membership roles. Why do physical educators join professional associations?
4. An oft-quoted remark is "Today is an era of specialization." Draw implications of this remark for the profession of physical education.
5. Define the terms *physical training* and *physical education*. Indicate how a physical education program would differ from a physical training program.
6. Discuss the meaning of the statement: "Physical education programs are concerned with all segments of the population."
7. Trace the history of sport in the United States from colonial days to the present.
8. Identify and discuss two movements that have been deterrents to the growth of physical education and two movements that have been catalysts to physical education programs.
9. What role has the President's Council on Physical Fitness and Sports played in the history of physical education?
10. Identify the four major objectives of physical education. Discuss the role and importance of each in physical education programs.
11. How can physical education gain greater recognition and respect in the future?

SELECTED REFERENCES

Bucher, C. A.: Administration of physical education and athletic programs, ed. 7, St. Louis, 1979, The C. V. Mosby Co.

Bucher, C. A.: Dimensions of physical education, St. Louis, 1974, The C. V. Mosby Co.

Bucher, C. A.: Foundations of physical education, ed. 8, St. Louis, 1979, The C. V. Mosby Co.

Bucher, C. A., and Thaxton, N. A.: Physical education for children: movement foundations and experiences, New York, 1979, Macmillan Inc.

Eitzen, S. D.: Sociology of American sport, Dubuque, Iowa, 1978, William C. Brown Co., Publishers.

Fox, E. L.: Sports physiology, Philadelphia, 1979, W. B. Saunders Co.

Gerber, E. W., and Morgan, W. J.: Sport and the body: a philosophical symposium, Philadelphia, 1979, Lea & Febiger.

Hackensmith, C. W.: History of physical education, New York, 1966, Harper & Row, Publishers.

Lucas, J. A., and Smith, R. A.: Saga of American sport, Philadelphia, 1978, Lea & Febiger.

Spears, B., and Swanson, R. A.: History of sport and physical activity in the United States, Dubuque, Iowa, 1978, William C. Brown Co., Publishers.

Ulrich, C.: To seek and find, Washington, D.C., 1976, AAHPERD.

Van Dalen, D. B., and Bennett, B. L.: A world history of physical education, Englewood Cliffs, N.J., 1971, Prentice-Hall, Inc.

Weston, A.: The making of American physical education, New York, 1962, Appleton-Century-Crofts.

Woody, T.: Life and education in early societies, New York, 1949, Macmillan Inc.

3 □ The challenge to become a leader in your profession

Courtesy Springfield College, Springfield, Mass.

There is an urgent need for dynamic leadership in the profession of physical education and sport. If this profession is to achieve its destiny, render its greatest public service, and achieve national exposure, well-trained and capable leaders are a necessity. Although there are leaders in the field today who are helping the profession to grow, a new group of leaders must continually emerge so that progress can be continued without interruption. Therefore, students who are currently in colleges and universities must prepare to assume the reins of leadership. If these students fulfill the requirements of such a role, the dividends will be great, not only for the profession as a whole, but also for them personally. This chapter is designed to show students why their leadership is needed, what is meant by leadership, what students are accountable for during their college days as well as after graduation, how professional organizations can help them as leaders, and finally, some tips that will help them to reach the top of their profession.

The field of physical education and sport is passing through a very critical period, accentuating the need for dynamic leadership. On the negative side, many changes are taking place throughout the nation. Economic uncertainties are resulting in austerity budgets. Programs are being curtailed or abolished altogether. Sources of energy are being depleted. Needed personnel are not being hired.

Although many problems exist, other national developments augur well for the profession. On the brighter side, there is increasing interest in health and physical fitness. According to the most reliable recent surveys, as indicated by the President's Council on Physical Fitness and Sports, approximately 55% of American adults, 18 years of age and over, participate in exercise and sport with some degree of regularity. About 90 million men and women, or double the number of 15 years ago, are involved. In addition, 30 million young people are engaged in out-of-school sports, 538,000 athletes participate in intercollegiate sports, and 6.45 million boys and girls are involved in interscholastic programs. College intramural sports account for 4.34 million participants, and college club and recreational sports involve another 1.41 million.

This public interest in fitness and sport has created many other opportunities. Books are being written. Politicians are becoming involved. New programs are being created. Television, radio, magazines, and newspapers are communicating the need for fitness.

This public interest in fitness and sport has also created one of the major problems facing the profession. The problem is reflected in the following questions: "Who is the rightful leader in the business of physical fitness?" "Who has the expertise for teaching sport skills?" "Who is the physical education expert?" "Is it the manager of the health spa who has little training in physical education?" "Is it the person who knows yoga but has no background in the biological and behavioral sciences?" "Is it the professional athlete whose qualifications are limited to exceptional playing skill in his or her sport?" "Who is the expert?" "Many vested interests are claiming to be the leaders, but who is the rightful leader?"

In the field of medicine, a person who pretends to have medical training and knowledge is called a *quack*. A quack often uses methods, medications, and gadgets in the diagnosis and treatment of disorders that are often untested and ineffective. A quack boasts of credentials, but in many cases the credentials are misleading or not legitimate. The quack capitalizes on the desire of many Americans for quick results and instant success. The quack is interested in money, not service.

There are also quacks in the physical fitness and sport industry. Examine the advertisements in some of the nation's popular magazines and notice the weight reducing, strength building, and spot reducing gimmicks and gadgets. If one took these advertisements at face value, the conclusion would be that it would be possible to be physically fit and have a beautiful, strong body in a matter of days, and without much effort.

A major challenge facing the professionals in physical education and sport is to be recognized publicly as the leaders in their field. This means separating the commercial interests and quacks in physical education and sport from the well-trained and professional-ly minded persons who have earned college degrees in their field of expertise. The public needs to recognize that the professionals are service rather than profit minded. The goal is not to make a sale for X number of dollars, but instead, to render a service—to help people become physically fit, learn sport skills, understand their bodily needs, have movement awareness, and improve their quality of life. Effective leadership is needed to help solve the problem of distinguishing the trained from the untrained practitioner in physical education and sport.

Leadership is needed in physical education and sport for other reasons also. Most physical educators are involved in group efforts, whether as part of a school, college, corporation, government department, or other affiliation. Uniting the efforts of member professionals and helping to make their group activity a productive, happy, and satisfying experience requires leadership. Regardless of where these trained professionals work, they want to be recognized for their expertise, be respected by their colleagues, and believe that they are in a dynamic and growing profession. This goal will not be achieved automatically. It will only occur as the profession demonstrates and articulates that the unique services it performs are in the public interest. This message must be disseminated throughout every part of the nation. Leadership is needed to accomplish this task. Leadership of a less visible kind is also required in the conduct of the many programs in physical education and sport that exist throughout the country in which physical educators deal with people directly. Here, the various members of an organization must be molded into an effective working group that is in harmony with the purposes of the organization.

Young people represent the future of the profession of physical education and sport. If leadership potential exists among the stu-

dents now preparing for this profession in the nation's colleges and universities, the profession will prosper. If the leadership potential does not exist among these young people, the profession will deteriorate.

WHAT IS LEADERSHIP?

The term *leadership* as used in this text represents the art of influencing people to work together harmoniously in the achievement of professional goals that they endorse. Leadership influences a person's feelings, beliefs, and behavior. In a sense, a leader is a person who can help a group to achieve goals with as little friction as possible, have a sense of unity, and provide an opportunity for self-realization. Leadership involves motivating and vitalizing the members of the profession to contribute a maximum effort. It taps vital resources and higher levels of achievement. It eliminates inertia, apathy, and indifference and replaces them with inspiration, enthusiasm, and conviction. It provides for self-fulfillment and satisfying endeavor. It results in power *with* the members, not power of the leader.

The leader should be very conscious of the need for self-realization on the part of each member of an organization or profession. Each individual needs to believe that he or she counts for something, is recognized, is somebody, and has a sense of worth. At the same time, the leader should recognize that each individual has different interests, urges, abilities, attitudes, talents, capacities, and creative powers. These traits must be taken into consideration by the leader who must show how not only the profession, but each individual in the profession, profits as a result of such an association. In addition, the practitioners should be involved in determining what the profession is trying to accomplish. In the final analysis, the test of leadership is determined by the number of people it enriches and helps to grow. It is a process of helping people to discover

themselves; it is not a process of exploitation.

Some personality characteristics of leaders include scholarship, intelligence, dependability, sociability, initiative, persistence, self-confidence, adaptability, insight, emotional stability, communication skills, cooperation, and knowing how to get things done. A general conclusion from an analysis of these characteristics is that leaders are made, not born, since the only inherited or partially inherited trait is intelligence, and the relationship of this quality to leadership is low. Therefore it is within the power of most students to develop the essential qualities for strong leadership.

Some qualities that students should develop if they wish to be leaders were set forth many years ago by Ordway Tead in his book, *The Art of Leadership*. In this case, they have been adapted to relate to leaders in the field of physical education and sport.

Physical and nervous energy

Leaders need both physical and nervous energy to cope with the many demanding hours of work required and the effort that is expended in the process. In addition, as Tead stresses, an effective demonstration of energy on the part of leaders begets energy on the part of followers. Energy is contagious. Leaders set the pace and are examples for others to follow. Furthermore, just as a banker should be a symbol of thrift and the clergy a symbol of sound values, leaders in physical education and sport should be symbols of what their field stands for—physical vitality, energy, and good health habits. To symbolize such qualities is an important way for leaders to advance their cause.

Sense of purpose and direction

Leaders must have conviction regarding what they espouse, what has to be done, and where they want to go professionally. The leader's goals are clear and definite, and the road ahead is clearly delineated. This conviction, sense of purpose, and direction requires knowledge and understanding of one's profession and the objectives that need to be achieved. Furthermore, the ability to support the worth of these goals scientifically is very important. Leaders must also be able to articulate the goals, not only in professional terms, but also in lay terms. To be able to dramatize these goals in simple, appealing ways will result in people more likely appreciating them.

Enthusiasm

The word *enthusiasm* comes from the Greek words that mean "possessed" and "inspired by some divinity." It refers to the quality of having vitality for one's purpose. Leaders not only have a strong belief in professional goals, but also a strong desire to further them. Leaders are excited about these goals and the profession that is trying to accomplish them. This feeling is so intense that it also results in exciting others. In other words, the effort expended by leaders gives off sparks that attract others to the cause. As a

Courtesy Keenan High School, Columbia, S.C. Photography by Charles McClary.

result, more and more persons begin to understand and support the cause that has been ignited in them by the leader.

Friendliness and affection

Leaders have a passion for people that is exemplified not by words but by action. Leaders are concerned about the well-being and happiness of other people and are aware of their desires and goals. The leader's affection for people is so great that it influences others. Affection begets affection. Too often people do not have any affection shown them. As a result, they are emotionally impoverished. When affection is shown, they respond in kind and often become followers. Leaders who have a passion for people know their names, make a deliberate effort to be friendly, and develop many personal acquaintances. The leader's friendliness and affection shows that he or she realizes that members of the profession are a means of ful-

filling the worthwhile cause with which all are associated.

Integrity

People must have trust in their leaders. They must know that their leaders are honest and reliable. They want their leaders to keep promises, be honest in their dealings, speak the truth, and say exactly what they mean. Leaders who have integrity act in accordance with the high expectations of their constituency.

Technical mastery

Just as teachers must possess technical mastery of the skills involved in teaching, so must leaders have a technical mastery of the organization or profession of which they expect or strive to be leaders. This means that leaders must know the processes by which goals are achieved and must understand how each person's task fits into the total

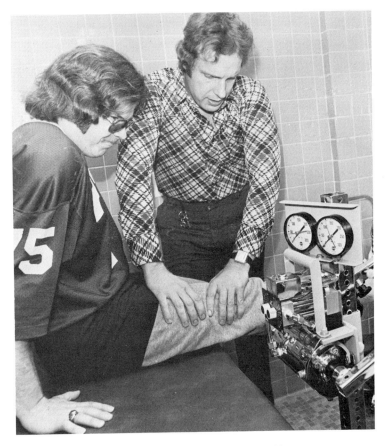

Courtesy Springfield College, Springfield, Mass.

enterprise. Leaders must be able to coordinate the various parts of an organization or the profession so that it is a unified whole. To accomplish this, leaders must promote teamwork, team spirit, and good human relations among all the membership.

Decisiveness

Leaders must get results. The goals of the organization or profession must be achieved. Therefore, decisions must be made, courses of action selected, and action taken. This requires courage as well as soundness of judgment. In fulfilling this responsibility, leaders must follow a sound procedure in arriving at decisions that will enhance the profession. One method is to recognize the problem, accumulate the facts, study the facts, develop alternatives, study each alternative, propose a solution, test the solution, and then make a choice. Once the choice has been made, leaders must stand behind their decisions.

Intelligence

The term *intelligence* is used here, not in the sense of an intelligence quotient, but in a way that relates to how the goals of the profession are accomplished. It refers to the ability to appraise situations and then be able to

Courtesy Westchester Co., N.Y., Department of Parks, Recreation and Conservation.

conceptualize the course of action that should be taken. Leaders who have this type of intelligence are able to sense relationships among various aspects of the enterprise, utilize past experiences when pertinent to solve present problems, and see a line of wise action that needs to be taken. Leaders who have this type of intelligence have imagination as well as sound reasoning powers.

Teaching skill

Good leaders are also good teachers in the sense that they set goals, pose problems, guide activities, and create interest. Leaders, like teachers, develop a feeling that the activity being accomplished is important and worthwhile. Leaders, like teachers, start where the member is, with what he or she knows and feels, and proceeds from that point. Leaders, like teachers, know that learning involves the whole organism—thinking, feeling and acting. Leaders, like teachers, act as guides for the learning experiences and thinking that takes place, supplying data and problems that make the learning process a meaningful experience.

Faith

Leaders have faith that the effort they expend in professional goal accomplishment is worthwhile and that their faith will inspire others. Leaders must have an inner conviction that they are involved in something that will make the world a better place in which to live and that the quality of life of people that it touches will be enhanced. As Tead pointed out, "The greatest leaders have been sustained by the belief that they were in some way instruments of destiny, that they tapped hidden resources of power, that they truly lived as they tried to live, in harmony with some greater, more universal purpose or intention in the world."

The above characteristics, when embodied in a leader, have an impressive effect on those with whom the leader comes in contact. The leader becomes a symbol for the cause that is being served. The leader gives prestige to the cause. Tead uses the leader in the field of religion as an example, "Go Thou and do likewise." "If I be lifted up, I'll draw all men unto me." In all professions, the outstanding leader is the embodiment of everything the profession stands for and is trying to achieve. As such, the profession is moved forward on his or her shoulders.

ACCOUNTABILITY AS A PROSPECTIVE LEADER

Simply stated, accountability means that people should be held responsible for their actions. In this case, the student, as a prospective leader, is accountable for certain things while he or she is in college and after graduation.

Accountability is characteristic of the times. More than half the states have enacted some type of accountability legislation involving education. These accountability laws provide for such things as testing personnel, evaluating programs, assessing student accomplishments, soliciting advisory board recommendations, utilizing cost-performance analysis, involving citizen appraisal, using performance-based objectives, and conducting systems analysis. Politicians and other public figures, as well as business executives, are also being held accountable for their actions.

Because accountability is a fact of life, this discussion will look at this subject from two frames of reference: (1) what is the college student accountable for who is preparing to be a leader in physical education and sport, and (2) what will he or she be accountable for as a leader after graduation from college?

Accountability as a college student

College students today are a different group from what they were 20 or 30 years ago. Today, students are not inhibited, want to be involved, do not agree with their elders and the establishment in many cases, want to participate in the decisions that affect their lives, and are committed to social change.

College students have certain rights that should be emphasized. However, if they want to be leaders in their profession, they are accountable for their actions. If a student is a prospective professional leader, it is disturbing when he or she asks to serve on a committee and then does not attend meetings. It is difficult to understand why a student who wants to be a leader requests time off from college to work in a political campaign and takes a vacation instead. It is hard to reconcile the fact that some young people are interested more in the grade than what they can get out of a course. A question is raised when students majoring in physical education profess an interest in the field but never participate in the club sponsored by the profession or join a professional association. Of course, there are examples of another kind, since most students are conscientious, dedicated, and responsible. However, more students are needed who are professionally involved in such ways as being active members of their college major's club, the Student Action Council of the AAHPERD, or devoting some of their free time to helping some worthy cause in their community. Students who are prospective leaders will become involved and will also help to get other students involved.

Students who are prospective leaders are also accountable for developing certain competencies during their college career. They need competencies they themselves believe are important, competencies their professors believe are important, competencies their profession believes are important, and competencies their future employers believe are important. For example, it is not enough to take a course in anatomy and physiology; the student must understand the human being as a functioning organism and be able to apply this knowledge of the science to his or her special field. It is not enough to take a course in communications; the student must understand the role of communications in influencing people in the achievement of goals of an organization or gaining public support for their profession. It is not enough to take a course in expository writing; the student must also develop the ability to write. Students are accountable for more than spending 4 years in college, taking a set list of courses, getting a degree, and telling someone they are educated. *They are also accountable for demonstrated involvement in the work of the profession and a mastery of many competencies.*

Accountability as a leader after graduation from college

In the second frame of reference, what will a student be accountable for after graduation when he or she hopefully becomes a leader in the profession? First, there will be accountability for the clientele with whom the leader is associated. This means that as a leader there will be accountability not only for the person who can score 20 points each game, but also for the person who can hardly throw the ball as high as the basket. There will be accountability not only for boys and men, but also for girls and women. There will be accountability not only for affluent people, but also for poverty-stricken people. There will be accountability not only for those persons who are in an optimum state of health, mentally and physically, but also for those who are physically, mentally, emotionally, or otherwise disabled.

The future leader in the field of physical education will be responsible for imparting knowledge and facts and developing skills. This leader will also be accountable for changing the behavior of those persons with whose welfare he or she is entrusted. This means not only providing persons with pertinent information regarding weight control, but also changing their eating habits so they lose weight. It also means not only quoting the findings of research studies regarding the importance of physical activity to health, but also changing their behavior so that activity becomes a regular part of their life-style.

The leader of the future will not only be accountable to those with whom he or she works directly, but also to the community and larger society. In respect to such accountability, it should be noted that the public has indicated that it is not going to pay taxes, build swimming pools, or pay high salaries unless physical education and sport can render some unique service. As one school board member said, who believed physical educators did not render any unique service, "Let's eliminate school buses and let the kids walk and run back and forth to school. In this way we will not only save gasoline but will also be able to do away with our physical education program."

An important responsibility of students looking forward to leadership roles is to be able to identify, define, articulate, and enunciate their profession's unique service to society. If physical education and sport is ever to become a great profession, if students are to have prestigious careers, and if the profession is to separate itself from quacks and hustlers, this work must be done.

The leader of the future will also be accountable to the profession. This means helping it to become strong and respected. It means raising standards and establishing and enforcing codes of ethical behavior for members of the profession. It also means that coaches and physical education teachers must have similar professional goals, women must work closely with men and men must cooperate with women, and students must appreciate the role of their professors and professors must involve the novice. United, the profession will be strong; divided, it will remain just an average profession. The profession needs to be characterized by a closeness and cohesiveness. A team spirit, camaraderie, and a feeling that "it's good to be a part of this profession," must prevail.

Finally, there is another person to whom each prospective leader is accountable. This is the most important person of all—oneself.

Students are no different than other human beings. They want to make something of themselves, achieve their destiny, do their thing, be recognized, and confirm the faith others have in them. Now is the time to start doing something about it. This means that they cannot think small; they must think BIG. It is possible for all students to make an outstanding contribution to their profession and to humanity. One of the greatest human tragedies is to see people suddenly realize that it is too late to accomplish goals they have dreamed about for many years. One often hears them say, "I wish I had known in college what I know now." "I feel trapped in my job." "I have a feeling there ought to be something more to life."

QUALITIES ESSENTIAL FOR PROFESSIONAL SUCCESS

Several years ago, I (one of the authors) tried to find the answer to success and interviewed and/or corresponded with 50 different people, including Eddie Rickenbacker, the outstanding aviator and airlines executive; Helen Hayes, the actress; and Chief Justice Warren of the Supreme Court of the United States. I asked each of these persons what he/she believed were the qualities that would help to guarantee success in life? In other words, what qualities were needed to be a leader in one's profession? The people who were surveyed provided several answers and suggestions, but five qualities were mentioned most often. The first quality was *intelligence*, and students have this quality or they wouldn't be college students. The second quality was *hard work*, and students have probably found out by now that the best things in life are not free, one has to work for them. The third quality was *health*, and students are in the business, so I assume they have this quality. The fourth quality was *respect for other people*. One of the strong points of most young people is their humani-

tarianism, their desire to help people. The fifth quality most frequently mentioned and probably one of the most important was *desire*. Students have seen persons who possess a strong desire and accomplish great things even though many obstacles were thrown in their path. The important thing was that these people kept their goals clearly in mind, were not sidetracked, and kept striving for what they wanted out of life.

Most young people have strong desires, and I am sure the students reading this text are no exception. They are not content to be a nonentity. They dream beyond the actual and think beyond their fingertips. In so doing, they are living up to the great law of nature, namely, that a person wants to become all that he/she is capable of becoming.

A few years ago, more than 2600 mourners filled Carnegie Hall in New York City to attend the funeral services of an 85-year-old impresario. The funeral was simple but impressive since it told what a great person this man was and what an outstanding success he had made of his life. Isaac Stern, one of his special protégés, played a Bach selection; Marion Anderson, whom this man had discovered in Paris in 1935, delivered the eulogy. Jan Peerce sang a selection of psalms. In the center section of the seats that line Carnegie Hall sat the celebrities whom this man had either discovered or helped, including Leonard Bernstein, Agnes de Mille, Van Cliburn, Roberta Peters, Robert Merrill, Renata Tebaldi, and Sir Rudolph Bing. Marion Anderson summed up this man's accomplishments in her eulogy: "He launched hundreds of careers and magnified thousands of others, and in the process he brought joy and a larger life to millions. He made not ripples, but waves. He went beyond his own shores."

You are not expected to be a Sol Hurok. All that is expected (and it is expected) is that you will make the best use of the things that are within your own power. An old man in one of Ibsen's plays had only one talent, the making of pie dishes, and only one ambition, to make a really excellent pie dish before he died. You may not have the fingers for turning a potter's wheel or the talent to be recognized throughout the world. But I am sure each of you believes that you have the ability to make your mark in physical education and sport or you would not be majoring in this field. You are entering the profession at a time when many professional problems exist that are most critical for your chosen field. On the other hand, you are living in an age that has much promise. This is a period when new ideas are being welcomed, innovative programs are in vogue, creativity is encouraged, and young persons are being provided opportunities to use their talents. This is the time when you can play a major role in shaping your profession. Do not lose this opportunity. Make something of yourself. In so doing, you will not only be a somebody, but you will also build a strong profession that can rightfully be called a full-fledged profession.

ROLE OF PROFESSIONAL ORGANIZATIONS IN LEADERSHIP

One of the requirements for gaining professional status is to have an organization that symbolizes and speaks for its membership and helps it to become self-regulatory. Such an organization is the American Medical Association, which speaks for the medical profession. Another organization is the American Bar Association, which speaks for the legal profession.

A profession that is self-regulatory has prestige and respect. The law profession, for example, is self-regulatory because it has the power to decide such things as the requirements for admission to the bar, rules regarding the suspension or exclusion of a member from practice, and the standards for ethical and unethical conduct.

Physical education should also be self-reg-ulatory. To achieve this autonomy, the profession must have a recognized organization that can and will speak for it with an authority that springs from and is granted to it by its membership. The organization must also be representative of the members in the field and have sufficient consensus to act authoritatively on their behalf.

The American Alliance for Health, Physical Education, Recreation and Dance is the most representative organization for physical education. Therefore, a question can be asked as to whether it meets the qualifications called for. Does this organization speak for all the physical educators in this country? In other words, does it speak for all physical educators in such places as schools, colleges, industry, and youth-serving agencies? Does it speak for coaches, exercise physiologists, instructors in YMCAs, and other specialists? Does it speak for the women as well as the men? Does it speak out authoritatively on the great issues of the day? Has this organization taken effective steps to cast out the intruders and the quacks? Has machinery been set up to enforce high standards of professional conduct? If the answer to these questions is "No," full professional status has not been achieved and work needs to be done. As a potential leader, you are challenged to help physical education and sport to become self-regulatory.

Several other purposes of professional organizations will now be discussed.

Provide potential leaders the opportunity to serve

Professional organizations have meetings, issue publications, promote desirable legislation, solve professional problems, and in many other ways attempt to upgrade and achieve the goals for which the profession stands. Most of this work is done by professionals in the field who volunteer their services. As such, many opportunities are provided for persons who desire to become leaders to serve in a variety of capacities. Also, professional organizations provide opportunities to meet other leaders in the field, better understand the issues with which the profession is struggling, and have a voice in how the organization is to be run. Young people should know that very few persons become outstanding leaders in the profession of physical education and sport unless they become involved with and actively participate in professional organizations.

Provide a means of unifying the profession

Members of a profession engage in a variety of specialized pursuits and have different ideas concerning professional priorities. These members are also located in different geographical areas. Some type of machinery is needed to coordinate their efforts and desires. An association helps to bring together persons in a profession who have different specialties, ideas, purposes, and viewpoints. It provides an opportunity to discuss the issues and reconcile differences. It provides a cohesive force for bringing together people engaged in the same type of work for the purpose of promoting their profession. As a result of such interaction, the profession gains cohesiveness and solidarity. Without professional associations, a field of endeavor would become stagnant and weak.

Provide a communication network

Professional organizations provide an internal and external communication network. Internally, it makes it possible for members of the association to be kept informed as well as to express their views on various issues. The communication network includes such elements as staff members in a central office, elected officers of the association, representatives in various districts and states, meetings, and journals, newsletters, and other publications. Externally, public pronouncements can be made regarding such matters as significant research that has been accomplished

by members of the association, legislation that is thought to be desirable and should be passed, special projects that are underway, and the pros and cons of public issues that relate to the work of the profession. Public support and funding can also be sought for a variety of projects that are important to the organization.

Provide for research

For a profession to grow, it must continually create new knowledge and provide better insight into its subject. Among other things, a professional organization can identify the areas and problems that need to be researched. It can also, through its committees, conduct and sponsor research that needs to be done.

Provide a legislative function

The professional organization must be alert to legislation that is being considered for passage at local, state, and national levels of government. It must weigh the merits of such legislation and determine whether it should be supported or defeated. The organization should also be instrumental in proposing new legislation that is vital to the life of the profession.

Provide an opportunity for fellowship

At the various meetings held by professional organizations, the opportunity is provided for persons with similar interests, skills, and vocational affiliation to get together. Such get-togethers afford opportunities for fellowship as well as for an exchange of ideas and a discussion of problems. This fellowship, in turn, provides a feeling of belonging for people who at other times during the year are separated from each other because they live in different sections of the country. When a person is not provided such an opportunity for fellowship, work sometimes becomes boring and one loses sight of the significance of his or her endeavors. Getting together with persons who are engaged in a similar type of work creates a feeling that one is engaged in an important and worthwhile endeavor. As a result, this in turn, provides an impetus and enthusiasm for one's work. The following are some organizations with which the leader in physical education and sport should be familiar.*

Amateur Athletic Union
American Academy of Physical Education
American Alliance for Health, Physical Education, Recreation and Dance
American College of Sports Medicine
American Corrective Therapy Association
American School Health Association
Association for Intercollegiate Athletics for Women
Canadian Association for Health, Physical Education and Recreation
College Sports Information Directors of America
Delta Psi Kappa
National Association of Intercollegiate Athletics
National Association for Physical Education in Higher Education
National Collegiate Athletic Association
National Education Association
National Federation of State High School Associations (Athletic)
National Intramural Association
National Junior College Athletic Association
National Recreation and Park Association
North American Society for the Psychology of Sport and Physical Activity
The Philosophic Society for the Study of Sport
Phi Epsilon Kappa Fraternity
Physical Education Society of the Young Men's Christian Association of North America
Society of State Directors of Health, Physical Education and Recreation
U.S. Collegiate Sports Council
Young Women's Christian Association of America

---

*For a detailed description of these organizations, please see Chapter 20 in Bucher, C. A.: Foundations of physical education, ed. 8, St. Louis, 1979, The C. V. Mosby Co.

A FINAL WORD FOR REACHING THE TOP OF YOUR PROFESSION

If a person is truly interested and committed to becoming a leader in the profession, it is possible to achieve this goal. At the same time, certain responsibilities must be undertaken and sacrifices made if success is to be assured. The following are some of the important requirements that must be met by the student who wants to be a leader in the field of physical education and sport.

Knowledge and dedication to the field of physical education and sport

A leader must have an excellent background in physical education and sport. This means possessing the various competencies that professors are trying to provide in the various courses that comprise the program. A superficial preparation will not do. Leadership requires a mastery of the knowledge, skills, and attitudes that are related to the biological, sociological, and psychological scientific foundations associated with this area of expertise.

A dedication to the field is also a necessity. This does not mean a casual interest that has developed because a student was a star athlete in high school or college. Instead, it means a strong desire and conviction that this profession is important because it represents a way of providing a useful and socially desirable service to society.

Area of expertise

A prospective leader should become a specialist in some area of physical education and sport such as elementary or secondary school physical education, college physical education, exercise physiology, biomechanics, motor learning, intramurals, or athletic administration. It is important to acquire all the information one can concerning this area of specialization. A prospective leader's objective should be to try and know more about his or her area of specialization than any other person. The goal should be to become recognized as a person who possesses the "know-how" in regard to the specialty. Various opportunities present themselves for gaining such recognition, including teaching, research, writing articles and/or books, and serving on professional committees.

Breadth of interest

Although specialization is important, one's learning should not stop there. A leader should also be cultured and well-rounded. This means it is important to know something about such fields as art, architecture, politics, travel, languages, economics, literature, and music. Since all of this knowledge cannot be gained in college, much of the work will need to be done on one's own. Among other benefits, such learning will help a person to carry on an intelligent conversation with other people. It is important for the student to recognize that as a leader he or she will not be limited to associating only with people in his or her specialty. Instead, there will be meetings with doctors, lawyers, business persons, politicians, and many other people in various occupations. Persons who are intelligent and cultured will make a better impression on those with whom they come in contact. Without it, they will, at times, be dull and boring.

Personality

One's personality is important. Leaders should have positive attitudes. They should reflect energy, drive, and ambition. They should have composure. They should possess poise, a diplomatic approach, and a sense of humor. They should also inspire trust and be likeable. Various physical characteristics also need attention. Obesity is a negative quality, particularly for the leader in physical education and sport. Dress and manners are important since they have to do with making an impression. Good posture and an image of self-confidence connote leadership qualities.

Articulation

Articulation is very important. One must know how to communicate effectively and use the English language properly. Leaders must be able to write and speak coherently. They are constantly in front of the public, making speeches, and communicating the goals of their profession. As such, they cannot afford to be weak in written or oral English.

DISCUSSION QUESTIONS AND EXERCISES

1. List and discuss five reasons why there is an urgent need for leadership in the profession of physical education and sport today.
2. Debate the question: "Resolved that physical education and sport does not have jurisdiction over its own domain."
3. Indicate the various places and situations in which leadership is needed today in physical education and sport.
4. Define the term *leadership* and list the personality characteristics that are qualities associated with leaders.
5. List eight qualities that should be developed by persons who desire to become leaders in their profession.
6. Write a 150-word essay on the topic: "The leader is a symbol for the cause that he or she serves."
7. What accountability does the student majoring in physical education and sport have when in college?
8. List and discuss the five qualities essential for professional success.
9. How can professional organizations provide opportunities for a person who wishes to become a leader in his or her profession?
10. Develop a formula that, if followed, would help a person to become a leader in his or her profession.

SELECTED REFERENCES

American Association for Health, Physical Education and Recreation: Developing democratic human relations, Washington, D.C., 1951, The Association.
American Alliance for Health, Physical Education, Recreation and Dance: HPER omnibus, Washington, D.C., 1976, The Alliance.

Anderson, W. G.: Analysis of teaching physical education, St. Louis, 1980, The C. V. Mosby Co.

Bucher, C. A.: Administration of physical education and athletic programs, ed. 7, St. Louis, 1979, The C. V. Mosby Co.

Bucher, C. A.: Dimensions of physical education, St. Louis, 1974, The C. V. Mosby Co.

Bucher, C. A.: Foundations of physical education, ed. 8, St. Louis, 1979, The C. V. Mosby Co.

Bucher, C. A., and Koenig, C. R.: Methods and materials for secondary school physical education, ed. 5, St. Louis, 1978, The C. V. Mosby Co.

Bucher, C. A., and Thaxton, N. A.: Physical education for children: movement foundations and experiences, New York, 1979, Macmillan Inc.

Dougherty, N. J., and Bonanno, D.: Contemporary approaches to the teaching of physical education, Minneapolis, 1979, Burgess Publishing Co.

Eitzen, D. S., and Sage, G. H.: Sociology of American sport, Dubuque, Iowa, 1978, William C. Brown Co., Publishers.

Fuoss, D. E., and Troppmann, R. J.: Creative management techniques in interscholastic athletics, New York, 1977, John Wiley & Sons, Inc.

McGlynn, G. H.: Issues in physical education and sports, Palo Alto, Calif., 1974, National Press Books.

Shivers, J. S.: Leadership in recreational service, New York, 1963, Macmillan Inc.

Siedentop, D.: Developing teaching skills in physical education, Boston, 1976, Houghton Mifflin Co.

Tead, O.: The art of leadership, New York, 1935, Whittlesey House.

Ulrich, C.: To seek and find, Washington, D.C., 1976, American Alliance for Health, Physical Education, Recreation and Dance.

4 □ Challenging professional opportunities for the future

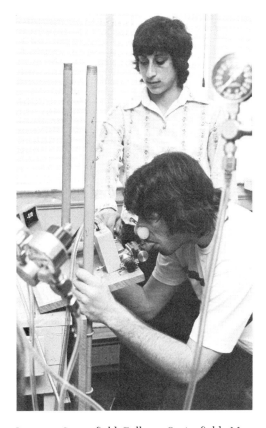

Courtesy Springfield College, Springfield, Mass.

The student who is majoring in physical education and sport in college, as well as persons already practicing in the field, want to know what professional career opportunities will be available in the 1980s. If they are aware of these opportunities, they will be able to prepare accordingly.

This is an era of specialization. Instead of preparing to be a general practitioner in physical education, the student who is look-ing toward the future may wish to specialize in one of the many areas of concentration within this profession. Furthermore, the physical educator who desires to get ahead in the field should know as early as possible what his or her specialized interests are. In addition, it is important for the student to determine whether or not he or she has the qualifications necessary to be a success in a particular area of specialization, as well as being aware of the number of job opportunities that are and will be available. A person may wish to specialize in exercise physiology but may have little inclination, for example, to study the biological sciences. In this case, it probably would not be wise to specialize in this area. Although motivation and interest are very important, ability and knowledge relating to the scientific foundations on which the specialization rests are more or equally important for success. Furthermore, the number of available positions must also be considered.

This chapter will discuss promising areas of concentration in which one can specialize in this profession and briefly describe some of the settings in which physical education and sport positions will exist in the 1980s.

SELECTED AREAS OF SPECIALIZATION WITHIN PHYSICAL EDUCATION

This section discusses several areas of concentration that have promise for the 1980s. It is not the purpose of this discussion to give an in-depth analysis of each area. Rather, the purpose is simply to familiarize students with the many opportunities and careers in which they can specialize. For a more detailed analysis of these areas of concentration, consult the references at the end of the chapter.

Administration of physical education programs

An area of specialization that requires expertise is that of administrator of a physical education program. This discussion refers to the role of an administrator in such positions as a chairperson of a high school or college physical education program or head of a physical education program in an organization. Athletic administration, because of its growing importance as a field of specialization, is discussed as a separate career later in this chapter.

Organizations are formed when people

band together for the purpose of accomplishing objectives that they would be incapable of attaining as individuals. Administration is the structure that holds an organization together, helps it function smoothly and efficiently, and helps it to achieve the goals for which it was established. Administration involves those individuals who mobilize and provide the resources to help an organization achieve its objectives. In some organizations, these individuals are called executives.

In the field of physical education, various types of programs require administrators who utilize and coordinate the human and material resources that are available to help the organization achieve its goals. A chairperson of a high school department, dean of a school, head of a division, or other administrative unit in physical education has the responsibility to lead, guide, and exercise the control needed to achieve the purposes for which the organization exists. The responsibilities of the administrator of a physical education program are in many respects very similar to those of the administrator in other professions. The main difference is in regard to the specialization and the tasks to be performed. The growth of programs in physical education and sport demonstrate the magnitude of organizational and management responsibilities that are necessary today and will continue to be in the future.

The qualifications needed by the person aspiring to the position of administrator of a physical education program include intelligence, scholarship, integrity, decisiveness, sense of humor, communication, and human relations skills. In addition, this person should be able to conceptualize, willing to accept responsibility, should understand the role of the behavioral sciences in administration, and have a command of technical skills associated with managing a physical education organization.

Duties and responsibilities for the administrator of physical education programs range from preparing and defending budgets, arranging schedules, and presiding over meetings, to planning, personnel management, facility management, preparing reports, and public relations.

The professional preparation needed to be an administrator of physical education programs should involve undergraduate and graduate work that includes experiences in such areas as personnel administration, finance, business administration, facility management, communications, psychology of human behavior, and sociology of institutions. Administrators should also have an internship experience in which they study firsthand how various administrative responsibilities are carried out in respect to such areas as budget preparation, public relations, and plant management.

The future outlook for administrators of physical education programs is promising for the person who has had extensive preparation, both in the field of physical education and in administration. To be qualified for most opportunities, one should be prepared for positions, not only in schools and colleges, but also in other agencies and institutions that have physical education programs. The trend today is in the direction of employing administrators who have special preparation and experience in the field of administration, rather than moving people within an organization who have little acquaintance with the field of administration into such positions. Administration is a science and needs people who possess expertise in this area of specialization.

Athletic administration

Sports represent a rapidly developing field. The interest in athletics from the standpoint of participation, as well as spectator interest, combine to produce one of the fastest growing segments of American life.

Athletic administration is a career for individuals seeking managerial positions within sport-oriented organizations such as schools, colleges, professional sports teams, sporting goods manufacturers, and leisure sports enterprises. Athletic administration may be involved with highly competitive sports, as well as intramural and other types of sport programs. Within athletic administration, several part-time positions often become full-time in a large sports organization such as general manager, business manager, controller, travel secretary, public relations director, director of ticket sales, and farm director.

The qualifications needed to be an athletic administrator include an understanding and expertise in the field of administration, knowledge concerning the structure and function of sports, and expertise in public and media relations. An athletic administrator must also have an understanding of such things as scheduling, contracts, personnel management, budgeting, advertising, sales promotion, purchasing practices, and care of equipment and supplies. He/she also must be able to meet, speak, and hold discussions with civic and alumni groups regarding the athletic program. The many changes that have taken place in sports in recent years require a well-informed and experienced individual with a sense of deep responsibility toward the position as director of athletics. Duties of the athletic director include scheduling and contracting events, securing officials for contests, game management, making travel arrangements, preparing and supervising the budget, taking inventory, public relations, and preparing annual reports.

Professional preparation for a position in athletic administration includes pursuing a degree program that includes experiences in such areas as managerial aspects of athletic administration, use and maintenance of facilities, financial accounting, psychology of coaching, legal aspects of athletic administration, communications, public relations, sportscasting, sportswriting, management information systems, and crowd control. An internship experience is also needed in which the student can see how administrative problems are handled in a practical, on-the-job situation.

The employment opportunities involved in the field of athletic administration are stable and labeled as fair to good for men according to most experts in the field. The growth in girls' and women's sports has greatly enhanced employment opportunities for women. With more leisure time available to the public and with the growth in the number of sport organizations, the field of athletic administration appears to be a fertile area of employment in the future for those persons who are well-prepared for such responsibilities.

Athletic training

The number of sport-related injuries has reached epidemic proportions. One estimate indicates that 17 to 20 million sports injuries occur each year. In light of the great number of these injuries, the need for athletic trainers is very evident. Qualified persons who serve in this capacity can help to prevent injuries, provide proper emergency care, and minimize the severity of injuries incurred in athletics. The expansion of competitive sports for girls and women dictates that qualified and certified athletic trainers are as necessary for girls' and women's sports as they are for boys' and men's sports. Furthermore, female athletic trainers are needed as much as male athletic trainers.

The qualifications for an athletic trainer are both personal and professional. Personal qualifications include poise, good health, intelligence, maturity, emotional stability, compassion, cleanliness, ethics, and fairness. Professional qualifications include a knowledge of anatomy and physiology, conditioning, nutrition, taping, methodology for preventing injury, and protective equipment. Furthermore, the athletic trainer should

have qualities that provide a harmonious and productive rapport with the team physician, coaches, athletic administrators, and the public in general. The trainer must be able to practice good human relations as well as protect the athletes' well-being.

Duties and responsibilities of the athletic trainer include the care and prevention of athletic injuries, helping with the development of a conditioning program in various sports, developing a liaison with physicians and athletes, seeing that safe athletic equipment and facilities exist, preparing and processing injury reports, reviewing physical examinations of athletes, administering first aid for injured athletes, and applying protective and injury prevention devices such as bandaging, strapping, and braces. Other duties include consulting with the coach as to when athletes may participate in a sport following an injury, supervising the training room and the supplies and equipment that are a part of this facility, teaching classes, and providing orientation in training procedures for coaches as requested and needed.

The National Athletic Trainers Association's (NATA) basic minimum requirements for the professional preparation of athletic trainers are recommended by most experts in the field. These standards include graduating from an approved undergraduate or graduate program that meets specific criteria set forth by the NATA, being a physical therapy degree graduate (such preparation meeting the specific requirements set forth by the NATA), or serving an apprenticeship that meets NATA specifications. Persons preparing for positions in athletic training should also be certified as such by the NATA. To do this, they must have proper training and pass the NATA certification examination. Important courses in preparing to be an athletic trainer include anatomy and physiology, physiology of activity, kinesiology, psychology, first aid and safety, nutrition, remedial exercises, health, techniques of athletic training, and advanced techniques of athletic training.

The career opportunities for the position of athletic trainer are excellent. Positions are opening up in college and professional sports. High schools are also beginning to recognize the importance and need for a person on the faculty with such preparation. The need for qualified female athletic trainers is also great. Probably the best way to get a position in an educational institution is to be certified to teach another subject, such as physical education. Athletic trainers are also hired in physical therapy clinics, health spas, and other places associated with physical fitness and sports.

Biomechanics

Biomechanics is the science that studies the results of internal and external forces on living bodies. It is that phase of physical education that explores the role of forces that cause or affect human motion. Furthermore, it investigates the result of such forces on geometric patterns of velocity, acceleration, and displacement. It is also concerned with the dynamics of the neuromuscular system. It incorporates aspects of engineering, physics, electronics, computer science, and mathematics with a knowledge of sport skills.

Persons with expertise in biomechanics work in such places as rehabilitation hospitals (sports medicine consultant), colleges or universities (professor), and private industry (sport equipment designer-consultant). These persons also work with professional athletic teams as consultants in the analysis of performance characteristics of professional athletes.

Persons who specialize in biomechanics as related to sport should have an interest in the design of protective equipment for athletes, the design of sports equipment such as determining the size of the dimples on a golf

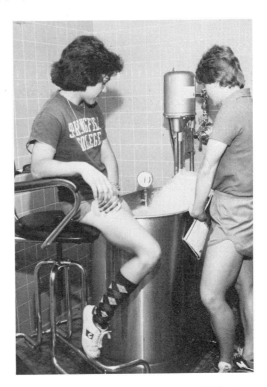

Courtesy Springfield College, Springfield, Mass.

ball, or sports performance analysis, research, or programming such as data gathering to determine the optimum point of contact of a ball with a bat or the optimum angle of takeoff of a high jumper. A person interested in biomechanics should also be mathematically inclined and interested in computer techniques, human engineering, cinematography, photoinstrumentation, and applied physiology. Such a person should also be inquisitive and want to find the solution to problems concerning human performance.

Duties and responsibilities of the person who specializes in biomechanics depend on the area of specialty. For example, some duties that might be performed in selected settings would be a *sports medicine consultant*—evaluate sport-related injuries with an orthopedist and physical therapist in a rehabilitation hospital, a *college professor*— design courses in or related to biomechanics, a *sport implement designer* in private industry—design research projects that test different types of equipment such as golf balls, or a *researcher in a sports medicine institute*—monitor programs of athletes to determine various factors that influence motor performance.

Professional preparation for the field of biomechanics requires work at both the undergraduate and graduate levels. One should have a sound background in physical education at the undergraduate level. Courses that might be taken at the graduate level include kinetic and kinematic analysis of human motion utilizing electromyography and stroboscopic-photographic techniques, advanced kinesiology involving an analysis of sport movements utilizing such devices as cinematography and electronic devices, and electromyographic kinesiology, which is designed to provide the theoretical background and practical application of electromyography to the study of human movement. Other courses could also include theoretical mechanics, neurophysiology, computer systems, advanced dynamics, applied physiology, and physiological psychology.

The future for specialists in the field of biomechanics is very promising. Job opportunities will increase as the public becomes more aware of the services rendered by such a specialist. The most dramatic increase may possibly be in the area of professional athletics and Olympic competition in which specialists will be needed in performance analysis. Positions in rehabilitation medicine are also on the increase as are positions in industry. Clinical research in physical and occupational therapy is relatively new and is expected to become much more important with the developing emphasis on justification of quality health care. Teaching positions at the college and university levels will also increase in the next 10 to 15 years.

Coaching

Coaching as a career exists in many organizations and in many sports. A coach may direct one person, such as a diver training for Olympic competition, or a well-organized team, such as a high school or professional football team. Coaches work in public and private educational institutions, including junior high schools, high schools, and colleges. They are also employed by such places as athletic clubs, Y's, national teams, the military, and professional sport teams. Women are also finding rewarding positions in coaching.

Qualifications for a coach include excellent technical knowledge and teaching and coaching skills in the sport to be coached. To receive an appointment to the best coaching positions in educational institutions, the following are important: experience with a successful background in the recruiting of student-athletes; ability to work with and communicate with students, faculty, and alumni; effectiveness in alumni relations in such areas as recruiting, fund raising, and other public relations activities; and ability to work within the framework of athletic conferences. For the beginning coach, playing experience and a degree in physical education will help in being appointed to a position.

Duties performed by coaches include recruiting players, establishing a training program, scheduling contests, conditioning participants, both mentally and physically, for competition, and maintaining good public relations. They also include keeping records of the training program, contests, expenses, and other matters; scouting new talent and other teams; providing for the safety of participants; taking care of correspondence on all team matters; updating of coaching skills through such means as clinics; and assisting in planning and conducting practice sessions. In addition, the duties include traveling with the team, being a guest speaker, providing for the medical health of participants, making

Courtesy Gannett Newspapers, White Plains, N.Y.

arrangements for trips, taking inventory, and supervising the care and maintenance of equipment and facilities.

Coaches are usually responsible for the entire scope of the program. They are usually directly accountable to the director of athletics and should work within the guidelines and philosophy of the school or organization where they are employed.

Ideally, the professional preparation of a coach should include a concentration in the field of physical education. However, in many cases this is not true, even among those persons who coach in educational institutions. The qualifications of many coaches is limited to playing experience. Physical education majors are often trained in such areas as coaching techniques, first aid, biomechanics, physiology, sport psychology, and other areas that can prove very helpful to the coach. Several years ago, the AAHPERD Division of Men's Athletics recommended that all states adopt a program requiring certification of interscholastic coaches. The areas recommended to be covered might well be a requirement for any coach regardless of the setting: medical aspects of athletic coaching, principles and problems of coaching, theory and techniques of coaching, kinesiological foundations of coaching, and physiological foundations of coaching. In addition to such formal educational preparation, coaches can do much on their own such as attending coaching clinics, reading professional periodicals, and observing games and other coaches.

The future outlook for coaching is competitive with the exception of girls' and women's sports. The emphasis on women's athletics today, with the increased publicity and exposure, has created many coaching opportunities. Fewer jobs for men will make competition greater for the positions that are available. At the same time, much depends on the sport one desires to coach. For example, soccer is growing rapidly and is a fertile area for coaching opportunities. Also, sports participation in this country is on the rise. Qualified persons who are skilled in sound educational teaching methods are needed. The student who has just graduated from college

Courtesy Jackson State University, Jackson, Miss.

might find a position as an assistant coach a valuable way to get experience before assuming a head coaching position.

Dance

This discussion is limited to dance in education because this specialty is a major concern in physical education. Dance, however, has other related areas in which careers exist, including dance critic, administrator, historian, therapist, choreographer, movement notator, recreation leader, and performer.

The career of the dance education teacher involves teaching within an educational institution or other organization. This type of teaching can range from rhythmic activities for children to more advanced work for persons who are preparing for a career as a performer or other specialty. Teaching opportunities, in addition to educational institutions, exist in such settings as private studios, special education programs, adult education programs, Y dance programs, and recreational dance programs.

Qualifications for the dance education teacher include optimum physical and mental health, patience, enthusiasm, creative

ability, as well as personal ability in the field of the dance, sensitivity to rhythm and form, knowledge of dance as an educational medium, understanding of the kinesiological aspects of human movement, skill as a teacher, knowledge of music, understanding of many dance forms, and ability to choreograph dances.

Duties of the dance education teacher include teaching game dances, rhythmic exercises, rhythmic gymnastics, recreational dance, folk dance, square dance, social dance, jazz, and modern dances. Persons trained in this field also produce dance concerts, choreograph school plays and operettas, and work with cheerleaders. Furthermore, they teach both theory and practice in ballet, musical comedy, theater dance, and ethnic dance (African, Spanish, Oriental). They also counsel persons majoring in dance and perform other routine duties associated with teaching.

The professional preparation recommended for dance education teachers includes a degree in education with concentration in the dance. Dance education teachers should be prepared and have experience in

Courtesy Springfield College, Springfield, Mass.

such areas as the historical background and function of dance together with an understanding of the interrelationship between dance and the other arts. They should also have a knowledge of the human body, basic movement concepts, form and analysis of rhythm and dance accompaniment, various forms of dance for different age levels, and principles and methods of teaching dance. They should also know the techniques of choreography, dance production, and the creative art process. Finally, it is necessary to demonstrate one's ability to teach dance in a student teaching assignment.

Dance as a medium of creative expression and physical activity is being stressed more and more. If the economy improves, demands for teachers in schools and colleges should increase. Dance in the schools does not usually require certification. In most cases, it is included as part of the physical education program, and therefore certifica-

tion is required in that subject area. If dance establishes its own identity and becomes a separate area for certification and subject in the curriculum, many more job opportunities will be created. It has accomplished this goal in many institutions of higher learning. The outlook for a career in dance is becoming brighter as the emphasis on the arts becomes more widespread.

Exercise physiology

Exercise physiology is the application of the principles of physiology to exercise or work conditions. It involves the study of the impact that exercise and work conditions have on the human body. It is concerned with such things as aerobic capacity, fatigue, and the manner in which the nerve impulse originates and is transmitted, together with the nature of the resulting action. It is concerned with the biochemistry of exercise, influence of various environmental factors on human performance, nutritional considerations, and pathophysiological conditions.

Qualifications for the exercise physiologist include a strong background in the biological sciences and a sound understanding of basic physiological principles. In addition to an undergraduate background, graduate work with specialization in exercise physiology is needed by anyone desiring to specialize in this field. Qualifications also include an insatiable curiosity for wanting to learn what happens to the body under various work and exercise conditions.

Duties and responsibilities of the exercise physiologist will vary with the area in which one specializes. Two services that the exercise physiologist performs can be used as examples. One service is to provide stress testing and the other is to improve the fitness level of one's clientele.

Stress testing is diagnostic and is designed to indicate the influence of exercise on the circulatory and other systems of the human body. The patient gets on a motor-driven treadmill, or stationary bicycle (ergometer), and exercises. Throughout this procedure, the patient's electrocardiogram (EKG), blood pressure, and heart rate are monitored. Oxygen consumption is also measured. The physiologist usually gives the stress test and the cardiologist interprets it, evaluates it, and prescribes the course of action for improvement. The test furnishes information concerning such things as the extent of any heart problems one may have, the person's cardiovascular fitness level, and the basis of the exercise prescription required.

The second service performed by exercise physiologists is exercise fitness training. This service involves determining the status of a person's cardiovascular efficiency and then improving the fitness level so that a greater amount of work can be performed with less energy expenditure, less strain, and more

Courtesy Nautilus, Scarsdale, New York.

confidence. On the basis of such things as the EKG, blood pressure, and maximal heart rate, the physiologist prescribes exercises that are designed to increase the cardiovascular capacity of the individual. The physiologist supervises the exercise program and periodically evaluates the progress being made. The program may also include lectures and advice on diet, cholesterol intake, and other factors. Of course, if the physiologist is at a college or university, he or she usually teaches classes and/or is involved in research projects.

Professional preparation of the exercise physiologist should include undergraduate courses in anatomy, histology, exercise physiology, kinesiology, and motor learning and graduate courses in applied anatomy and physiology, exercise and health, exercise testing and training, research training in ap-

Courtesy Westchester Co., N.Y., Department of Parks, Recreation and Conservation.

plied physiology, and statistics. It is also helpful to take courses in nutrition, neuropsychology, cell biology, and electromicroscopy.

Exercise physiology is one of the fastest growing branches of physical education today. Position openings exist in cardiac rehabilitation centers, private industry, cardiology units of hospitals, and colleges and universities.

Adult fitness

Several years ago, a national adult physical fitness survey conducted for the President's Council on Physical Fitness and Sports indicated that the physical fitness of adults was inadequate. It also showed that the adult population of America, in particular, needed more and better physical education programs as much or more than any other age group. Such programs, it has been pointed out, can delay the aging process, deter the onset of degenerative diseases, and enhance the quality of life for Americans. As a result of such information, the stress on adult fitness has increased by leaps and bounds.

The emphasis on adult fitness has, in turn, resulted in an increase in health clubs, industrial fitness programs for employees, and services provided by Y's and other groups to upgrade the fitness of the adult population. Also, national campaigns have and are being conducted that are aimed at encouraging adults to become more physically active.

Qualifications and the professional preparation needed for persons who desire to specialize in adult fitness programs suggest a sound physical education program at the undergraduate level and graduate work that places a heavy emphasis on exercise physiology. In addition, a person should understand the makeup of the human body and have a knowledge of the aging process, the impact of various health practices on the aging process, communications, and human relations. A strong background in psychology and sociology is also helpful.

The best professional preparation for the area of adult fitness is to pursue the training that the exercise physiologist follows. In addition to general education and physical education courses, it is also helpful if other courses could be taken, such as biology of aging, sociology of aging, health and aging, fitness and therapeutic programs for the adult population and elderly, and recreation programs for the adult population. A practical experience that involves working with adults first-hand is also a necessity.

The duties and responsibilities of the specialist in adult fitness varies with the position (see the sections on industrial fitness and exercise physiologist for more details). In general, duties involve helping and advising adults in the assessment of their own physical fitness, prescribing a fitness routine for developing and maintaining physical fitness, providing exercise advice, and supervising and conducting various types of physical activity programs.

The future looks bright for employment in adult fitness programs. An increasing number of employment opportunities exist in programs for the elderly, health clubs, nursing homes, Y's, retirement homes, recreation departments, and other special agencies that serve the adult population. These programs need physical educators trained in special types of exercises and programs for adults.

Industrial fitness

Industrial fitness programs are on the increase. As such, it is being discussed as a separate career area although it also logically fits under the title of adult fitness.

An increasing number of research studies show the advantages of having physically fit employees. The results of these studies indicate that employees who are fit stay on the job longer, rise faster and higher in the firm, seem to think more clearly, get along better with their co-workers, and generally get more out of their jobs.

General qualifications needed by those persons wishing to specialize in this area of physical education should include an understanding of human anatomy and physiology, the ability to diagnose and evaluate cardiovascular disorders and symptoms that would preclude strenuous exercise, the ability to prescribe exercise programs based on individual needs, a knowledge of diet and nutritional factors, the ability to operate testing machines and equipment needed to evaluate an individual's health status, a background in physical education, and a basic understanding of first aid.

Duties and responsibilities include those that have been listed for the exercise physiologist and adult fitness. In addition, the following can be mentioned: informing and motivating employees to be physically fit, including the benefits of regular participation in physical activity programs, providing factual and accurate information as to why the employer is offering the program, working closely with the medical staff, providing a variety of physical activity programs that meet sound physiological and sociological objectives, and conducting periodic evaluations.

Professional preparation should consist of a background in physical education and at least a master's degree in exercise physiology (see the sections on adult fitness and exercise physiology).

Exercise programs, such as the employee fitness programs, can produce desirable physiological as well as psychological changes in those persons who participate actively and regularly. Better physical fitness and the favorable modifications in coronary risk factors should, in theory, lead to less heart disease among employees as well as improve their sense of well-being. Industry recognizes that it is paying a high price for physical inactivity in such forms as compensation, health insurance, and absenteeism. As a result, it is beginning to realize that it must make a commitment to fitness. Therefore, the future for a career in industrial fitness is very encouraging. Big business wants to meet the physical and health needs of its employees, because today, more than ever before, it is good business.

Specialist in physical education for handicapped persons

Laws such as P.L. 94-142 have indicated that society now recognizes its responsibility to educate and provide for handicapped persons. Indeed, physical education as a required educational experience is specifically written into the text of the law. The resulting demand for specially trained physical educators to work with handicapped persons is increasing rapidly. Also, financial support is being provided by the government to train physical education personnel to work with handicapped persons and to conduct research and demonstration projects in this area. Some of the handicaps these persons have include mental retardation, visual impair-

ment, difficulty in hearing, physical disabilities, emotional problems, perceptual-motor learning disabilities, and cerebral palsy.

The qualifications for physical education teachers who wish to work with handicapped persons includes an understanding of the person with the handicap, as well as other handicaps, their causes, and treatment. They should like to work with persons who need special help and should be able to establish a good rapport with them to instill confidence in their work. The physical educator should appreciate the various mental and emotional problems that confront a handicapped person and the methods and procedures that can be followed to cope with these problems. The physical educator must in some ways be a psychologist, creating interest and stimulating motivation toward physical activity for the purpose of improvement. The physical educator should also be sympathetic to the advice of medical personnel. The physical educator must be interested in the medical, psychological, or other examinations of handicapped persons and be interested in working with physicians, psychologists, social workers, or other specialists in developing a program that best meets the needs of the disabled person.

The duties of a physical education teacher who works with handicapped persons depends on the type of handicap and the capacity in which the physical educator serves, that is, as a resource person, teacher, or professor. As an example, some duties of a teacher of mentally retarded persons would include building physical fitness by improving such qualities as strength, muscle tone, and endurance; developing habits of correct body mechanics in motor activities; having the persons experience activities that involve movement of the entire body, developing body awareness, and improving such gross motor skills as running, skipping, throwing, catching, and kicking. Other duties include

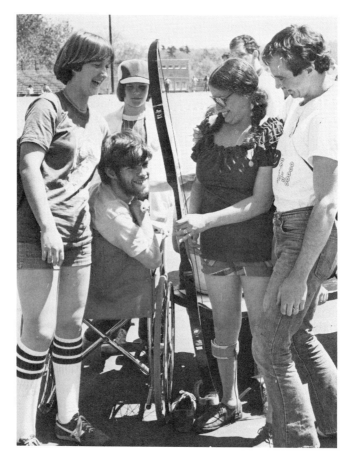

Courtesy Springfield College, Springfield, Mass.

developing skills and coordination to play modified games, supervising participation in a wide range of activities, providing individualized instruction, presenting game concepts, rules, and techniques in a way that the handicapped persons will understand, and seeing that, as far as possible, special equipment is used when needed. Skills should be taught in a slow and repetitious manner that will be helpful to the mentally retarded persons.

The professional preparation of the specialist in physical education for handicapped persons includes an understanding of the philos-ophy of special education and physical education, a knowledge of human growth and development, both normal and abnormal, an acquaintance with specific types of handicapping conditions that affect motor performance, a realization of the contribution that physical activity can make to the total growth and development of handicapped persons, modifying physical education activities to meet the needs of each person, and understanding the trends regarding physical education for handicapped persons. The professional preparation also includes experiences associated with methods of teaching physical education activities for handicapped persons, perceptual motor and physical fitness diagnosis and assessment, behavior management, nature of handicapping conditions or diseases, formulating individualized prescriptions, proper use of special equipment and facilities, psychology of mental retardation and other handicaps, and measurement and evaluation. This specialty also requires many opportunities to work directly with handicapped persons.

There are many employment opportunities for teachers of physical education of handicapped persons, resource specialists, and college professors who train persons to work with the disabled. There are many employment opportunities, not only in schools and colleges, but also in industry and in special organizations that serve persons with specific handicaps, such as blindness and mental retardation.

Teaching in elementary, middle, and secondary schools, colleges, and universities

More than two million men and women teach in private and public institutions and at various educational levels from nursery school to the university. Qualifications for teaching include the desire to work with people, being a scholar, having a sense of humor, and being in good physical and mental health. Physical educators, in particular, need a sound background in the foundational sciences and should possess some degree of motor ability. An undergraduate degree is required as a minimum for teaching at any level, and master's and doctoral degrees are required for teaching at higher educational levels.

Duties for the physical educator vary at each educational level, but most include teaching various types of physical activities, providing movement experiences, imparting knowledge about the human body and the importance of regular physical activity and other desirable health habits, counseling, coaching, research, performing administrative functions, measurement and evaluation duties, and community responsibilities.

Professional preparation of the teacher of physical education in general includes courses in general education, such as English and psychology; studies in the professional foundations, including methods of teaching and the philosophy of education; and concentration in the area of specialization, including such courses as anatomy and physiology and motor learning. Another requirement is student teaching, which enables the student to experience an actual teaching experience before graduating. Some physical educators desire to concentrate in areas of specialization that have already been discussed, such as coaching, athletic administration, and physical education for handicapped persons. In such cases, the professional preparation will, in addition to general physical education requirements, include courses in the area of specialization.

For the person who wishes to teach in a professional preparation program at the college level, graduate work is a requirement. Areas of specialization include the handicapped, motor learning, biomechanics, history and philosophy of physical education, behavioral foundations of sport, and exercise physiology. Persons who wish to teach activity courses and/or coach at the college level can also benefit from graduate work.

The future of the teaching profession depends on one's area of specialization. Faculties are stable in both schools and colleges because of current economic conditions. Teachers and professors are staying in their positions longer, and fewer new faculty members are being hired. Therefore, one should select an area of concentration with care. Although there is always room for an outstanding teacher, the best opportunities at present are physical education for handicapped persons at precollege levels and such specialties as motor learning, exercise physiology, handicapped, and biomechanics at the college level.

SELECTED SETTINGS IN WHICH PHYSICAL EDUCATORS RENDER PROFESSIONAL SERVICES

Physical education and sport programs are conducted in a variety of settings. Some of the more popular settings that will be fertile areas for employment in the 1980s are discussed below.

Educational institutions

Traditionally, schools, colleges, and universities have represented the settings in which the largest number of physical educators sought employment. This fact continues to be true; however, the number of new positions that will be available is limited by the uncertain economic conditions of the country.

Educational institutions include such settings as nursery and elementary schools, middle schools, junior high schools, senior high schools, 2-year and 4-year colleges, and universities. These institutions may be either public or private. Educational institutions have many different types of programs, including physical education activity programs; intramural, extramural, and varsity athletic programs; adapted and/or physical education programs for handicapped persons; and professional preparation programs. These programs offer many different types of physical activities including movement education, aquatics, games of low organization, individual and team sports, dance and rhythmic activities, gymnastics and formal-type activities. Higher education also has professional preparation programs in such areas as motor learning, exercise physiology, biomechanics, administration, and behavioral aspects of sport.

Educational institutions are an important consideration as a setting since more than 60 million Americans are engaged full-time in some aspect of the educational process. There are more than 16,000 school districts, nearly 90,000 elementary and secondary schools, 3000 junior colleges and 4-year colleges and universities in the United States. A college degree is required for employment in most educational institutions. In some cases, particularly at the college and university level, graduate degrees are also required. Most states also have certification requirements for teaching in the public schools.

Industry

An estimated 50,000 industrial firms are engaged in some type of recreational or fitness program for their employees. Why? Because management is recognizing that physical fitness represents a prudent investment in the health, vigor, morale, and longevity of the men and women who are the company's most valuable asset. By helping to prevent heart attacks, disabilities, and premature retirements, fitness programs save money.

Industry has found that there are many benefits derived from industrial fitness programs, including cardiovascular benefits resulting from the modification of primary coronary risk factors (obesity, smoking, and tension) as a result of physical activity. The alleviation of low back pain resulting from muscular deficiency is another benefit. Other benefits that have been found in some studies include better emotional stability, better control of diabetes, reducing the disability associated with some respiratory system disorders, and better control of blood pressure. Other studies have shown that employees have increased work performance, more positive reactions to work, better stamina, feelings of better health, reduced stress and tension, improved self-concept, more adequate sleep and rest, and greater feelings of accomplishment.

Various types of industrial fitness programs exist including those that provide educational programs through seminars, brochures, and other materials; programs using facilities outside the industrial plant that are used by employees on their own time or in which the employer provides the total program including facilities, leadership, medical clearance, and time off for employees to engage in the program.

For any industrial fitness program to be successful, there must be an interested and enthusiastic employer, outstanding leadership, employee education, medical approval, proper objectives that can be met with adequate resources, and a variety of physical activities. The program must also be readily accessible for the employees. Examples of companies that have interesting industrial fitness programs include Boeing, Chase Manhattan, Exxon, Firestone, General Foods, Goodyear, Kimberly-Clark, Pepsico, Texaco, and Xerox.

Health clubs

The health club industry has grown very rapidly during the last 10 years. One estimate places the number of health clubs in the United States between 2500 and 3500. This number is increasing each year. The revelation for many people of the importance of physical activity to optimum health and the desire on their part to have a good body image have contributed to this growth. Businesspersons, housewives, and people from all walks of life are becoming more and more interested in their personal health, and many look to health clubs for help. The exercise machines, swimming pools, attractive surroundings, and other facilities that health clubs frequently provide, plus instructors to supervise physical activity, furnish the opportunity to get this help. Many persons also find it difficult to exercise by themselves.

They prefer to engage in physical activity with other people who have the same fitness goals they do. Most health clubs provide such a setting.

Health clubs have facilities that afford resistive-type exercise and other equipment and services such as treadmills, stationary bicycles, small swimming pools, whirlpools, saunas, steam rooms, cold plunges, oil baths, nurseries for mothers to leave their children, and locker and shower areas. Programs consist of a variety of formal and informal classes and activities, including classes in calisthenics, jogging, nutritional guidance, ballet, and yoga.

A person must be selective when joining a health club because some are "fly-by-night" organizations and are only concerned with making money. Customers are frequently attracted to clubs by misleading advertisements. Men and women are promised results that will never happen and are asked to sign contracts that lock them into an extended period of membership. Some clubs do not have well-trained instructors. Other clubs want instructors who sell memberships as their primary responsibility. They are not as concerned with the instructor's expertise in physical education. Therefore, health clubs should be carefully evaluated to determine those that offer acceptable services, leadership, and programs.

Service organizations

Service organizations, such as the Young Men's Christian Association, Young Women's Christian Association, Young Men's Hebrew Association, Young Women's Hebrew Association, and Catholic Youth Organization, as well as the armed forces, American Red Cross, and settlement and neighborhood houses, are settings in which physical education programs exist. Physical activities normally represent an important part of their programs since they are concerned with the health and physical fitness of their members. The financial support of many of these organizations is achieved through such means as membership dues, United Way drives, and contributions from philanthropic individuals. These organizations commonly have physical educators on their staffs who provide leadership for their physical activity and sport programs.

Many of these organizations have excellent facilities for conducting physical and sport activities including gymnasia, swimming pools, exercise rooms, and play areas. Program activities frequently include bowling, judo, sailing, softball, dance, basketball, floor hockey, gymnastics, arts and crafts, music, teen club, swimming, ceramics, sculpture, and pottery. These organizations also sponsor athletic leagues and contests for various community groups. Programs often provide for preschool, teen, adult, and family memberships.

Youth organizations

Some organizations are focused primarily on young people, including Boys Clubs of America, Girls Clubs of America, Boy Scouts of America, Girl Scouts, American Youth Hostels, Inc., Camp Fire Girls, 4-H Clubs, Future Farmers of America, and Pioneer Youth of America. These organizations provide programs designed to develop qualities in young people that will make them better adults and citizens. They encourage the development of skills and habits that promote such qualities as optimum health, strong character, and the worthy use of leisure time. As a result, physical and other activities constitute an important part of their programs. Some of the activities commonly provided are swimming, basketball, fencing, camping, gymnastics, dance, as well as arts, crafts, drama, singing, trips, photography, and projects associated with various special interest groups. Facilities vary for these organizations from swimming pools, gymnasia, lockers and

showers, library, arts and crafts room, staff meeting rooms, secretarial offices, and camps to a vacant room in a building with limited space that has been provided by some community-minded person.

Government and welfare agencies

There are opportunities for physical educators to render their professional services at all levels of government. At the federal level, the President's Council on Physical Fitness and Sports is an example of a governmental agency that creates opportunities for physical educators to render services through its various sponsored projects. At the state level, departments of education, councils on fitness, sports authorities, and various social agencies frequently employ physical educators. Veterans Administration and other government hospitals utilize services of physical educators in the rehabilitation process for their patients. At the village, county, and city level of government, park, recreation, and conservation departments and agencies utilize professionals to organize their sports, fitness, and game programs. For example, the Parks, Recreation and Conservation Department of Westchester County, New York, has a $6 million budget. Among its various responsibilities are the supervision of five county golf courses, many parks with swimming pools, and athletic programs that involve thousands of participants each month. Summer, fall, winter, and spring athletic, camping, and outdoor education activities involve hundreds of employees on a full-time basis. In addition, many more persons are employed on a part-time basis. Many cities also have recreation programs that have large athletic and other forms of physical activity programs for citizens of all ages.

Physical education and sport organizations

Physical education and sport organizations are another area in which physical educators are employed. Some of these are closely associated with educational institutions. There are national professional physical education and sport associations such as the American Alliance for Health, Physical Education, Recreation and Dance, National Collegiate Athletic Association, and National Federation of State High School Associations (athletic). Some states have their own professional physical education and sport associations with executive secretaries and other personnel on a full- or part-time basis. In some larger cities, professional personnel administer school athletic leagues. At the national level, the United States Olympic Committee is an example of an organization that is not as closely connected with educational institutions, but is expanding so that the United States may successfully compete in international competition.

At the professional sports level, there are highly organized establishments in such sports as baseball, basketball, football, soccer, tennis, and golf. Examples of these organizations are the New York Yankees, Professional Golf Association, and the U.S. Lawn Tennis Association. These organizations need personnel to help in the organization and administration of their vast enterprises. Millions of dollars are involved in the running of professional sports, and trained personnel in the field of athletic administration are needed to carry on the day-to-day operations that are a part of this work.

Centers for elderly persons

Elderly persons constitute a significant segment of our population. In 1980, there were 25 million persons 65 years of age and older. In the year 2000, there will be 32 million, and in 2020, there will be 45 million. They are insisting on such things as lower taxes, better health care, more say in government, and centers that provide physical and social opportunities. As a result, centers

for elderly persons, as well as fitness programs for this segment of the population, are becoming more commonplace throughout the nation.

There is increasing scientific evidence of the importance of physical activity and diet as a means of slowing the aging process. For example, Dr. Harold Elrick, a graduate of the Harvard Medical School and a specialist in metabolic diseases and problems of the aging, has done much research in this field. Based on his research findings, Dr. Elrick, in a report to the United States Sub-Committee on Aging, indicated some of the characteristics and requisites for maintaining one's fitness and mental vigor in later years: (1) daily, prolonged physical activity, (2) diet low in calories and animal (saturated) fats, cholesterol, and salt, and (3) a well-developed, slender musculature. Dr. Elrick also pointed out that elderly persons who engaged in distance running had physical and mental vigor, low incidence of hypertension and cardiovascular disease, and low blood cholesterol, were slender, and possessed a well-developed musculature. He stressed that any body function that is not used continually, mentally or physically, will gradually deteriorate. He also indicated that a well-designed exercise program involving endurance activities is a part of the life-style of long-lived population groups.

David A. Leslie, Director, Teletoes Demonstration Project in Iowa City, Iowa, conducted a study at the senior citizen center in the Oaknoll Retirement Residence. The project was called TOES (The Oaknoll Exercise Society). From this study, it was shown that an exercise program adapted to the needs of elderly persons can result in many physical, mental, and social benefits for the participants. Those persons who were involved felt better, slept better, had fewer aches and pains, and possessed a better self-image. Leslie stressed that trained physical educators were needed to lead these programs if the participants were to achieve the greatest benefit from them.

Elderly persons, whether they live in nursing homes, participate in programs at senior citizen centers, are a part of an organized governmental recreation program, or are provided for in other places, represent a segment of the population to whom physical educators can render professional services in the future.

DISCUSSION QUESTIONS AND EXERCISES

1. What implications does the age of specialization have for the person preparing for a career in physical education?
2. List five areas of specialization within physical education and the qualifications for each.
3. What college courses should be taken by a person desiring to become a specialist in (a) athletic administration, (b) athletic training, and (c) dance education?
4. What is meant by the term *biomechanics?* Where can a person who has specialized in the area of biomechanics find employment?
5. Discuss the various duties performed by a coach. Describe the preparation that a coach should have to perform these duties.
6. Why does the area of exercise physiology offer an attractive employment possibility today?
7. List and discuss some of the reasons why you believe adult physical fitness represents a promising area for specialization today. What professional preparation is needed for one who desires to specialize in this area?
8. Discuss the implications of P.L. 94-142 for physical education for handicapped persons. What qualifications are needed and what duties are performed by a person who works with mentally retarded persons?
9. List and discuss the employment potential for five different settings in which physical educators can render their professional services?
10. What are some of the difficulties concerned with being employed by a health club?
11. Why do elderly persons represent an attractive area of employment in the future?

SELECTED REFERENCES

Broyles, F. J., and Hay, R. D.: Administration of athletic programs—a managerial approach, Englewood Cliffs, N.J., 1979, Prentice-Hall, Inc.

Bucher, C. A.: Administration of physical education and athletic programs, ed. 7, St. Louis, 1979, The C. V. Mosby Co.

Bucher, C. A.: Foundations of physical education, ed. 8, St. Louis, 1979, The C. V. Mosby Co.

Bucher, C. A., and Koenig, C. R.: Methods and materials for secondary school physical education, ed. 5, St. Louis, 1978, The C. V. Mosby Co.

Bucher, C. A., and Thaxton, N. A.: Physical education for children: movement foundations and experiences, New York, 1979, Macmillan Inc.

Drowatzky, J. N.: Motor learning—principles and practices, Minneapolis, 1975, Burgess Publishing Co.

Fait, H. F.: Special physical education—adapted, corrective, developmental, Philadelphia, 1978, W. B. Saunders Co.

Fordham, S. I., and Leaf, C. A.: Physical education and sports—an introduction to alternative careers, New York, 1978, John Wiley & Sons, Inc.

Fox, E. L.: Sports physiology, Philadelphia, 1979, W. B. Saunders Co.

Gallon, A. J.: Coaching—ideas and ideals, Boston, 1974, Houghton Mifflin Co.

Klafs, C. E., and Arnheim, D. D.: Modern principles of athletic training, ed. 5, St. Louis, 1981, The C. V. Mosby Co.

Miller, D. I., and Nelson, R. C.: Biomechanics of sport, Philadelphia, 1973, Lea & Febiger.

Northrip, J. W., Logan, G., and McKinney, W.: Introduction to biomechanic analysis of sport, Dubuque, Iowa, 1979, William C. Brown Co., Publishers.

Sabock, R. J.: The coach, Philadelphia, 1979, W. B. Saunders Co.

Schurr, E. L.: Movement experiences for children, Englewood Cliffs, N.J., 1980, Prentice-Hall, Inc.

Telford, C. W., and Sawrey, J. M.: The exceptional individual, Englewood Cliffs, N.J., 1977, Prentice-Hall Inc.

5 □ The future of physical education and sport

Courtesy Springfield College, Springfield, Mass.

Human beings have always been interested in the future. Toward the beginning of Shakespeare's *Macbeth*, Banquo and Macbeth are engaged in conversation and speculating about what the future holds for them. Banquo says to Macbeth, "If you can look into the seeds of time, and say which grain will grow and which will not, Speak to me . . ." Times have not changed. Today, people are still interested in the future. For example, more than 200 Think Tanks, such as the Rand Corporation and the Hudson Institute, seek to unravel the mysteries of the years ahead.

Why is the future important to most human beings? Dr. Bernard Aaronson and his associates at Princeton attempted to find the answer by using posthypnotic suggestion. He gave each of the subjects the following instructions: "Time is divided into three categories: the past, present, and future. When I wake you, the future will be gone. There will be no future." The results of this experiment were startling. Some of the subjects experienced behavior changes that normally might result after taking a powerful drug such as LSD. They lost their motivations and anxieties. They were discouraged, unhappy, and despondent. Later, Dr. Aaronson, again using hypnosis, indicated to the subjects that there was an expanded future. They not only had the past and the present, but also a tomorrow. The results this time were entirely different. The subjects were happy. They had anticipation. They looked forward to tomorrow. To them, the future represented challenges, opportunities, hope, and fulfillment.

What is going to happen in physical education and sport in the future? How can we predict so that planning can start today? The Chinese proverb says, "To prophesize extremely difficult—especially with respect to the future." Yet, many persons are predicting what will happen in the future. Daniel Bell, Arthur Clarke, Alvin Toffler, Herman Kahn, Edward Cornish, and Stephen Rosen do so by using different methods such as trend extrapolation, scenarios, and expert advice. Some people have been very accurate in their forecasts:

Dateline 1932: Aldous Huxley wrote, in his book, *Brave New World:* "The Director . . . continued with some account of the technique for preserving the excised ovary alive and actively developing . . . actually showed them how the eggs were inspected for abnormalities, counted and transferred to a porous receptacle; how this receptacle was immersed in a warm bouillon containing free-swimming spermatozoa. . . ."

Dateline July 25, 1978: Almost 50 years after Huxley's book came off the press, Louise Brown was born in England—the first test-tube baby, the first child in history to be conceived outside the womb.

Dateline 1945: Arthur C. Clarke, who has written more than 40 works of fiction and nonfiction (*2001: A Space Odyssey*), predicted the establishment of worldwide communication satellites.

Today: Clarke's predictions are a reality as programs are televised to us by satellite from all over the world.

Dateline January 7, 1929: Buck Rogers and his rocket ships were launched as a comic strip that appeared in 38 newspapers across the country. The number quickly jumped to 450. Buck became the hero of a radio series in 1932 and later a television series.

Today: Buck Rogers' new escapades in the 25th century seem much more within the realm of possibility as a result of what our space program has accomplished.

Of course, all prognosticators have not been as accurate in their predictions.

Dateline 1901: Rear Admiral George Melville, Chief Engineer of the U.S. Navy, said, "If God had intended man should fly he would have given him wings. . . . The airship business is a "fake" and has been so since it was started 200 years ago."

Dateline 1903: (2 years after Melville's prediction) the Wright brothers pioneered the first powered, controlled, sustained flight of an airplane.

Dateline 1957: George Romney, former Governor of Michigan and President and Chairman of the Board of American Motors, predicted that in 1980 the Nash Rambler would be the most popular automobile in America.

It should also be noted that some of the predictions people make may be true at the time they are made, but they are not known immediately by the average person. For example, the idea of frozen foods originated in 1908, but frozen foods were not introduced to the public until 1923. Television was conceived in 1884 but was not seen by most consumers until 1947—a time lag of more than half a century.

Although there have been and will be errors in forecasting, it is still very important to try to predict what will happen in the years ahead. Why? Because all of us are going to spend our lives in the future. Why? Because the future to some extent is known and to some extent can be controlled. Why? Because it can affect our beliefs and assumptions. We can anticipate problems. We can plan. Why? Because people shape the future. The Manhattan Project in World War II and the space program in the 1960s show this to be true. Why? Because one of our largest and most successful corporations has found that "Staying a little ahead is the best way to keep up." One scientist has stated that "An important reason for studying the future is not so we can learn what may happen, but rather to help us decide about what kind of a future we want and develop ways to achieve it."

Furthermore, we in physical education and sport should not start too late in our planning. Like the mother who asked a noted educator, "When should I start the education of my youngster?" "How old is your child?" the educator asked. "Five years old," the mother responded. "My God, lady, hurry, rush home, get started right away," came the reply, "you've already lost the best 5 years." If persons in physical education and sport do not become involved in planning for the future soon, they too will have lost some of the best years for accomplishing this task.

Although forecasting the future of physical education and sport is difficult, it is important to try to accomplish this assignment by following Daniel Bell's premise. He indicates that time is not an "overarching leap" from the present to the future. Instead, it has its origins in the past, incorporates the present, and extends into the future. By using imagination and insight, combined with a knowledge of facts concerning the past, present, and what futurists, scientists, and experts predict for the future, it is possible to forecast what will happen in the field of physical education and sport in the years ahead.

A basic assumption that will be used in forecasting future developments in physical education and sport is to recognize that rapid change is characteristic of our way of life. For example, people who are 40 years of age or older have witnessed the entrance of the atomic age, the space age, and the computer age. They have seen more than 80 new nations appear on the face of the globe, the world population doubled, and the gross world product doubled and then redoubled. As C. P. Snow, the British scientist, said, "The rate of change has increased so much that our imagination can't keep up."

Next, recognizing that change is ever present, certain areas can be identified in which change has occurred and is occurring and that lend themselves to a better understanding of future developments in physical education and sport. Three areas that have implications for physical education and sport are (1) the habitable universe, (2) the art of medicine, and (3) conceptualization of the physical dimension of the human body.

THE HABITABLE UNIVERSE

Two elements that relate to a habitable universe are transportation and communication. Each has a bearing on where people live in the universe and how they communicate with each other. Therefore, it is interesting to look at each historically, to see what futurists predict, and, finally, to draw implications for physical education and sport.

Transportation—past and present

Historically, the means of transportation have gradually increased the speed and distance that people can travel. When early human beings wanted to get from one location to another, they walked. They had to depend on their own means of locomotion. If they wanted food, shelter, and protection from the elements they had to depend on their own resources. Then came the invention of the wheel, which led to greater mobility. The adaptation of the wheel to carts, buggies, wagons, and other vehicles increased the range of human mobility. Yet this means of transportation still restricted people to a small geographical area. Most people did not travel far beyond their home and lived their entire lives in the communities in which they were born.

About 200 years ago, the steam engine was invented and eventually resulted in chugging railway trains and paddle wheel steamboats. As a result, people increased their mobility. More recently, buses, automobiles, and airplanes have made travel possible for everyone. Today, modern means of transportation enable us to travel to any part of the world in a matter of hours.

Transportation in the future

Tomorrow the transportation picture will be so improved that today's travel will appear decadent by comparison. The future will see automated highways replacing today's expressways. Cars will be hooked electronically into a buried cable at various highway intersections and fed smoothly into the moving stream of traffic. Hover trains will run along guide rails and attain speeds of up to 300 miles per hour. Commercial hydrofoils will travel 40 knots on top of our waterways. Rosen points out that Dr. Robert Salter, head of physical sciences for the Rand Corporation, envisions a tubecraft system capable of carrying passengers between New York City and Los Angeles in 21 minutes. These vehicles, driven by electromagnetic waves, will travel through deep underground, airless tunnels at nearly 14,000 miles per hour, much as a surfboard rides the ocean waves.

The work of the astronauts has laid the basis for the future in respect to space travel. According to Arthur Clarke, people who are living today will be able to buy a ticket to the moon at a price equivalent to the present round-the-world jet flight. Rockets that launch present systems will be replaced by the space shuttle.

The July, 1976, issue of *National Geographic*, visualizes the outcomes of a serious proposal that was developed by a group of 30 engineers and social and physical scientists. They describe what a typical colony in space will be like. Ten thousand people, their mission to build more colonies, will live under artificial gravity in an encircling tube called a *torus*. The torus is divided into six separate sections each of which has supermarket, farming, and residential areas, and such facilities as theaters, sports arenas, schools, and libraries. Sunlight is filtered and dispersed by means of mirrors that can be tilted to produce an 8-hour night every 24 hours. Farming is very productive as a result of controlled sunlight, an unfailing water supply, ample fertilizer, equable temperature, and a somewhat higher carbon dioxide content in the air. The crop yields are many times what they are on earth.

A second area of the habitable universe that will be an especially exciting place to live in the future is underwater. Since more than two thirds of the planet's surface is covered with ocean, there will be sufficient room to construct many underwater communities. Rosen also indicates how scientist William Backley has developed a submerged capsule equipped with observation ports that is a model for future underwater communities. A superstructure to the capsule has a helicopter landing pad and docking facilities for surface craft. The capsule is held in place by anchors and is made stable by a concrete mat suspended beneath the unit. An airlock and elevator offer easy access either to the ocean floor or to the surface. Backley's work represents a model for the construction of a future underwater colony that will have residential areas, farming, and other facilities comparable to those that will exist in space.

Communications—past and present

The history of personal communications shows that great progress has been made since early times. If early human beings wanted to talk with someone, they walked to where the person was and spoke face to face. Later, messages were sent by code—beating drums, waving flags, and sending smoke signals. As the years passed, the letter, telegraph, and telephone came into use.

Historically, public communication has taken the form of newspapers, books, and lecture tours. Then, in the early 1920s small crystal set radios came into use. At first they used earphones, and then loudspeakers were added. More recently, in the 1940s, television came into use and revolutionized public communications. There are now more than 700 television stations, 73 million black and white television sets, and 54 million color television sets in the country. Television reaches 75% of all the households in America. There are more homes with television sets, according to the April, 1979 issue of *Futurist* magazine, than with toasters, electric coffee makers, or telephones. About 14 million United States households have cable television (20% of the total).

Communications in the future

As in transportation, the changes taking place and that will take place in the future in communications will be dramatic. Kahn, of the Hudson Institute, points out that there will be two-way pocket phones; three-dimensional photographs, movies, and television; and computers that will match, simulate, or surpass many human intellectual abilities, including some aesthetic and creative capacities. Computers will be used as teaching aids with one computer giving simultaneous, individual instruction to hundreds of

students at their own console and topic, at any educational level from elementary to graduate school. Laser beams will be used to reduce the size of data signals submitted, and as a result, an entire library of 20,000 volumes can be stored on an 8 × 10 inch piece of nickel foil. Many magazines, pamphlets, and books will be in the form of small packs of cards that are easy to store.

The magazine, *Changing Times*, predicts two-way television that will enable a person to shop, participate in surveys, do banking, and pay bills without leaving home. There will be telephones equipped with a device that redials numbers automatically after a busy signal. Arthur Clarke indicates that we will be able to do 90% of our business electronically.

According to *Futurist* magazine, television will show great growth in the years ahead. By the year 2000, there will be 2200 television stations in the United States, and large cities will have 15 to 20 channels. Eleven million households, virtually every town with a population of over 2500 persons, as well as many rural areas, will also have cable television. Programs will include many public service programs, educational courses, sports programs, and community debates. Producing programs for syndication will increase greatly.

Television games will be very popular. They are currently available to one million households. By 1982, they will be available to eight million households. This number will grow to 42 million by 1987 and to over 80 million by 2022. Games will be played over cable television and will utilize two-way communications and permit individuals to compete against a computer and/or against human opponents. There will also be many tournaments scheduled in which viewers can test their skills against other players.

As one can readily see, conceptualization of the habitable universe has changed dramatically. It is greatly different from the time of Columbus, when many persons thought the world was flat, to the present day when human beings have landed on the moon, space capsules have landed on distant planets, and Cousteau and others have probed the ocean depths. This conceptualization of the future habitable universe and the rapid changes that are occurring means that education and the professions must prepare human beings for greater mobility and for a different way of life that will be a reality in the future.

Implications of the future habitable universe for physical education and sport

Physical education and sport programs will be provided in new and different settings. Skills and instructional strategies will benefit from technological advances, and home telecommunications will represent a major area of program concentration.

Space colonies and submarine communities will be a reality in the future, probably much sooner than we think. Remember, unleashing the power of the atom took only 4 years, and putting a man on the moon took only 8 years. As such, programs for these new settings in physical education and sport should be on the drafting board now. Meetings should be held with experts in the physical sciences, marine biology, space program, and others so that more will be known about life in space and underwater and the type of programs that will best contribute to such an existence. Conditions that simulate space and underwater living should be established in our laboratories, and experiments should be conducted so that we know what types of activities are most adaptable to such a way of life. Professional conferences should be held concerning the role of physical education and sport in space and underwater. Futurist committees should be appointed, brainstorming sessions should be held; doctoral students should be encouraged to do studies on these new frontiers.

Unrealistic? Farfetched? Too remote? Preposterous? Not at all. Arthur C. Clarke says, "When a distinguished scientist states that something is possible, he is almost certainly right. When he states that something is impossible, he is probably wrong."

As a result of the increased mobility of the population, the range of skills taught will need to be broadened. Human beings will need skills that can be utilized in various locations—in the mountains, deserts, cities, space, underwater, as well as in various parts of the world. A variety of skills should be provided, many more than at present, to provide suitable choices for people wherever they want to live.

Skills will be able to be taught much more scientifically and effectively in the future. In addition to utilizing basic concepts of motor learning, motor development, and biomechanics, such technological advances as more sophisticated computers, video feedback, three-dimensional pictures, television, and robots will be used extensively.

The subject matter of physical education and sport will receive greater emphasis in the future so that human beings can better adapt to the many changes taking place in the universe. The new communications technology will facilitate this task. Computer memory systems, microprocessors, and knowledge retrieval will make it possible for each person to have access to updated research regarding the impact of physical activity on his or her biological, psychological, and sociological welfare.

In educational institutions, computer systems linked with television in a new science called Telematics, will measure students' performance against learning models. Students will be given preliminary tests at computer terminals and then, based on these tests, given assignments to carry out. If the student is successful, further work in the form of problems will be assigned, but if the student does poorly, further assignments will be given. In some cases, the student will be referred to an instructor for coaching. When assignments are completed, the computer will provide feedback to the student. This program will react to each student's work individually, constantly evaluate the student's performance, and provide problems that are needed by the student at various stages in the course.

Physical education and sport will play a prominent role in television in the future. The greatest growth will take place in cable television, which will be available to most households. Physical education will syndicate many programs that will be shown in various parts of the country. These syndicated programs will include clinics that demonstrate the step-by-step approach to developing skill in dance, sport, or physical education activity. Lectures and experiments relating to such areas as exercise physiology will be taped for distribution. Demonstrations of methods by which one's physical fitness can be assessed and various exercise-type programs for conditions such as low-back pain resulting from muscular weakness will be shown. Programs will be directed toward all segments of the population, whether they be children, young people, adults, elderly persons, or handicapped persons.

A major aspect of programming in cable television will be many games and tournaments in which individuals can compete against the computer or against other persons within the system to test their skill or merely to relax and enjoy a leisurely activity. Tournaments will be held periodically in such sports that lend themselves to television. With the growth of communication satellites, there will be international as well as national competitions. Physical education and sport television programming will be conducted by professionals rather than by persons who have little training or understanding of the science of movement and the relation of physical activity to health.

THE ART OF MEDICINE

The art of medicine has changed since early times and continues to change. As a result, physical education and sport will be affected in the future.

The art of medicine—past and present

The art of medicine has changed from early times when sickness was thought to be caused by evil spirits, the help of the gods was solicited, superstition prevailed, and there was reliance on magic, incantation, and guesswork. Human beings have made progress over the years in acquiring and applying scientific knowledge to advance health and lengthen life.

Contagious diseases are being brought under control by drugs and modern medical knowledge. The Black Death that swept across Europe between 1347 and 1361 and killed 3 out of 5 people in the city of Florence, half the population of Italy, two thirds of the students at Oxford University in England, and 25 million people throughout all of Europe, will never occur again.

The United States has benefited from this medical progress. There were 100,000 cases of smallpox in 1921, but in 1972, the U.S. Public Health Service recommended that routine smallpox vaccinations be discontinued because there had not been a case of smallpox in the United States since 1949. In 1954, there were 38,476 cases of poliomyelitis (1368 deaths), but in 1969 no fatalities from polio were recorded. Communicable diseases have been brought under control, but in their place heart disease, cancer, and stroke are the killers.

More than 30 years ago, some doctors wrote books on the benefits of avoiding exercise. Times have changed. Dr. Lawrence Lamb points out that in the past half century, 75% of the presidents of the United States (beginning with Woodrow Wilson and excluding President Kennedy because of assassination) had atherosclerotic (fatty deposits) disease, causing strokes, heart attacks, and death. Lamb blames such deaths on changes in our life-style characterized by horseless carriages, inadequate physical activity, cigarette smoking, and the ingestion of rich food and alcohol. As a result of this changed life-style, Lamb concludes that our fitness level has deteriorated.

The medical profession over the years has done an excellent job in eradicating tuberculosis, pneumonia, scarlet fever, and polio. Now they realize that something must be done if the health of the nation is to be improved. Dr. Kenneth H. Cooper indicated in 1977 that the leading causes of diseases in men and women 35 to 54 years of age were related to such things as obesity, insufficient exercise, alcohol, and diet. The President of the American Medical Association says that 90% of the factors that determine a person's health are related to such things as exercise, diet, smoking, and drinking.

Today there is strong support for the position that a major way to advance the health of the American people will result only from what individuals are willing to do for themselves. The Public Health Services Forward Plan for 1977-1981 stresses that the emphasis in the future should be on preventive medicine. Another fitness expert says, "We are killing ourselves slowly but just as surely as by cancer or crime. The villains are ourselves, our willingness to succumb to the technological advances causing the sedentary lifestyle."

Lamb indicates that fitness is an important aspect of self-help medicine. He says, "The doctor cannot exercise for people. Yet such habits as these have nearly wiped out the wonderful achievements that medicine has made in the past half century." He goes on to paraphrase the late President Kennedy's remarks by saying: "Ask not what your doctor can do for you, but what you can do for yourself."

Norman Cousins, in his book, *The Anatomy of an Illness*, tells how he was at death's door with what his doctors termed a *fatal disease*. He was listed as a "terminal case" and given only a short time to live. However, he was determined to get well. He developed a positive attitude, worked closely with his doctor, and tried every way possible to mobilize his body's natural resources to resist the disease. Gradually he improved and got well primarily from what he claims was the result of his body's own healing powers. As Dr. Schweitzer would say, "He carried his own doctor inside him."

Today the medical profession is interested in self-help medicine. As a result, it is becoming more interested in physical education and sport. An increasing number of psychiatrists, for example, are making exercise and diet basic components of treating problems such as chronic lethargy, mild depression, and pervasive feelings of boredom and frustration. Doctors cite numerous beneficial effects for patients who engage in a strict exercise regimen, including improved sexual performance and less compulsion to any form of gluttony—eating, smoking, or drinking. "People in good condition feel better about themselves. But it's even more than self-image—people whose bodies are in shape have a great sense of well-being," said Dr. Norman Tamarkin, a psychiatrist.

Research conducted by medical personnel supports the need for physical exercise. Dr. Ralph S. Paffenbarger, Jr., professor of epidemiology at Stanford University School of Medicine, reported on his research study. The substance of his report appeared on the front page of the *New York Times*, November 29, 1977. The results show that of the 17,000 individuals studied, those who participated in intense physical activities for at least 3 hours a week and who expended a total of 2000 calories each week through exercise experienced a protective effect against coronary heart disease, a protective effect even if the individual had other characteristics such as high blood pressure or overweight that increase the risk of heart disease.

Dr. Kenneth Cooper and other medical doctors have founded clinics. The Preventive Medicine Institute—Strang Clinic in New York City, world-renowned for its work in cancer, heart disease, and stroke prevention, now has a Health Action Plan for Physical Fitness that includes self-assessment and various types of exercise programs. Institutes of sports medicine and athletic trauma are becoming commonplace and are staffed by medical doctors and physical educators. Industrial physical fitness programs, particularly for executives, are in vogue and are usually under the supervision of medical personnel and have exercise physiologists on their staffs. On the recommendation of some medical doctors, some insurance companies are starting to give discounts to people who do not smoke and who exercise regularly.

The art of medicine in the future

The future will place more and more stress on self-help and preventive medicine. The health of the nation will depend on each individual's willingness to do something about his or her own health. As a result, the life that is saved may be his or her own. Physical education and sport, since they are concerned with providing people with the knowledge, skill, resources, and qualities that contribute to good health, will play an active role, along with the medical profession, in self-help medicine.

Implications of the art of medicine for physical education and sport

Physical education and sport will become more closely associated with the medical profession. Today 90% of the factors that affect a person's health relate to what the individual does for himself or herself. In the fu-

ture, the percentage of factors will be even greater as communicable diseases are further brought under control. A person's health will largely be determined in terms of exercise, diet, smoking, drinking, and other habits that affect an individual's well-being. In light of this development, the medical profession will devote more and more of its efforts to preventive medicine. As this happens, doctors will become increasingly interested in the role that physical education and sport play in preventive medicine. Just as members of the medical profession are presently involved in industrial fitness programs and in sports medicine, their work in the future will involve them increasingly in school, college, agency, and other programs of physical education and sport. Eventually, the medical profession may desire to incorporate physical education into their ranks as a branch of the medical profession.

The formal physical education curriculum in the future will stress knowledge and skill. The stress in physical education and sport will be on preventive self-help medicine, particularly in respect to knowledge and skill. The basic purpose of such programs will be to provide the consumer with a knowledge about the human body and the skills essential to proper movement and participation in various sports and physical education activities. In addition to knowledge and skills, there will be short exploratory courses in various activities simply for the purpose of orienting students as to how knowledge and skills may be applied.

Each person will be responsible for his or her own well-being. By providing the necessary knowledge and skill, education will have fulfilled its primary responsibility. The wherewithal has been provided to enable each person to contribute to his or her own fitness. Whatever physical activity is engaged in will be done mainly on the person's own time. School will be a place to impart knowledge and teach skills, not to engage in physical activity for its own sake. In respect to physical fitness, schools will show ways that it can be assessed, developed, and maintained. However, as far as developing this quality, it will be up to the individual person. The school will periodically evaluate each individual to determine how well the knowledge and skill have been applied. Remedial help will be given when insufficient progress has been made.

The life-styles of most people will change in the years ahead. As scientific studies are continued and their findings reveal the importance of proper health habits, the life-styles of most people will gradually change. The increase in the number of adults who quit smoking, reduce their alcohol consumption, and engage in exercise will be significant.

Although there will be ample amounts of energy over the long term in light of fossil fuels, solar and thermal energy, and nuclear power, the short-term will present problems that are associated with short supply of energy resources. As a result, there will be more and more emphasis on self-energizing activities, such as hiking, swimming, walking, and bicycling. Furthermore, research will indicate how bicycling and other means of transportation provided by one's own muscle power can reach higher speeds and thus be utilized in place of fuel-consuming vehicles.

The emphasis in the future will be on all segments of the population. Children, youth, young adults, and elderly and handicapped persons will have physical education and sport programs in which to participate. To provide for each individual's well-being from the time of birth to the time of death, there will be one director of physical education and sport for the total school-community program. This director will be responsible to a community board that includes representatives from the board of education, medical profession, and other elements of the popu-

lation. It will also provide for better progression in the program of activities. It will involve programs in movement education, intramurals, athletics, as well as all kinds of recreational activities. When an industry is located in a community, employees will also be included. Employees will be given time off during the workday, and all employees will be included in the program. In many cases, industry will subsidize these programs.

There will also be an emphasis on a record system that represents an up-to-date file on each individual's physical education and sport history from birth until death. The computer makes such a record system possible. These records will contain the various physical education and sport activities engaged in, physical fitness test results, physical strengths and weaknesses, skills learned, and other matters that relate to such a history. Such records will help to ensure better progression in the administration of activities, less overlap and repetition in the activities offered, progress that the individual is making in becoming physically educated, and other matters that will help in counseling and guiding each person in the achievement of individual and professional goals.

CONCEPTUALIZATION OF THE PHYSICAL DIMENSION OF THE HUMAN BODY

In many instances, past history does not provide much support for the physical dimension of the human body as something to be optimally developed, respected, nourished, and utilized in the accomplishment of educational goals. Historically, the physical body has been of secondary importance to the mind and the spirit.

Conceptualization of the body—past and present

Even during Greek times, when gymnastics was stressed and the Olympic Games originated, the development of the body was not thought compatible with intellectual growth. In his classic, *The Republic*, Plato indicated that the body has "less of truth and reality" than the soul, and therefore, what serves the body's needs is less true and real than what serves the soul's needs. "Physical culture," Plato argued, "must be kept subordinate to intellectual culture, lest the lower activity obstruct the higher. Worst of all . . . (excessive care of the body) is prejudicial to learning of all kinds and to thought and meditation."

Aristotle said that physical and intellectual education must not be carried on simultaneously. The two different sorts of work tend naturally to produce different and indeed opposite effects. Physical work clogs the mind, and mental work hampers the body.

Asceticism, the doctrine that prevailed during the early Christian era, proclaimed that through self-torture and self-denial a person can be disciplined to reach a high state, spiritually and intellectually. The adherents to this doctrine persecuted the body under the thesis that by such self-mortification the spirit would be strengthened. Indeed, the body was termed a lion chained to the spirit-mind.

The Brawnville Papers, published in Boston in 1869, contained a letter from a disgruntled observer to members of The Athletic Club in his community who planned to include gymnastics for women in their program. Using the Bible as a frame of reference, the writer asks the question: "Where in the Bible can you find the least authority for gymnastics? The Apostle Paul said, "Exercise thyself rather unto Godliness, for bodily exercise profiteth little; but Godliness is profitable unto all things." He went on to indicate that it was a great shame and a scandal that young ladies would be so negligent of propriety to expose their ankles. "The Apostle Paul," he continued, "would not allow women to appear in public with their heads uncovered to say nothing of exposure of their ankles."

Puritanism, a doctrine that was brought to America by the Pilgrims, embraced austerity and frugality and, at the same time, gave free rein to the development of the idea of fear of play.

Kern explains how man's relation to his physical body in the last 150 years is one of the great tragicomedies of social history. He points out how in the nineteenth century the bourgeoisie abhorred the body. "Suddenly, decent people were too good for their bodies; too rational, too prudent, too dignified, too serious. The body was a brute that linked the bourgeoisie to the lower classes, which were hardly better than partially tamed animals. Accordingly, they put the body in a cage: corsets and crinolines for women, cylindrical black tubing for men." The corset, Kern suggests, was not so much a fashion as a form of self-mortification. In the styles of the 1830s, skirts were lengthened to the floor, concealing even the ankle. The body was inundated beneath layers of petticoats, the bonnet covered the head, shawls concealed the upper part of the body, and the wire-framed crinoline hid the rest.

Pleasure was illicit, therefore forbidden to husbands and wives. The bourgeoisie never took off their clothes—even in the conjugal bed. The body was for production—not pleasure.

The turn of the century saw a change in the conceptualization of the physical body as the physical culture movement emerged. It became fashionable to hike, enjoy the fresh air, and bicycle. Around 1900, Isadora Duncan reasoned that the source of all physical movement was located in the solar plexus and not at the base of the spine, as classical ballet had taught. Her "liberated" movements became a symbol of the liberation of the body sought by the advocates of the physical culture movement.

Kern points out how the Nazi physical culture movement, characteristic of Germany's pre–World War I days, was designed to cultivate physical excellence on a national scale. The Hitler Youth and Strength Through Joy organizations stressed, "Your Body Belongs to Your Nation."

The field of art reflected the change in the conceptualization of the body. In the years preceding World War I, the Expressionists depicted nudes in widely exaggerated shapes and positions. After the war, brightly colored and more revealing paintings began to appear.

The literature of the post-war years shows the emancipation of the flesh. As Kern points out, "D. H. Lawrence described the bodies of Connie and Mellors in *Lady Chatterly's Lover* as if he were giving Europeans their first lesson in anatomy."

Interest in the physical body resulted in a more scientific explanation of how disease could be prevented and health achieved. There were major advances in anatomy and physiology, preventive medicine, sanitary laws, nutrition, pharmacology, and disease control. As these developments occurred, life expectancy also increased. For example, Haley points out that the mean life expectancy in 1841 in London was 37 years. Today, in London, it is nearly double that figure.

One corollary of the increased interest in the care and nurture of the human body saw an emphasis on physical education and sport. The American Association for the Advancement of Physical Education, a forerunner of the AAHPERD, was founded in 1885. George Barker, Hartvig Nissen, Amy Morris Homans, Dudley Sargent, Edward Hitchcock, and William Anderson articulated the worth of their field. Gymnasiums were constructed. A normal school for teachers was founded. Tennis, golf and other sports were introduced from abroad. Basketball was invented by James Naismith. There was a crew race between Harvard and Yale. Williams

Courtesy Lincoln University, Jefferson City, Mo.

played Amherst in baseball, Rutgers battled Princeton in football. The number of states that enacted laws regarding physical education increased from 17 in 1919-1921 to 29 in 1930. The number of institutions preparing physical education personnel increased from 20 in 1918 to 139 in 1929.

Today, the body is no longer neglected. Care is taken to determine how it can best be preserved, be most productive, and give the most pleasure. Clothes are revealing to display the beauty of the human form. Education is giving it a higher priority. The body is no longer considered evil. Play is no longer considered a sin.

Sports play an important role in society today. According to the President's Council on Physical Fitness and Sports, millions of young people and adults are engaged in sports. Athletic participation by girls alone is over 2 million. Since 1970, the number of girls participating in interscholastic athletic programs has increased by 600%.

Current interest in the human body, physical fitness, and physical education and sport has led to the creation of specialties within physical education such as exercise physiology, anatomy, biomechanics, dance, motor learning, motor development, sports psychology, and sports sociology. These specialties are striving to be recognized for their expertise. As such, some have their own professional associations, meetings, and professional journals.

There is much interest in fitness today. As a result of this interest, physical fitness is becoming a multimillion dollar business. Entrepreneurs associated with health spas, exercise salons, and weight-reducing clinics are invading the field of physical education. Thousands of charlatans proclaim they have the secrets to good health, physical fitness, skill, and movement analysis and development.

Conceptualization of the body in the future

There has been a dramatic change in the conceptualization of the human body since the days of asceticism, puritanism, and the bourgeois attitude of the Victorian era. However, the future will provide even more dramatic changes. The body will continue to be the focus of attention of the medical profession, physical educators, and businesspersons. The body will be recognized as one of the strongest forces in the world. More and more the need for self-help medicine will be recognized. More and more it will affect the economy through such extensions of the body as clothes, cosmetics, and jewelry and the desire of people to have a desirable physical self-image. It will affect how additional hours of leisure will be spent, particularly in respect to the need for activities in which the body is used as a vehicle of expression. It will play a more important role in helping human beings possess sound mental, physical, and social health. It will affect education as the public appreciates and better understands that a neglect of the well-being of the body will endanger the well-being of the mind.

The publication, *Planting Seeds for the Future*, indicates that technology will gradually enable people to live longer, eventually for 200 years or more, and thus create a whole new world of healthy, hearty Methuselahs. This increased life span will be made possible as researchers uncover the secrets to longevity. Body organs will be replaced, including the use of the bionic heart, deactivated genes will be switched back on to renew cell tissue, destructive cellular garbage produced by the body or lipofuscin build-up will be prevented, diet will be controlled, prosthetics and cyborgs will bring the $6 million man closer to reality, and lowering body temperature will add many years to human life.

Kahn and Wiener predict that simple techniques will be developed that will affect one's appearance, body build, and physical fitness. Extensive and permanent cosmetological changes including physique, complexion, and skin color will take place, and there will be new techniques for keeping physically fit and acquiring physical skills.

Rosen indicates that scientists have found that human behavior seems to be affected by the combined influence of three internal biological clocks or rhythms. The three types of cycles are physical, emotional, and intellectual. These cycles can be traced from high to low points at various periods during a person's life. The physical cycle runs for 23 days and determines strength and physical capabilities. The emotional cycle runs for 28 days, and the intellectual or mental cycle runs for 33 days. Results of a study by behavior researcher Hans Schwing suggests that subjects are prone to accidents and are low on good common sense when the physical and emotional cycles reach zero days or neutral points. Lows and highs are not dangerous but are days of stress and attentiveness, when a cycle is changing direction.

Toffler points out that rapid change and new techniques will create many health problems in the future. Since the pace of a person's life is closely related to health, since change requires considerable adjustment, and since there are limits to adaptability, health problems will occur. Among these problems will be that excessive activation of the endocrine system will lead to wear and tear on the human organism.

The conceptualization of the human body has changed markedly from early times and it will change even more in the future. Instead of mind-body dualism, the unity of the two has been recognized and steps are being taken to develop both to their fullest potential. Instead of advocating self-mortification the emphasis is on self-nurture. Medical attention is focused on the conditions necessary to prevent disease rather than on the disease itself. Instead of the body being a brute, it is now a pet. Instead of play being a sin, it is increasingly becoming a part of everyone's life-style.

Implications for physical education and sport

Physical education and sport will gain much support in the future from the increased interest in the human body. The scientific knowledge gained from the research suggests that the ingredients and care needed to maintain the organic system will result in a greater emphasis on programs and activities with which physical education and sport are concerned. The stress on self-help preventive medicine will link us more closely with the medical profession. School and community programs will be interwoven to bet-

ter serve the entire population. The stress on fitness will continue, the life span of human beings will increase, and there will be more leisure, all of which will provide an added boost to these fields. Physical education and sport will become an important part of the life-styles of people everywhere as well as a more important part of education. Specialization within physical education and sport will continue to prevail.

Physical education and sport in the future will establish jurisdiction over its own domain. Physical educators will be recognized for their expertise and become the publicly recognized leaders in their field. They will achieve this recognition by providing themselves with the proper credentials—credentials that separate them from the intruder, the quack, and the imposter. The proper credentials are in the form of a systematic, organized knowledge base—a scientific rationale that describes the worth of their field and the unique service they provide. This knowledge base:

1. Supports the art and science of human movement as it relates to sport, dance, play, and exercise
2. Synthesizes the various subdisciplines, such as exercise physiology, into a unified discipline that relates to our programs as an integral whole, rather than in a piecemeal, unorganized, insignificant, and haphazard pattern
3. Documents the fact that sport, dance, play, and exercise foster human growth and development
4. Leaves no doubt in the public's mind that the kinesthetic sense can influence cognitive and affective behaviors in addition to motor behavior
5. Shows that a better human being will result by developing a proper relationship of body, senses, mind, and spirit

Sports will take on some new dimensions in the future. Since the American people like excellence in performance, professional sports will continue to grow rapidly in the years ahead. The economic rewards in terms of the sales of supplies and equipment, gate receipts, and television advertising will also provide the catalyst for this growth. This growth of professional sports will result in less spectator interest in high school sports as more and more professional sports events are televised. College sports will continue to thrive since it represents a recruiting ground for the professionals. Professional leagues for women will be created in most of the major spectator sports. In some cases, there will be coeducational professional sports competition. New and modern facilities will make it possible for sport contests to be conducted under the most optimum conditions. Conditions such as those that occurred in the 1979 World Series between Pittsburgh and Baltimore, when it was 30 degrees and rainy, will not occur. Climate will be controlled, and games will be held under a translucent dome. Players will be selected scientifically. As part of this selection process, biological rhythms of players will be recorded to determine who should be on the starting team on a particular day. As a result, many injuries will be eliminated as well as better performance assured. Also, participants will know that losing often results from having fewer capabilities on certain days than others.

The future will continue to accent specialization as physical education and sport become fragmented into many specialties and subcultures. Exercise physiologists, motor learning experts, sport psychologists and sociologists, and those who specialize in biomechanics and other areas will try to separate themselves from the rank and file of general physical educators and coaches. Each will have its own professional association that will grow in number. Each will hold its own professional conferences. Each will strive to be recognized for its own worth. Each will meet periodically and have its own publications. Instead of being known as physical educators, each will constitute a separate profession such as the profession of exercise physiology or the profession of sport sociology. To retain its membership in light of this development, the AAHPERD will find it necessary to provide many additional services and exposure that these subcultures can see and recognize as helping them to grow and prosper. The present structure of an alliance will fill short-term needs, but eventually, unless the structure is changed, people in these specialties will leave the parent organization.

DISCUSSION QUESTIONS AND EXERCISES

1. Why is the future important to human beings? Why is planning for the future important?
2. What evidence is there to show that the future can be shaped by human beings?
3. Explain the meaning of the statement, "The future has its origins in the past, incorporates the present, and extends into the future."
4. Discuss five examples in which change is characteristic of today's way of life.
5. Outline the history of transportation together with future prospects and the implications it has for physical education and sport.
6. How can sophisticated computers and television improve the teaching of physical skills?
7. Prepare a list of programs involving physical education and sport that could be syndicated and shown on cable television.
8. What is meant by self-help medicine? Why has this concept developed? What implications does it have for physical education now and in the future?
9. How has the concept of the physical dimension of the human body changed from ancient times until the present?
10. What are some predictions for the future in respect to physical education and sport?
11. Describe the unique service that physical education should render in the future based on self-help medicine.
12. How can physical education establish jurisdiction over its own domain?

SELECTED REFERENCES

"The best is yet to come," Time 114:27, July 16, 1979.

Branley, F. M.: Energy for the 21st century, New York, 1975, Thomas Y. Crowell Co.

Bucher, C. A.: Administration of physical education and athletic programs, ed. 7, St. Louis, 1979, The C. V. Mosby Co.

Bucher, C. A.: Foundations of physical education, ed. 8, St. Louis, 1979, The C. V. Mosby Co.

Cornish, E. S.: Planting seeds for the future. Prepared for Champion International Corporation, Stamford, Conn., by the World Future Society, 1979.

Edson, L.: The search for a bionic heart, New York Times Magazine, October 21, 1979.

"The forecasting mind," Futurist, June 1979.

"Forecasting your lifestyle," Science Digest, October, 1977.

"George Orwell's vision of the future—pro and con," Futurist, April 1979.

Haley, B.: The healthy body and Victorian culture, Cambridge, Mass., 1948, Harvard University Press.

"Home telecommunications in the 1980s," Futurist, June 1979.

Huxley, A.: Brave new world, New York, 1932, Modern Library.

Kahn, H.: The next 200 years, New York, 1976, William Morrow & Co., Inc.

Kahn, H., and Wiener, A.: The year 2000, New York, 1967, Macmillan Inc.

Kern, S.: Anatomy and destiny, Indianapolis, 1976, The Bobbs-Merrill Co., Inc.

Lamb, L. E.: Fitness: the hidden health factor. Speech presented at the President's National Conference on Physical Fitness in Business and Industry, October 5, 1972, Washington, D.C.

"The 1980s—problems, promises, and surprises," Changing Times 33, January 1979.

"Now the '80s," Newsweek, November 19, 1979.

Rosen, S.: Future facts, New York, 1976, Simon & Schuster, Inc.

Rostow, W. W.: Getting from here to there, New York, 1978, McGraw-Hill Book Co.

Toffler, A.: Future shock, New York, 1970, Random House, Inc.

Watson, J. W.: Living together in tomorrow's world, New York, 1976, Abelard-Schuman.

Welsh, R., editor: Physical education—a view toward the future, St. Louis, 1977, The C. V. Mosby Co.

Part two

GUIDELINES FOR
PROFESSIONAL GROWTH

6 □ Developing a sound philosophy of physical education and sport

Courtesy Springfield College, Springfield, Mass.

Prospective physical educators may wonder whether or not philosophy can help in such practical matters as conducting a program or coaching a team. For example, can philosophy help a person to determine what the objectives of the program should be, what activities to offer, or what teaching methods to use? Can it help the coach select the proper offensive or defensive strategy? Can it aid in the selection of rules and regulations? Some physical educators with little or no experience might answer "No" to these questions, concluding that philosophy is for "scholars" in their ivory towers of learning. Others, with many years of service, may believe that the experience they have acquired over the years will suffice in guiding them in the conduct of their programs or in the coaching of their teams.

Those physical educators who do not believe that a well-thought-through philosophy is important are not justified in their thinking and attitude. This belief is based on the observation of programs conducted by individuals who are not guided by a sound philosophy of physical education. Such programs are frequently characterized by a lack of purpose, duplication of activities from year to year, and improper teaching methods.

A sound philosophy of physical education does not in itself ensure an effective physical education program. It does, however, provide proper guidance for those physical educators who have the necessary education and technical training. Preliminary to having a sound philosophy of physical education, the effective physical educator will first have developed a sound philosophy of life and education.

WHAT IS PHILOSOPHY?

Philosophy has been defined as a "search for a comprehensive view of nature, an attempt at a universal explanation of the nature of things"[1] and as "that branch and method of human inquiry that is concerned with the triadic relationship of ontology, epistemology, and axiology, or, in simpler, but not so comprehensive terms, reality, truth, and value."[2]

Philosophy is defined in this text as an area of systematic study that seeks to help people to better understand themselves in relationship to their universe and is a logical and introspective method of searching for truth, reality, goodness, and beauty. As such, philosophy gives a person a logical basis for actions and provides guidance and direction for making personal and professional decisions.

ALTERNATIVES TO PHILOSOPHY

According to Hansen,* some individuals who question the need for philosophy insist that the scientific method, as well as other modes of inquiry, will prove just as effective in providing guidance for effective action. A brief examination of some of these other modes of inquiry will serve to underscore the importance of philosophy.

Belief

To some people, a strong belief constitutes an adequate philosophy. One often hears individuals say with conviction, "I believe that everyone who really wants to work can get a job." Oftentimes, this statement is made without the realization that some people really want to work, but because of the realities of the economic situation, cannot find a job. The statement that is based on mere belief without supporting evidence or logical reasoning usually tends to be supportive of existing prejudices. This is the most unreliable kind of statement and does not offer real guidance for action.

Common sense

Those persons who govern their lives and actions by the common sense approach are simply extending their failure to act on the basis of such aspects of philosophy as rational inquiry and intellectual reflection. Human beings should use their intellectual capacities to think through the solution to problems, rather than rely on common sense. To use common sense as a basis for selecting physical education activities, for example, is untenable. This common sense approach does not include systematic, rational, logical, and creative thinking that underlies the philosophic approach.

1. Weber, A.: History of philosophy, New York, 1925, Charles Scribner's Sons, p. 3.
2. Hansen, K. H.: Philosophy for American education, Englewood Cliffs, N.J., 1960, Prentice-Hall, Inc., p. 97.

*These alternatives to philosophy were borrowed from Kenneth H. Hansen (see Selected References [Chapter 6]).

Logic

Decision making that is based on logic is a very attractive alternative to philosophy according to some persons. Even though logic is a division of philosophy and offers one means of rational thinking, it is simply a technique and is much too narrow to use as the total basis for making decisions. For instance, a person might develop a logical reason why every student should participate in athletics. However, the philosopher, as a result of rational inquiry, might question the value of athletics for all students. It might be discovered that some students might have other more important needs than participation in athletics. Logic must be used in conjunction with the total field of philosophy rather than as a mode of inquiry in itself.

Scientific inquiry

The scientific method is considered by some to be the ultimate method of inquiry when attempting to solve problems or uncover truths. The scientific method is a viable mode of inquiry, since it is characterized by such rigorous processes as carefully defining a problem, becoming familiar with all knowledge related to the problem, controlling and analyzing the variables associated with the problem, and reaching a valid conclusion based on the results of a careful and thorough analysis of the data. However, philosophy is needed to help determine the ultimate use that is to be made of scientific discoveries. Henderson stressed the need for the use of both science and philosophy in education more than 30 years ago when she reasoned that "the science of education is needed to discover the best means and techniques for achieving the goals which philosophy of education has helped us to see as our objective."[3] Dewey spoke of the interrelatedness of science and philosophy from a standpoint of values. When science is used, according to Dewey, and action based on that use occurs, some value judgments must be made. He concluded that in these instances "there are . . . philosophical implications, since philosophy is a theory of values to be achieved and to be rejected."[4]

THE NEED TO HAVE A PHILOSOPHY

Individuals in today's complex, materialistic, technological, and highly mechanized society are faced with many difficult problems and decisions. A philosophical approach to solving these problems and reaching rational decisions will be helpful. Philosophy provides individuals with a rational basis for examining the universe and society and their place in it. It evaluates the actions of human beings in light of ethical and moral values. Philosophy seeks to determine the truth. It provides a continuing search for the essence of existence. Philosophy seeks to provide solutions to these and other problems.

The major concerns of philosophy can be summarized in the following three questions: What is reality? What is truth? What is of value? Philosophy serves to guide individuals in their search for reality, truth, and value. Statements by Dewey and Hansen pinpoint the role and importance of philosophy. Dewey observed:

Philosophy is not a special road to something alien to ordinary beliefs, knowledge, action, enjoyment, and suffering. It is rather a criticism, a critical viewing, of just these familiar things. It differs from other criticism only in trying to carry it further and to pursue it methodically. . . . Men thought before there was logic, and they judged right and wrong, good and evil, before there was ethics. Before there was ever anything termed metaphysics men were familiar with distinctions

3. Henderson, S. V. P.: Introduction to philosophy of education, Chicago, 1947, The University of Chicago Press, p. 17.

4. Dewey, J., and Childs, J. L.: The underlying philosophy of education. In Kilpatrick, W. H., editor: The educational frontier, New York, 1933, D. Appleton-Century Co., p. 289.

of the real and unreal in experience, with the fact that processes whether of physical or human nature have results, and that expected and desired results often do not happen because some process has its path crossed by some other course of events. But there is confusion and conflict, ambiguity and inconsistency, in our experience of familiar objects and in our beliefs and aspirations relating to them. As soon as any one strives to introduce definiteness, clarity, and order on any broad scale, he enters the road that leads to philosophy.[5]

Hansen has indicated the unique features of philosophical inquiry with this statement:

. . . It should be apparent that the methods of philosophy are not really so much different from the methods of other kinds of inquiry and thinking except that they are perhaps broader in their scope, deeper in their probing, more searching in their self-criticism, and productive of a greater degree of personal commitment to a course of action.[2(p. 10)]

DIVISIONS OF PHILOSOPHY

Philosophers have devised various divisions of philosophy to examine questions related to reality, truth, and value. Metaphysics, epistemology, and axiology are the three main divisions of philosophy. Logic, a separate philosophical science, deals with questions relating to the nature and forms of valid reasoning. Since it deals with knowledge and reasoning, logic will be included under the main division of epistemology.

Metaphysics

Metaphysics is concerned with the nature and structure of reality. Questions in metaphysics might be cosmological, dealing with the cosmos or universe; ontological, related to the nature of existence; or theological, re-

lated to the nature and existence of God. The following are questions that would be in the province of metaphysics: What is the ultimate nature of being or existence? What is real? What is the nature of God? Is there a single substance of which all things are composed? Is there a natural order to the universe?

Epistemology

Being concerned with the search for ultimate knowledge, epistemology examines the nature of knowledge itself. To search for this knowledge, four questions present themselves: (1) What is the source of knowledge? (2) What is the standard for evaluating such knowledge? (3) What is the relation between ideas and things? (4) What are the forms of valid reasoning? The first three questions are the province of epistemology, and the last question is dealt with by logic.

Axiology

Axiology is the division of philosophy through which philosophers consider the ultimate worth of things. The three ultimate values are truth, goodness, and beauty. Axiology technically deals only with truth, but through ethics (a subdivision of axiology), problems of the good life are examined, and through aesthetics (another subdivision of axiology), the nature of beauty is examined. Axiology seeks to discover the truth about all three of the ultimate values if this philosophic province is viewed in its broadest connotation. In essence, axiology seeks to determine the true purposes of a people in a particular society.

THE IMPORTANCE OF A WELL-THOUGHT-THROUGH PHILOSOPHY OF PHYSICAL EDUCATION AND SPORT

A well-thought-through philosophy of physical education and sport is important for the following reasons.

5. Dewey, J., quoted by Winn, R. B., editor: John Dewey: dictionary of education, New York, 1959, Philosophical Library, Inc., pp. 100-101.

Explains the worth of physical education and sport

Philosophy is a process through which individuals search for truths, reality, and values. Through philosophy, physical educators are able to study the meaning, nature, importance, and source of values in physical education. Philosophy guides the physical educator in determining the aims, objectives, principles, and content of physical education and provides a logical means of determining whether physical education is providing worthwhile services in the education of human beings.

Provides a guide for one's actions and decisions

To plan and conduct a program intelligently, a clear idea of what one is planning for and the best methods of achieving these objectives are needed. Another requisite is a sound value system to have some basis for actions. A well-thought-through philosophy provides the necessary guidance and direction of one's actions and decisions by seeking to find answers in a logical manner to questions related to program objectives, content, and methods of operation.

Leads to improvement of educational practices

When educational practices are based on intuition, common sense, or emotional whim and fancy, they are not sound. However, when educational practices are based on a well-thought-through philosophy, they are much more likely to be correct and functional. This is especially true if physical educators develop their philosophies in a rational, logical, and systematic manner and if they represent the best interests of all human beings. Such a process will enable physical educators to assemble scientific facts and apply workable theories to support their decisions regarding aims and objectives of the pro-

gram, activities, instructional strategies, and the like.

Provides a basis for relating physical education to general education

Since philosophy determines ends as well as the means to achieve ends, it provides direction and guidance in establishing objectives and determining outcomes based on sound principles and values. Philosophy can also act to explain the relationship between physical education and education in general. For instance, one of the goals of general education is to develop the total person—physically, mentally, socially, and emotionally. A philosophy of physical education that espouses the "holistic" concept of development also aims to develop the total person. By relating the philosophy of physical education to that of general education, the education of all students will be enhanced.

It is very important for physical educators to develop programs whose goals are consistent with those of general education. These programs must be based on sound principles and logical reasoning and guided by a sound value system. With such a philosophical underpinning, programs of physical education will complement programs of general education in providing for the optimal development of human beings.

Provides a means of professional growth and development

Philosophy is validated by experimentation and scientific inquiry. One's philosophy of physical education should be based on scientific information and principles. Such a process leads one to continually study, reflect, and reason logically. Therefore, one grows both professionally and personally. Philosophy is inextricably associated with scholarship. Bookwalter states that excellence in scholarship will lead to a more acceptable philosophy, and a sounder philosophy will reveal problems and uncover gaps in the field of learning.[6] Intellectual curiosity will be stimulated by the realization of problems and gaps in knowledge, and such curiosity will result in inquiry in the form of research. When facts and new knowledge are arrived at through the scientific process, problems are solved and the gaps leading to greater knowledge and better understanding are filled. The improved scholarship helps to validate and clarify philosophy. The search for a sound and validated philosophy embraces scholarship and thus increases personal and professional growth and development in the process. It is a never-ending process of investigation, discovery, change and/ or modification, and adaptation to new situations and information.

SCHOOLS OF PHILOSOPHY

At various times throughout history, different schools of philosophical thought have been evident. A total of five philosophical positions are discussed below. The first four are classified as traditional philosophies (idealism, realism, naturalism, and pragmatism) and the fifth, existentialism, is labeled as a contemporary philosophy.

Idealism

The philosophy of idealism has a long history. The Greek philosopher Plato is considered to be the father of idealism. He expounded some of the key concepts of idealism over 2000 years ago. Other major adherents of idealism have been Aristotle, John Locke, Immanuel Kant, and George W. F. Hegal. Charles H. McCloy and Mable Lee are physical educators who have espoused idealist concepts.

Idealists believe that the "idea" of a thing and not the thing itself signifies ultimate real-

ity. The mind is the most important faculty in understanding the real world. They place great stress on reason and the scientific method in seeking knowledge of the universe. Although idealists place great importance on the mind, they do not overlook the importance of a person's spiritual development. Idealists think that reality is spiritual rather than physical.

Believing strongly in the powers of the mind, the idealist insists that true knowledge consists of universals or ideals that are eternal and purposeful. This truth or knowledge is discovered by an individual through thought processes, including intuition and insight as well as rational thought. Truth remains the same even though human beings change. Truth should be used for the purpose of developing the individual.

Values, to the idealist, are eternal and are interpreted by people as a function of ideas through their intellectual powers. By being able to exercise free will, individuals can choose between such values as good or evil, right or wrong, love or hate, and freedom or restraint. Since human beings are fallible and have the power to rationally distinguish between various alternatives regarding values, they may incorrectly interpret such values. According to idealists, however, the values themselves do not change.

The overall objective of idealist physical educators is to develop the ideal person. Such a person would be nurtured through the use of the mind and the exercise of creative powers for reasoning and reflective thinking. This person would be intelligent, totally fit, spiritually secure, and morally strong. In other words, objectives would be selected that would aid in the development of the total person. The curriculum would consist of activities and experiences to achieve these objectives. Furthermore, the curriculum would be "idea" centered. The teacher would use a variety of teaching methods including the traditional method (in

---

6. Bookwalter, K. W.: This matter of promotion, 67th Proceedings of the National College Physical Education Association for Men, Washington, D.C., January 1964, American Association for Health, Physical Education and Recreation, pp. 1-5.

which demonstration of the ideal would be stressed), student projects, discussion periods, and individual demonstrations by students. The method or methods that would help students to reach their full potential would be used.

Realism

Realism, like idealism, has its roots in Greek tradition and thought. Some of the concepts of realism were a direct revolt against certain tenets of idealism. Some of the philosophers who were associated with idealism were also those who helped to shape realism. For instance, Aristotle was identified with idealism, but he is also considered the father of realism. Some of the basic thoughts of Aristotle were in conflict with those of his great teacher, Plato. One example of this difference in thought is the belief of Plato that change is unintelligible because it is chaotic, whereas Aristotle finds order—especially direction—in change.

Other major adherents of realism have been St. Thomas Aquinas, René Descartes, Benedict Spinoza, John Locke, Immanuel Kant, Johann Herbert, Bertrand Russell, Alfred North Whitehead, George Santayana, and William James.

It should be indicated from the outset that there are several subdivisions of realism. Two of the most prominent are rational realism and natural or scientific realism. This section will not discuss the specific differences of each subdivision, but rather will focus on the main concepts of most realist philosophers. Modern realism, it should be reemphasized, is a revolt against certain aspects of idealism.

Realists believe that true reality exists in the natural laws of the universe or physical world and does not depend on the human mind for its existence. For human beings to exist to the fullest, according to realists, they must seek to understand and live by the laws of the natural world.

To the realist, truth or ultimate knowledge is obtained through the scientific method and other objective means. Subjective methods of searching for truth, including personal and emotional approaches, are not accepted as proper. While human beings may be able to think and reason about things in the real world, what they think must be in accordance with reality or such thought will be illusory.

Realists are similar to idealists in their view that values are permanent. Unlike idealists, however, realists believe that something is good or right only if it corresponds to the laws of the natural world; if it does not conform to the natural laws that determine reality, it is wrong.

The traditional objectives of physical fitness, neuromuscular skill development, organic development, and social development are sought by those who espouse the philosophy of realism. The ultimate objective or aim is to provide those activities and experiences that will enable students to understand and adjust to the immutable laws of the real, physical world. The curriculum of realist physical educators would be scientific—an emphasis on progression, with subject matter sequentially arranged and activities based on valid principles—and would be taught in a scientific manner. Required courses would abound in this type of curriculum. The traditional method of explanation and demonstration by the teacher and practice by students would be used by realist physical educators. They would use drills extensively and would teach skills that have been determined to be correct by the scientific method and proved useful through philosophical inquiry.

Naturalism

Naturalism is the oldest philosophy as far as the history of philosophy in the western world is concerned. Thales, who lived during the early part of the sixth century B.C., is considered the father of naturalism. Other major adherents of naturalism are Leucippus, Epicurus, Lucretius, and Democritus of the ancient world and Thomas Hobbes, Jean Jacques Rousseau, Herbert Spencer, Alfred North Whitehead, and George Santayana of more modern times.

It is interesting that Butler, a philosopher of education, would not classify Rousseau as a naturalist because of his deistic metaphysical beliefs. However, Butler included Rousseau in his list of naturalistic philosophers because "while his metaphysical beliefs were not naturalistic, his glorification of Nature has had the effect of promoting naturalism, particularly in politics and education."[7] Rousseau fashioned most of his ideas about naturalism in his treatise on the proper education of Emile.

Naturalism contains many of the ideas and concepts of realism and pragmatism. Some books omit a discussion of naturalism as such and include the key concepts of this philosophy under the rubric of realism. Naturalists believe that true reality is found in nature. The physical world, with all its material things, is sufficient for human beings to find ultimate reality. Scientific methods are considered the best means of discovering truth about the knowledge of nature. Religious truths are also derived from nature, according to the naturalists. For Rousseau, in fact, nature was his God. The philosophy of naturalism holds that nature is the source of everything of value; no values can exist outside of nature.

The overall objective of naturalist educators is to help students learn to adapt to the natural laws of the universe. Such general objectives as self-realization, social development, physical and skill development, and

7. Butler, J. D.: Four philosophies and their practice in education and religion, New York, 1968, Harper & Row, Publishers, p. 62.

mental development are important objectives for naturalists.

The physical education curriculum is designed to encourage free exploration on the part of the students. Activities would be offered that coincide with the growth and development of each student. Therefore, the curriculum would stress progression and sequential development of activities. Furthermore, activities would be selected that foster natural movements in students. Gymnastics, dance, and free play activities would predominate. Outdoor education such as orienteering and individual challenge-type activities such as those in Outward Bound programs would be stressed by naturalists. The physical educator would act as a guide and facilitator in helping students to develop their inborn talents. The problem-solving methods of movement education would be used as the teaching approach. Students would be helped to develop their powers of inductive reasoning in solving problems. All teaching procedures must be in accordance with the laws of growth and development in programs conducted by naturalists.

Pragmatism

Pragmatism is a modern philosophy and, more specifically, a modern American philosophy. However, it has its roots in ancient philosophy. The earliest appearances of beliefs found in the pragmatism of today occurred in the teachings of Heraclitus. Other pragmatists include Francis Bacon, Auguste Compte, and the American philosophers Charles Pierce, William James, and John Dewey.

Experience and change are two key words in pragmatic philosophy. Reality for pragmatists is the knowledge that something works in practice. In Burke's words "experience is the master criterion, the source of truth, the only reality; all else is unknown and unknowable."[8] Since experience varies from person to person and constantly changes, reality must be considered as ever-changing by pragmatists.

From the foregoing statements about experience being the ultimate reality for pragmatists, it is obvious that pragmatists also express the notion that knowledge is discovered through experience. To the pragmatist, truth is transient; it changes as new knowledge is discovered through experience. Whatever proposed solution to a problem that works in a given situation is considered to be right or true at that moment. A pragmatist considers the scientific method the best means of obtaining knowledge in the search for truth.

According to pragmatists, values, like truth, change with experience. Values are created by human beings through meaningful actions and the examination of their experience. Something is considered good, for example, if it is successful in practice. Pragmatists believe in the democratic process in determining value systems. They would contend that a practice is bad and would eschew it if it were unsuccessful in group practice.

To help students solve the problems of life as they presently exist is the ultimate aim of the pragmatic educator. A very important objective of pragmatic physical educators in helping to achieve this aim is the development of social efficiency in students. They are very concerned with aiding students in their ability to get along with one another in group situations. Other objectives of pragmatic physical educators are teaching problem-solving skills, developing creativity, and teaching the "why" of physical education.

The curriculum would consist of activities and experiences to aid the students in preparation as members of society. Team sports that stress cooperation and social adjustment would be emphasized by pragmatic physical educators. Activities such as dance, outdoor experiences including camping, boating, mountain climbing, rappelling, orienteering, fishing, and some individual and dual sports would also be a part of the curriculum. The teacher would act as a guide and would use the problem-solving approach to achieve the objectives of the program. Through movement education methods, students are encouraged to think and arrive at their own solutions to problems. The ability to apply these solutions to everyday living is the essence of pragmatic philosophy.

Existentialism

There is no question about existentialism being a modern philosophy. However, there is disagreement regarding its beginning. Some maintain that modern existentialism began with the nineteenth century theologian and philosopher, Soren Kierkegaard who insisted that one must take a "leap of faith to God" if one is truly to become a Christian. Others maintain that it was Friedrich Nietzsche (who lived from 1844 to 1900) and his proclamation that "God is dead" who ushered in modern existentialism.

There is also divided opinion among educators and philosophers as to whether or not existentialism belongs to a school of philosophy in the normal sense. Some existentialist philosophers contend that it is not a school of philosophy with one categorical set of beliefs in the traditional sense. Kaufman, reflecting the prevailing views of several writers on existentialism, has written that it "is not a philosophy but a label for several widely different revolts against traditional philosophy."[9] To give an example of his statement,

8. Burke, R. K.: Physical education and the philosophy of pragmatism. In Davis, E. C., editor: Philosophies fashion physical education, Dubuque, Iowa, 1963, Wm. C. Brown Co., p. 7.

9. Kaufman, W. A.: Existentialism from Dostoevsky to Sartre, New York, 1956, World Books, p. 11.

Kaufman has also indicated that "the three writers who appear on every list of 'existentialists'—Jaspers, Heidegger, and Sartre—are not in agreement on essentials."[9] The one thing that these and other existentialist philosophers have in common is their view of the extreme importance of the individuality of human beings or, to borrow again from Kaufman, "their perfervid individualism."[9]

Notwithstanding the uncertainty regarding the start of existentialism and the divided opinion about its place in the philosophical schools of thought, existentialism has had and continues to have a profound influence on twentieth century thought. Physical education teachers should become familiar with this philosophical position and use whatever positive contributions that it can make to the profession.

Existentialists maintain that true reality exists only as the individual person is able to live an individual and authentically human existence. Each person must face the real world and make decisions based on his or her inner convictions. Each person must also be responsible for his or her actions—these actions and consequences thereof are an individual's reality.

As the existentialist sees it, truth is determined by each individual. The truth in knowledge is thus determined by experience, intuition, and feeling as expressed by the individual; it is not received by any external reality. In essence, truth must be lived, according to existentialists.

The actions of each individual, from the existentialist's point of view, result from inward reflection. Such values as good or bad, right or wrong, beautiful or ugly are determined by each person. Consequently, each person is responsible for establishing his or her own system of values; a person must also live with the consequences of his or her actions. Furthermore, there is no one from whom to seek help in making value judgments and other decisions; we are "condemned to be free" in Sartre's opinion.

Van Dalen expressed the overall objectives of education as viewed by existentialists when he wrote:

The existentialist elevates the individual to a position of central prominence, for he contends that self-determination is the ultimate objective of pedagogical attention. Education is to awaken the student to a knowledge of his moral self. It is to make him understand that the responsibility for choosing what he will become and for living with what happens as a result of his decisions rests with him alone.[10]

In addition to the objectives indicated above, the development of creativity, a positive self-image, and intellectual curiosity are other important objectives of the existentialist physical educator. In a true existentialist's program of physical education, there would actually be no other objective than "to participate for the sake of participation." The idea would be to participate in physical education activities so each individual could find his or her authentic existence or being. To provide some guidance and direction, however, the teacher is encouraged to consider the objectives that were presented.

The curriculum, in the existentialist program, would consist of a variety of activities so that students would be able to choose those that develop their individuality. Although individualized activities would predominate, group activities would also be provided. Students would be able to determine how they might fit into a group and yet maintain their individuality. The idea in providing group and competitive activities is to prepare students to live in a world in which they are

---

10. Van Dalen, D. B.: Philosophical profiles for physical educators. In Bucher, C. A., editor: Dimensions of physical education, St. Louis, 1974, The C. V. Mosby Co., p. 51.

alone and must compete with others. Gymnastics, dance, and self-testing activities, among others, would be stressed in an existentialist physical education class. These activities would be designed to develop creativity, self-determination, and individuality.

The existentialist physical educator would use guided discovery and problem-solving methods in his or her classes. The objective would be to get the students to examine alternatives, make decisions, and be responsible for the consequences of their actions. To get students to the point of self-reliance, the teacher would use guided discovery methods. As soon as students demonstrate their ability to handle responsibility, they would be given such responsibility.

EDUCATIONAL PHILOSOPHIES

Five general philosophies have been discussed and some of the concepts of each can be applied to education in different ways. In fact, many of these philosophies have played a major role in shaping educational thought and practice throughout history. However, several educational philosophies have been developed to deal specifically with the problems and conduct of educational thought and practice. Philosophers of education usually state their philosophical beliefs in the context of broad cultural orientations. These educational philosophies (progressivism, perennialism, essentialism, and reconstructionism) will be briefly identified at this point.

Progressivism

Progressivism is a philosophy that is based on many of the concepts and principles of pragmatism. This educational philosophy is also identified by some as instrumentalism and experimentalism. Two of the leading proponents of progressivism were William James and John Dewey.

Progressivism is said to have resulted from certain educators' rebellion against the formal approach to education that was traditional in European schools. Theodore Brameld, a noted philosopher of education, expressed the feeling that progressivist thoughts are characteristic of more than opposition to authoritarianism and absolutism in its many forms. He believes that there is also a group of progressivists who share beliefs that are positive and remedial. Brameld states that "the latter are expressive of man's confidence in his own natural powers, particularly his self-regenerative power to face continuously and to overcome satisfactorily the fears, superstitions, and bewilderments of an ever-threatening environment."[11]

Progressivists view education as inherently a social experience, with students at the center of learning. Cooperative effort is stressed instead of competition, and the democratic process is practiced by progressive educators. Furthermore, progressivists encourage students to actively participate in the decision-making process involving curriculum and related areas of the educational program. Problem-solving methods of instruction are used by progressive educators, and the teacher acts as a guide and facilitator. The child is taught to be an independent, self-reliant thinker.

One of the chief criticisms of progressive educators is the permissive atmosphere in their classrooms. Although some teachers are overly permissive and allow children to disrupt the educational process, this practice is not consistent with true progressivist ideals. It must be admitted, however, that there are weaknesses as well as assets in progressivist thought. Brameld summarized these assets and liabilities in the following statement:

. . . progressivism is: Strong in scientific method—weak in concern for the concrete and comprehensive outcomes of this method. Strong in teaching us how to think—weak in teaching us

11. Brameld, T.: Philosophies of education in cultural perspective, New York, 1955, The Dryden Press, p. 93.

the goals toward which to think. Strong in characterizing as well as encouraging active intelligence—weak in estimating and counteracting the forces and restrictions that block its effective operation. Strong in encouraging individual self-expression and individual action—weak in integrating these successfully and powerfully with group self-expression and group action. Strong in tolerance of varying belief—weak in conviction or commitment to needed positive beliefs. Strong in the processes of ongoing, dynamic experience—weak in agreeing upon the products of such experience. Strong in believing that the present is important and real—weak in believing that the future is equally important and real. Strong in delineating the complexities and pluralities of experience—weak in fusing these into comprehensive, appealing, purposeful designs.[11(p. 92)]

In terms of educational practice at present, progressive beliefs are not in evidence. The trend in many schools is "back to basics." However, since one of its major themes is change, progressivism will continue to exert a felt influence on education. For instance, when some new idea is proved successful in the classroom, it will be instituted regardless of whether it is considered "basic."

Perennialism

Perennialism is based largely on the concepts of realism as expounded by Aristotle and later by St. Thomas Aquinas. Unlike progressivism, which is based on the changing nature of things, perennialism rests on the concept of an unchanging and constant universe. Some of the practices of this philosophy are also based on idealistic concepts and principles. For example, perennialism assumes that the basic, or essential, characteristic of people is their ability to reason. One of the leaders of this philosophy in contemporary America was Robert Hutchins, the former president of the University of Chicago.

The task of education, according to perennialists, is to help people rise above the natural world and strive toward the eternal destiny that awaits them. Even though students have free will, they are not encouraged to question the authority and actions of teachers. Moreover, they are warned that they must be willing to suffer the consequences of their actions when such consequences are contrary to the wishes of the teacher.

Education is based on principles and concepts that are permanent and unchanging. The curriculum in a perennialist school is constant and universal. It includes subjects such as art, philosophy, music, and literature; great books from the past are used to instruct students in this liberal tradition. Teaching methods stress the traditional lecture and demonstration. The perennialist teacher believes that time is wasted by permitting students to explore and experiment and thus would not use problem-solving methods of instruction. Rather, they would teach the great lessons of the past by example and precept. Individualization of instruction is not a part of the teaching strategy of perennialist teachers; they teach the same material in the same manner to all students.

Perennialism has been criticized as being too regressive and a threat to democracy. In judging perennialism unacceptable as a philosophical position, Brameld observed:

. . . as a philosophy of culture, perennialism has been adjudged as regressive, not in any invidious sense, but in the precise sense that it would solve the problems of modern civilization by restoring the kind of absolute standards that governed ancient and medieval civilizations.

. . . it invites the restoration of hierarchial structures and controls rather than the establishment of democratic ones. [Also], the principles that are supposed to serve as infallible guides are to be those finally established, not primarily through the public and experimental process that is the genius of democracy, but through the operation of a metaphysical wisdom that, by definition, defies this process.[11(p. 12)]

Essentialism

Essentialism is an outgrowth of idealism and realism. It also shares some of the concepts and beliefs of perennialism. Thus, it might be considered eclectic in its orientation. Adherents of essentialism include Thomas Briggs, Frederick Breed, Henry Broudy, Herman Horne, and William Brickman, former editor of *School and Society.*

The main position of essentialism is that there is a core of knowledge, skills, and values that are essential for all people to learn. Essentialists also maintain that learning involves hard work and the application of discipline. The teacher must set firm controls so that students will put forth the effort necessary to succeed in learning this difficult but essential core of material. If the student puts forth the necessary effort to succeed, interest will be heightened. However, students must be directed by the teacher to learn the essential material even though interest in it is low; effort is more important than interest. Mental discipline is maintained in the schools of essentialists through traditional methods such as drill and recitation. Logical organization and presentation of course materials is stressed, and the scientific method is used to arrive at data, with emphasis placed on the physical sciences.

Critics of essentialism maintain that the traditional methods of teaching, reliance on the teacher for authority and discipline, emphasis on prescribed subject matter, and refusal to acknowledge the interest of students militates against the development of independent thinking and acting human beings. This, these opponents say, is inimical to the democratic process and true learning.

Reconstructionism

Reconstructionism is an outgrowth and extension of pragmatism and progressivism. It maintains that the major purpose of education is to "reconstruct" society to meet the cultural crisis of our time. To achieve this goal, the school must reinterpret the basic values of western society in the light of the scientific knowledge presently available to human beings. Probably the most prominent spokesperson for reconstructionalism is Theodore Brameld. He has written several books expressing his points of view on this philosophy.

According to Morland's interpretation of reconstructionism, "It is the philosophy of culture that would use the manifest possibilities of group experience to re-make the culture according to a specific design where the ideals of democracy become factual realities on a global scale."[12] Social learning is at the center of all reconstructionist teaching. This and other principles were outlined by Kneller as the basic principles of reconstructionism:

> The main purpose of education is to promote a clearly thought-out program of social reform; education must undertake this task without delay; the new social order must be 'genuinely democratic'; the teacher should persuade his pupils democratically of the validity and urgency of the reconstructionist point of view; the means and ends of education must be refashioned in accordance with the findings of the behavioral sciences; and the child, the school, and education itself should be shaped largely by social and cultural forces.[13]

The reconstructionists would use concepts and ideas from other philosophies to achieve their aim of reshaping society in terms of democratic ideals. For example, they borrow the various tools of measurement from essen-

12. Morland, R. B.: A philosophical interpretation of the educational views held by seven leaders in American physical education. In Bucher, C. A., editor: Dimensions of physical education, St. Louis, 1974, The C. V. Mosby Co., p. 55.
13. Kneller, G. F.: Contemporary educational theories. In Kneller, G. F., editor: Foundations of education, New York, 1963, John Wiley & Sons, Inc., p. 115.

tialists so that a scientific view of human nature can be understood and subsequently used to reconstruct society in accordance with this information. Reconstructionism also recognizes the need for logical clarity and for a steadfast and clear picture of world order and purpose as articulated by perennialists.

The reconstructionist curriculum contains material and courses that will enable teachers to impart the most generous and humane values of the culture, all designed to rebuild the social structure. It is a futuristic curriculum, emphasizing preparation for life in a "reconstructed" society. Social self-realization is the predominate goal in the curriculum designed by reconstructionists. Adults as well as young people are encouraged to participate in education. The community-school concept is a reconstructionist idea.

Teaching strategies for reconstructionists are varied; however, they stress group discussion, debate, and dialogue in a democratic atmosphere. Role-playing is also emphasized as a teaching strategy. Students are given opportunities to make group decisions about curriculum matters, but the teacher makes forceful arguments for the acceptance of the reconstructionist point of view. Like progressivists, reconstructionists act as guides and facilitators. "In the area of physical education, little time is devoted to competitive interscholastic sports; emphasis is, rather, on intramural games, the dance as both a recreation and art form, and other shared activities."[14]

Like other philosophies of education, reconstructionism has its critics. For instance, it is criticized for relying too heavily on the behavioral sciences for validated information when there are many disagreements among these scientists regarding their findings.

Kneller voiced the "scientific criticism" in this way: "Science has yet to answer the questions, 'What are the 'best' values for men to accept?' and 'What social institutions best aid their realization?' The boast of reconstructionism, that it is based on reliable scientific knowledge of human behavior, is only partially valid."[13(p. 119)]

It is also believed by some people that this "utopian" society with democratically determined ideals, which is sought by this "radical" philosophy of education called reconstructionism, is not possible in a pluralistic society such as the United States. Even Brameld, the chief spokesman for reconstructionism, admits that it does not have a large following of adherents. He expressed optimism, however, that this philosophy is catching on in other parts of the country. He states: "Especially does this appear to be the case in parts of Europe and Asia where awareness of the forebodings of disaster as well as the foretokens of hope seems at times to be more acute than in our own culture."[11(p. 14)]

In a recent re-examination of reconstructionism, Brameld noted that this philosophy was considered by many critics as a maverick among educational theories for several reasons. He cited features of reconstructionism such as stressing the importance of Marxian theory in education, the insistence of distinguishing between indoctrination and conviction, accepting mythologizing in education in a nonpejorative sense, and accepting the concept of social–self-realization as the major features of this philosophy with which critics are uncomfortable.

Brameld still expressed hope for the objectives of reconstructionism, regardless of whether or not the philosophy itself survives. Speaking of a "reinvigorated period of democratic renewal and militancy" caused by a renewed student radical movement, Brameld said, ". . . it may well transcend its preceding

---

14. Brameld, T.: Patterns of educational philosophy, New York, 1971, Holt, Rinehart and Winston, p. 480.

period by much more mature, future-directed, social–self-realizing programs of global action across many nations."[15]

THE PHILOSOPHY OF SELECTED EDUCATORS AND PHYSICAL EDUCATORS

Morland[12(pp. 54-57)] gathered quotations from the writings of 96 educators and philosophers and assigned them to various educational philosophies according to their philosophical beliefs. He also compared the ideas of physical educators with those of the educational philosophers. Morland formulated four points of view toward each of six general areas with 20 subareas that were used for the basis of comparative analysis of the two groups of educators. These areas included the general philosophical orientation, views on specific aspects of the educative process, type of curriculum, administration, role of the school in society, and aims of edu-

cation. Table 1 contains a listing of educational philosophers and physical educators according to their philosophical orientation.

Seven leaders of physical education were chosen by Morland: Thomas D. Wood, Clark W. Hetherington, Jesse Feiring Williams, Jay B. Nash, Charles H. McCloy, Mable Lee, and Elmer D. Mitchell. Morland emphasized that individuals were selected who showed evidence of varied backgrounds in their professional preparation as well as in their teaching careers. However, each of the leaders was a recipient of the Gulick Award, which indicates that an educator has made outstanding contributions to the profession. Other leaders could have been chosen, but they were not because of their close association with one or more of the leaders who were chosen.

As indicated in Table 1, the majority of the educational philosophers are adherents of essentialism and perennialism (7 persons are associated with each of these two philosophies). Five educational philosophers are associated with each of the other two philos-

15. Brameld, T.: Reconstructionism as a radical philosophy," The Educational Forum **62**:75, November, 1977.

Table 1. Categorization of selected educational philosophers and physical educators according to their educational philosophy

Progressivism	Essentialism	Perennialism	Reconstructionalism
Educational philosophers			
Boyd H. Bode	William C. Bagley	Mortimer J. Adler	I. M. Berkson
John L. Childs	J. Donald Butler	William Cunningham	Theodore Brameld
John Dewey	Frederick S. Breed	Robert M. Hutchins	Kurt Lewin
William James	Henry S. Broudy	William McGucken	Karl Mannheim
William H. Kilpatrick	Michael Demiashkevich	Jacques Maritain	Lewis Mumford
	Herman H. Horne	John D. Redden	
	Rupert C. Lodge	Francis A. Ryan	
Physical educators			
Thomas D. Wood	Charles H. McCloy		
Clark W. Hetherington	Mable Lee		
Jesse F. Williams			
Elmer D. Mitchell			
Jay B. Nash			

Table 2. Summary of responses of leading American physical educators indicating their philosophical position*

Idealism	Realism	Pragmatism
116 (20%)	99 (17%)	277 (49%)

*The analysis is based on the total of 572 responses for the 12 areas by all 49 respondents.

Table 3. The extent of apparent individual eclecticism

Number of philosophical positions checked	Number of respondents	Percentage of the total group
4	21	43
3	23	47
2	4	8
1	1	2

ophies (progressivism and reconstructionalism). Five of seven physical educators are adherents of progressivism, and the other two are associated with essentialism. None of the physical educators were classified as either perennialists or reconstructionists.

Bair[16] also conducted a study in which he identified the philosophical beliefs held by selected leaders in American physical education. Fifty-two leading American physical educators were chosen for the study. All of the selected physical educators were Fellows of the American Academy of Physical Education. Thirty-five of the physical educators were chosen on the basis of recommendations of three staff members of the Department of Health and Physical Education at the University of Southern California who were active members of the American Academy. Seventeen additional leaders were chosen on recommendation by two or more of the initial 35 leaders selected. Forty-nine (94%) leaders returned the completed checklists and were included in the final analysis of the data (Table 2).

Four philosophies were used by Bair in his study. In addition to the traditional philosophies of idealism, realism, and pragmatism, Bair included aritomism. Only the first three philosophies (idealism, realism, and pragmatism) are analyzed in this book, since

16. Bair, D. E.: An identification of some philosophical beliefs held by influential professional leaders in American physical education, unpublished doctoral dissertation, Los Angeles, 1956, University of Southern California.

42 of the 49 respondents checked statements representing those philosophical positions.

By far the greatest number of respondents were adherents of pragmatism, with 277 (49%) of the 572 total responses having been checked for the 12 areas that represent this philosophical position. Next in terms of total responses was idealism with a total of 116 responses. Only 99 responses were checked for the 12 areas of realism.

Bair was also interested in the extent of eclecticism among the leading physical educators (Table 3). The data indicate that 21 of the 49 respondents checked statements representing four different philosophical positions; 23 respondents checked three positions; and four respondents checked two positions. One person checked responses relating to only one philosophical position, which indicated that this physical educator was not eclectic at all. This is rare, but it is the epitome of achievement in philosophy. There was no indication by Bair as to the particular philosophical position of each respondent.

ESTABLISHING A PERSONAL PHILOSOPHY

Developing a philosophy of physical education, just as a philosophy of life, is a consuming, tedious, and often difficult task. Oftentimes, such a quest is never completed. But each person should be "somewhere on the journey," to use Zeigler's terminology, to the arrival of a personal and professional philosophy. As Zeigler has reminded us:

No matter which stage of philosophical development you may have achieved presently—the "ostrich stage," the "cafeteria stage," the "fence-sitter stage," the stage of early maturity, or the stage of philosophical maturity—you may find it necessary to retrace your steps before you can truly build your own personal philosophy logically, consistently, and systematically.[17]

Although it is difficult to think through and indicate your philosophy in a logical and systematic manner, the process should be attempted. The goal is to move through the various stages until you arrive at the stage of philosophical maturity—a personal philosophy. This personal philosophy will provide the guidance and foundation on which a professional philosophy rests.

In addition to providing guidance and direction for one's actions and acting as the foundation on which to build a professional philosophy, the development of a personal philosophy serves several other purposes. The importance of a well-thought-through philosophy was discussed earlier in this chapter. By way of summary, developing a philosophy serves the following important functions: it forces one to think logically, critically, and analytically about life, people, education, and physical education; it explains the worth of physical education and sport; it provides a basis for relating physical education to general education; and it provides a means of professional growth and development.

There are several approaches to developing a philosophy. Following is a personal outline and brief discussion of a procedure for developing a philosophy of physical education for school programs. The same procedure may be used to develop any type of philosophy.

A step-by-step procedure for developing a philosophy

The basis for developing this philosophy was what Morris describes as the "Outside-In" or deductive method.[18] The specific steps involved in this procedure are outlined, and then directions and suggestions are provided for the development of each step.

1. Think through logically, analytically, systematically, and comprehensively your personal views on reality (metaphysics), truth or knowledge (epistemology), and value (axiology).
2. Indicate the educational theory to which your convictions will lead.
3. Indicate what you think should be the aims of education.
4. Indicate what you think should be the functions of the school in a democratic society.
5. Indicate the concrete practices and behavior patterns you would use in teaching as a result of the educational theory you espouse.
6. Compare what you have done in the previous steps and the ideas you have established with the general philosophies and the educational philosophies or theories described in this chapter.

Step 1. Each of the steps in this process of developing a well-thought-through philosophy is important and requires careful attention. The first step takes on added significance, however, because it is the foundation on which your entire philosophy rests. Your personal views on metaphysics, epistemology, and axiology must be comprehensively and clearly developed. Because each of these divisions of philosophy is related, a logical, consistent development of ideas regarding them is important to the proper development of later stages of your philosophy. If you allow yourself to develop incompatible ideas by de-

17. Zeigler, E. F.: Physical education and sports philosophy, Englewood Cliffs, N.J., 1977, Prentice-Hall, Inc., p. 239.

18. Morris, V. C.: Philosophy and the American school, New York, 1961, Houghton Mifflin Co.

veloping eclectic viewpoints on these areas, you will encounter problems later. For example, it would be incompatible to adhere to the views of both realists and pragmatists concerning value. Whereas realists believe that values are permanent and unchanging, pragmatists believe that values change with experience. There are many other incompatible ideas of realists and adherents of other schools of philosophy. You must be careful not to embrace incompatible ideas from different philosophical positions.

How does one go about preparing for this first step in building a philosophy? As in developing a philosophy, there are several means of preparing oneself for developing ideas regarding reality, truth or knowledge, and values. A starting point might be to read what philosophers have said about these questions and problems. This reading might be related to a college course in philosophy and/or the philosophy of education. You should also think about and apply these questions to experiences that you might be having in your personal life. From all of these activities, a basic foundation should emerge on which to build a comprehensive and clear philosophy.

Step 2. Once you have developed a set of compatible ideas regarding reality, truth, and value so that you can classify yourself into one of the schools of philosophy, you may then proceed to step two. This step involves the development of the educational theory that follows from your fundamental convictions. At this point, you may use the information in this chapter or an educational philosophy textbook to help you. The point is to get a book that indicates the basic philosophies from which educational philosophies have been developed or to which they are connected. By following this procedure, you may then indicate your educational theory by examining your general philosophical ideas. If you have ideas that are mainly pragmatic, for instance, you would probably be

considered a progressivist or even a reconstructionist in terms of educational philosophy. The same careful, analytical, and comprehensive assessment of your position is as necessary at step two as it was in the first step. Your views regarding the various divisions of educational philosophy must be compatible and consistent.

Step 3. If you have been rigorous and comprehensive in carrying out the tasks of the first two steps, it should be fairly easy to state what you think should be the aims of education. Aims or purposes of education have been stated by various individuals, groups, organizations, and philosophers. They have differed according to the philosophical persuasion of the person or group making such statement of aims. The stated purpose of education by essentialists would be to transmit those enduring aspects of our social heritage and the verified knowledge of the past. On the other hand, progressivists believe that education should help students to discover the qualitative experiences that will lead to the good life.

You might examine several statements of aims or purposes of education (such as the Cardinal Principles of Education, the statement of aims by the Educational Policies Commission, and professional groups of educators) to determine those aims that are consistent with your educational philosophy. The importance of basing your educational views on a critical assessment of your philosophical views is reemphasized at this point. Butler especially emphasized the importance of establishing a carefully thought-out value system when he wrote that ". . . we must have a value theory if in turn we are to embrace aims or functions for education which will stand up against the ravages of time and the challenge of the uneducated of all levels and ages."[7(p. 495)]

Step 4. This step should be a natural outgrowth of the previous one. Once having developed the aims or purposes of education, it should be easy to state the functions of the school in helping to achieve these aims. You may use your experience as a student, the knowledge you have gained from courses in the foundations of education, and any other means at your disposal to increase your knowledge of the various functions of schools in different societies. In the final analysis, the functions that you hold for schools should be consistent with your philosophical ideas. The school, as one of many social institutions, should be viewed as one vehicle for helping to achieve the aims of education. These aims of education should have been based on your views of reality, truth, and value. The interconnectedness of the ideas is very important, and they must be compatible.

Step 5. Now you are ready to indicate the specific behavior patterns and techniques you would use in the classroom or gymnasium as a result of your ideas of educational theory. What kind of curriculum would you develop? What kind of teaching methods would you use? What kind of evaluation techniques would you use? All of these, as well as other questions, should be answered at this point. Students or teachers with very little experience will have to rely on what their teachers have taught and how they have behaved in the classroom when working out this step.

It is very important in this step as in other phases of the development of your philosophy that you be consistent in connecting the various stages in a logical and harmonious manner. Study carefully your ideas on philosophical questions related to reality, truth, and value. Compare these ideas to educational questions related to the aims of education, the values of the school in this process of education, and the specific strategies you would use to accomplish your ultimate goals. Another example is provided to stress the importance of compatibility of ideas among the various stages of philosophy development. The teacher of realistic philosophical inclination would probably not use problem solving as a method of teaching or subject matter of social experience as the major curriculum material since these are antithetical to the ideas of most realists, in terms of general philosophy, and most essentialists, in terms of educational theory. These types of practices would be consistent with the philosophy of pragmatists and the educational theory of progressivists.

Step 6. This is the final and summarizing step. You should be aware, however, that if your views on aspects of philosophy or educational theory or practice in the various stages are too incompatible, it may be necessary to rethink aspects of your philosophy. There should be a consistent relationship between ideas at each stage and among ideas in the various stages. In speaking of the importance of a logical and consistent movement from philosophy to educational theory to practice, Morris said:

. . . in the degree to which you can draw a deductive argument from your philosophic position to your educational theoretical position to the kinds of specific behavior patterns you feel a teacher would follow according to such a view, in that degree you will have put down a complete "work paper" for the next stage.[18](p. 469)

The next step to which Morris referred was the comparison of the kinds of teaching behavior the teacher exhibits with the deduced behaviors according to the various stages of philosophy development. Since this book is for students majoring in physical education, this stage is not necessary here. You can compare your actual teaching practices with your philosophical position and your educational theoretical position once you begin teaching. At this point, you should have developed a comprehensive philosophy.

Although the deductive method proposed by Morris was for the development of a philosophy of education, it can be used to develop a philosophy of physical education. By thinking through each step with physical education as the focal point, a philosophy of physical education will be developed that is consistent with the basic goals and objectives of general education. An example of the use of this process in developing a philosophy of physical education is presented next.

AN EMERGING PHILOSOPHY OF PHYSICAL EDUCATION FOR SCHOOL PROGRAMS

I shall attempt to present a description of my personal philosophy of physical education for programs in schools. My personal philosophy has helped me to clarify my thinking about the main aims or purposes of education, the function of the school in society, the relationship of physical education to general education, and whether my teaching is based on sound philosophical ideas and educational theory. Furthermore, it is hoped that my statement of philosophy will help students who are majoring in physical education and beginning teachers to think about their philosophy of physical education in a logical and comprehensive manner.

In terms of what is real, I believe that true reality is to be found in the experience and nature of human beings, even though it is constantly changing because of the changing social, political, economic, and religious conditions and situations. As individuals begin to understand and account for the impact of cultural forces on human beings, they will develop the type of culture that is best suited for humanity.

I believe that knowledge comes from both sense experience and the insight of reason. Truth can be established by the scientific method, problem solving, and intuitive thinking, or a combination of these. Truth or knowledge, like reality, is transitory; it changes as circumstances and conditions change. Knowledge should continually be revised and updated as new experiences and

information dictate. Human beings should seek the truth to enable them to develop as social beings in a democratic society.

Human beings are capable of making value judgments because they have free will. In fact, it is vitally necessary that these value judgments be made. It must be realized, however, that certain actions and behaviors are better for human beings than are others. Through group experience, one can determine those values that may be used as a starting point for making value judgments. Determining what is good or right, for example, should reflect the effect such actions might have on the group as well as the individuals in the group. An action would be considered good if it were to work out in practice.

Before indicating my beliefs about physical education in particular, I think that some statement about the central purpose of education is necessary. I believe that the aim or goal of education is to transmit the desirable cultural traits of a people and to equip them with the necessary skills, knowledge, and total fitness to enable them to discover new truths that will make for a satisfying and productive life in a democratic society. The Educational Policies Commission, expressing the same sentiments about the purpose of education, indicated in 1946 how this aim might be achieved. This group wrote:

. . . This involves the dissemination of knowledge, the liberation of minds, the development of skills, the promotion of free inquiries, the encouragement of the creative or inventive spirit, and the establishment of wholesome attitudes toward order and change. . . .[19]

To achieve this central purpose of education, all people should be developed to their optimum level of ability—physically, mentally, emotionally, and socially. I believe that

---

19. Educational Policies Commission: Policies for education in American democracy, Washington, D.C., 1964, National Education Association and American Association of School Administrators, p. 60.

the four groups of objectives (self-realization, human relationships, civic responsibility, and economic efficiency) stated by the Educational Policies Commission in 1938 and reiterated in 1961 are worthy for today's education. The widely used "taxonomic system" developed by Bloom[20] and Krathwohl and co-workers,[21] which is divided into three domains (cognitive, psychomotor, and affective) provides an excellent framework for communicating instructional objectives.

The school should unite with other agencies in the community (churches, community centers, hospitals, and others) to achieve its central mission. However, the school should be the most vital and vibrant learning and resource center in the community. It should provide services for all persons, including the community—the young and old, the rich and poor, and the healthy and disabled.

Physical education, I believe, can aid in the development of the "total person." Specifically, the purposes of physical education are to develop individuals who: (1) use their bodies efficiently and effectively in movement situations generally and in sports and games specifically, (2) develop the necessary skills for participation in leisure time activities, (3) develop a positive attitude toward self, others, and physical activities, (4) understand, appreciate, and value physical activity as an adjunct to healthful living, and (5) are socially well-adjusted.

I believe that the purposes and specific objectives of physical education can be achieved with a competent professional educator who offers a variety of activities and experiences for people. These activities and experiences should be based on sound principles of growth and development and the re-sultant needs, interests, and capacities of each individual. Furthermore, I believe that the "why" of physical education should be taught in addition to the skills and fitness activities. Teaching the "why" of physical education means teaching the cognitive aspects as well as the psychomotor and affective-social aspects. For example, I would teach the students about the worth of physical education in their overall school program and especially about the values of physical activity to their total development. The sequencing of curriculum material would be based on the present level of student achievement, and the principle of progression—from simple to more complex—would be stressed. I would teach concepts rather than isolated skills and knowledge.

In addition to the instructional program, I would have an intramural, extramural, and varsity athletic program. I believe also that physical education should be adapted to meet the special educational needs of individuals with handicapping conditions, such as those with impaired vision or hearing, low fitness levels, obesity, and so on. I also believe that coeducational activities should be offered at all levels.

In the elementary school, I would stress the development of basic movement skills. These skills would include locomotor, non-locomotor, and manipulative skills and would be developed in a movement education environment. The specific structure of the program would conform to Laban's Theory of Movement, which stresses four major components: body awareness (what can the body do?) spatial awareness (where does the body move?), qualities of movement (how does the body move?), and relationships (with whom or what does the body move?).*

At successive grade levels, I would apply these skills to specific sport forms such as

20. Bloom, B. S., editor: Taxonomy of educational objectives, Handbook I: cognitive domain, New York, 1956, David McKay Co., Inc.

21. Krathwohl, D. R., and others: Taxonomy of educational objectives, Handbook II: affective domain, New York, 1956, David McKay Co., Inc.

*A complete discussion of the development of these components has been provided in another source (Bucher and Thaxton, 1979).

dance, gymnastics, tennis, field hockey, and so forth. As stated previously, I believe that students should also be aided in the development of objectives in the cognitive and affective/social domains as well as the psychomotor area.

Varsity level sports competition would not be provided for students at the elementary school level. I would stress play days and sport days and intramural sports for those students in the upper elementary grades. The main part of the program in the elementary school would be instruction in movement skills and opportunities for the development of social self-realization. The program of sports at the junior high school level would stress intramural and extramural activities, deemphasizing large crowds, excessive traveling, and expensive awards. When varsity sports are offered at the junior high school level, the program would be adapted to meet the needs, interests, and developmental level of boys and girls. Varsity sports would be provided for youngsters at the senior high school level. The emphasis in this program would be on helping the persons with superior skill levels to display those skills in socially acceptable activities. This would be an educational sports program rather than a commercial venture. (Refer to Chapter 11 for a complete discussion of various guidelines for the conduct of sports programs.)

I believe that several teaching styles should be tried to develop students to their optimum level of ability. With some students, a more direct approach might be necessary; with others a more informal approach might prove more successful. I would strive to move toward the discovery method (described by Mosston) in my teaching. As students become more mature in making decisions, they would be allowed increasingly more freedom in directing their own education. I do not interpret this as meaning that I, as a teacher, would cease teaching once students were able to direct their own learning

at a more independent level. On the contrary, I would help the students to reach even greater heights in learning by challenging them with more complex concepts. For example, as soon as individuals mastered the requisite skills, they would be challenged to improvise novel movements and create unique and new movement patterns.

Finally, I believe that the physical education program must be expanded beyond the boundaries of the school if all of its objectives are to be met. For instance, instruction in golf, equestrian arts, swimming, and other specialized activities might best be taught by specialists who are not affiliated with schools, if they have the necessary personal qualities and professional competencies.

DISCUSSION QUESTIONS AND EXERCISES

1. Define philosophy. Discuss the limitations of each of the alternatives to philosophy (belief, common sense, logic, and scientific inquiry).
2. Write a position paper on the topic: "The importance of a well-thought-through philosophy of physical education."
3. Identify and discuss the three major divisions of the discipline of philosophy.
4. List and discuss the key concepts of the five schools of philosophy presented in this text.
5. Compare and contrast idealist and existentialist teachers in terms of their choice of objectives and methods of teaching physical education.
6. List and discuss the key concepts of the four educational philosophies presented in this text.
7. To arrive at the truth, what means would each of the following utilize: idealist, realist, naturalist, pragmatist, and existentialist.
8. Prepare a paper outlining and discussing the essential differences in philosophy between Mable Lee and Jesse Fearing Williams and between Charles McCloy and Thomas D. Wood.
9. Assume that you are a debater and have been assigned the affirmative side of the topic: "Resolved: that physical education should be required for all college students." Present a se-

ries of written arguments setting forth your position on this topic. In arriving at the arguments to support your position, use philosophy and the alternatives to philosophy as modes of inquiry and ask the class to critique each set of statements as to their effectiveness in convincing them of your position.

10. Outline and discuss the six essential steps in developing a philosophy. Apply this process to the development of your personal philosophy.

11. Based on a reading of the description of the philosophy of one of the authors of this text, indicate the philosophical (both general and educational) orientation of that person.

12. Using the material in this chapter as a starting point, develop your philosophy of physical education. Present your statement of philosophy to your class and ask them to react to it.

SELECTED REFERENCES

Bair, D. E.: An identification of some philosophical beliefs held by influential professional leaders in American physical education, unpublished doctoral dissertation, 1956, Los Angeles, University of Southern California.

Brameld, T.: Patterns of educational philosophy, New York, 1971, Holt, Rinehart and Winston.

Brameld, T.: Philosophies of education in cultural perspective, New York, 1955, The Dryden Press.

Brameld, T.: Reconstructionism as a radical philosophy, The Educational Forum **62:**67-76, November 1977.

Brameld, T.: Toward a reconstructed philosophy of education, New York, 1956, The Dryden Press.

Broudy, H. S.: Building a philosophy of education, Englewood Cliffs, N.J., 1954, Prentice-Hall, Inc.

Brubacher, J. S.: Modern philosophies of education, New York, 1969, McGraw-Hill Book Co.

Bucher, C. A., editor: Dimensions of physical education, St. Louis, 1974, The C. V. Mosby Co.

Bucher, C. A.: Foundations of physical education, ed. 8, St. Louis, 1979, The C. V. Mosby Co.

Bucher, C. A., and Thaxton, N. A.: Physical education for children: movement foundations and experiences, New York, 1979, Macmillan Inc.

Butler, J. D.: Four philosophies and their practice in education and religion, New York, 1968, Harper & Row, Publishers.

Cobb, R., and Lepley, P. M., editors: Contemporary philosophies of physical education, Columbus, Ohio, 1973, Charles E. Merrill Publishing Co.

Davis, E. C.: The philosophic process in physical education, Philadelphia, 1967, Lea & Febiger.

Davis, E. C., editor: Philosophies fashion physical education, Dubuque, Iowa, 1963, William C. Brown Co., Publishers.

Dewey, J.: Philosophy of education, Totowa, N.J., 1966, Littlefield, Adams & Co.

Durant, W.: The story of philosophy, Garden City, N.Y., 1927, Garden City Publishing Co.

Hansen, K. H.: Philosophy for American education, Englewood Cliffs, N.J., 1960, Prentice-Hall, Inc.

Henderson, S. V. P.: Introduction to philosophy of education, Chicago, 1947, The University of Chicago Press.

Kaufman, W. A.: Existentialism from Dostoevsky to Sartre, New York, World Books, 1956,

Kilpatrick, W. H., editor: The educational frontier, New York, 1933, D. Appleton-Century Co.

Kneller, G. F., editor: Foundations of education, New York, 1963, John Wiley & Sons, Inc.

Kneller, G. F.: Introduction to the philosophy of education, New York, 1964, John Wiley & Sons, Inc.

McCloy, C. H.: Philosophical bases for physical education, New York, 1940, F. S. Crofts and Co.

Morris, V. C.: Philosophy and the American school, New York, 1961, Houghton Mifflin Co.

Osterhoudt, R. G.: An introduction to the philosophy of physical education and sport, Champaign, Ill., 1978, Stipes Publishing Co.

Park, R. J.: The philosophy of John Dewey and physical education, The Physical Educator **26:**55-57, May 1969.

Patterson, A., and Hallberg, E. C.: Background readings for physical education, New York, 1967, Holt, Rinehart & Winston.

Slusher, H. S.: Man, sport and existence, Philadelphia, 1967, Lea & Febiger.

Van Dalen, D. B.: Philosophical profiles for physical educators, The Physical Educator **21:**3-6, October 1964.

Van Dalen, D. B., and Bennett, B. L.: A world history of physical education, Englewood Cliffs, N.J., 1971, Prentice-Hall, Inc.

Webster, R. W.: Philosophy for physical education, Dubuque, Iowa, 1965, William C. Brown Co., Publishers.

Weiss, P.: Sport, a philosophic inquiry, Carbondale, Ill., 1969, Southern Illinois University Press.

Whitehead, A. N.: The aims of education, New York, 1967, The Free Press.

Williams, J. F.: The principles of physical education, Philadelphia, 1964, W. B. Saunders Co.

Winn, R. B., editor: John Dewey: dictionary of education, New York, 1959, Philosophical Library, Inc.

Zeigler, E. F.: Physical education and sport philosophy, Englewood Cliffs, N.J., 1977, Prentice-Hall, Inc.

7 □ Toward a scientific basis for teaching physical education and sport

Courtesy Springfield College, Springfield, Mass.

With the present emphasis on increased productivity of teachers and simultaneous demands for educational accountability, several attempts are being made by educators to improve the teaching-learning process. Some of the suggested means of improving student learning are to apply research findings to teaching practice, to use the systems approach in education, and to use the scientific basis for teaching. Information has been presented on the first two suggested approaches in other chapters of this text. This chapter will discuss the rationale for using a more scientific basis for teaching physical education and ways in which such an approach might be accomplished.

DEFINITIONS

Definitions and explanations will be given for the terms *learning*, *teaching*, and the *teaching-learning process*. An indication will also be made of the importance of the physi-

Courtesy Jackson State University, Jackson, Miss.

cal education teacher in the teaching-learning process. Finally, as a preface to the discussion of the scientific basis for teaching physical education, a clarification will be made to distinguish between the art and the science of teaching.

Learning

Learning is a change in behavior that results from instruction, study, practice, past experience, or any combination of these variables; learning is *not* a change in behavior that is a result of maturation or a temporary change in the learner. An example of learning that adheres to this definition is that of a student who is not able to perform a handspring before entering the class but who masters this skill during the class. The learning of the handspring may have been the result of instruction by the teacher, practice by the student, study of the mechanics of the handspring in a book, observation of another student performing the skill, or a combination of these methods.

Teaching

Teaching may be defined as those actions by the teacher and/or learner that make learning more successful than it would be without such teaching. Although it is recognized that learning can occur without a teacher being present, teachers can facilitate the acquisition of knowledge, skills, and attitudes. For example, a student may be able to learn to hit a ball, perform a dance step, or play tennis. However, such learning should be enhanced if the teacher structures a proper learning environment, helps the student to analyze the components of the skill, and provides the necessary feedback to help the student correct mistakes and/or reinforce correctly learned skills. Learning in the affective and cognitive domains can also be facilitated by teacher input.

The teaching-learning process

A combination of actions of the teacher and learner and a reciprocal interaction between the two comprise the teaching-learning process. Some of the actions occur before class (planning lessons, structuring the environment for effective and efficient learning), some occur during the class (presenting the learning tasks, arranging time for practice, providing feedback), and some occur after class (evaluating what was accomplished and using such evaluative material to aid in future planning).

THE IMPORTANCE OF THE TEACHER OF PHYSICAL EDUCATION

Physical education teachers are important for three reasons: (1) they determine the kind of educational environment that is provided for students, (2) they determine whether new program ideas will be successful and whether research findings will be implemented, and (3) they are role models for students.

Teachers are responsible for the kind of educational environment that is provided for students

The responsibility that teachers have to plan and structure an educational environment for optimal learning is of singular importance. The type of learning environment and the teaching approaches used in a class are important variables that affect the outcome of learning by students. A research study by Martinek, Zaichkowsky, and Cheffers[1] illustrates the important role teachers assume in affecting student learning. These authors sought to determine the effects of a physical education class in which the teacher made all of the decisions and a class in which the teacher and students shared in the decision-making process. It was concluded that a teacher-directed approach is best for the development of motor skills and that a sharing approach has a positive effect on the development of positive self-concepts. The results of this study are consistent with the findings of other research studies on this topic; they all demonstrate the effect of teacher influence on student learning, thereby demonstrating the importance of the teacher in the teaching-learning process.

Teachers determine whether new program ideas will be successful and whether research findings will be implemented

The second reason why teachers are important is two-fold—their ability to determine the success of a program and their willingness or unwillingness to apply the findings of research to the practice of physical education. These factors are related to the major responsibility of teachers discussed in the preceding paragraph, that is, the shaping of the educational environment. The impact that teachers have on the success of a new program was noted by Stern and Keislar:

> No matter how sound its theoretical base, no matter how richly supported with resource materials and audiovisual devices, if an innovation is imposed authoritatively on the teacher, with no attempt to develop understanding and enlist support, it will not succeed.[2]

The importance of physical education teachers because of their ability to shape the quality of education can be further illustrated by their attitude and acceptance of a mandated program idea. For example, coeducational classes are required as a result of Title IX. Some physical educators who are not receptive to the idea of coeducational classes will not prepare and teach those classes with the same dedication, enthusiasm, and competence as they would if they favored coedu-

1. Martinek, T. J., Zaichkowsky, L. D., and Cheffers, J. T. F.: Decision-making in elementary age children: effects on motor skills and self-concept, Research Quarterly **48**:349-357, May 1977.

2. Stern, C., and Keislar, E. R.: Teacher attitudes and attitude change: a research review, Journal of Research Development in Education **10**:64, Winter 1977.

cational classes. Therefore, the program quality in these classes is diminished.

Like their refusal to support innovative program ideas for which they are not enthusiastic, teachers' refusal to apply the findings of sound research can also dilute the quality of a program. Consider, for example, a physical education program in which the teacher spends an inordinate amount of class time talking, whereas research indicates that students learn by doing.[3] (See Chapter 9 for more information on this topic.)

Teachers are role models for students

Besides their value as shapers of educational environments for optimal learning and their influence on the quality of education by their actions regarding innovative program ideas and their utilization of sound research findings, physical educators are also important because they act as role models for students. The type of example physical education teachers set for students influences them greatly. A physical educator who is obese and who exhibits poor health habits such as excessive drinking, smoking, and keeping an unclean appearance does not act as a good role model for students. Because physical education teachers also teach about such personal health and health habits, they should serve as a positive example to students that these aspects of living are important.

Teachers act as role models whether or not they intend to do so. Realizing the importance their role modeling has on students, teachers should become conscious of their status as role models. Moreover, they should make sure that the role models being displayed are consistent with their intended roles. Wescott, in an article documenting the fact that physical educators and coaches act as role models for students, states that:

Physical educators and coaches have two important responsibilities: (1) to model desirable behavior in areas such as personal health and health habits, personal fitness and activity habits, sportsmanship, discrimination, honesty, fairness, and responsibility; and (2) to reinforce students and athletes who do likewise.[4]

The fact that teachers and coaches act as role models for students is not so important in itself; the important point for teachers to remember is that the effect they have on students may be strong or weak, positive or negative. It would be most desirable if physical educators and coaches could exert a strong, positive influence on the personal and social behavior of their students and athletes. Wescott[4(pp. 31-32)] offers several suggestions for teachers and coaches to enable them to be better role models and exert strong, positive influences on desirable traits in students.

ACCOUNTABILITY OF PHYSICAL EDUCATION TEACHERS

The inflationary economic conditions of today and the poor performance of some students in basic subject areas are two reasons why school officials and the public have increased their demands for greater accountability of teachers. In education and physical education, accountability means being responsible for the achievement of stated goals and objectives. Teachers must also demonstrate, in a convincing way, that what they are teaching has value. At a time when educational budgets are tight, administrators are constantly looking for ways to cut back. Subjects that are considered "frills" are being dropped from the curriculum. In some schools, physical educators are being dismissed. It is therefore urgent for teachers

3. Thorndike, E. L.: Human learning, New York, 1931, Johnson Reprint Corp.

4. Wescott, W. L.: Physical educators and coaches as models of behavior, Journal of Physical Education and Recreation **50**:32, March 1979.

and administrators in physical education to inform school administrators and the public about the value of physical education as a school subject.

The broad goal of physical education programs is to develop physically educated individuals. While this goal is worth achieving, it is much too broad; it is a long-term goal. Specific, short-term performance objectives must be developed. In addition, instructional objectives must be designed to measure the degree to which students are meeting these performance objectives on the way to the ultimate goal.

Even with specific, measurable objectives teacher accountability will not be possible without appropriate and valid evaluation instruments.* The evaluation procedure should be designed to assess only those objectives that teachers are responsible for meeting. Administrators must realize that there are variables other than those in the gymnasium or classroom that affect student learning and performance. In holding teachers accountable for student achievement, administrators must also ascertain the effect of those nonschool factors (influence of peers and home environment and time students spend in preparation for school, for example) on student performance. Physical educators must not be held accountable for students' failure to accomplish certain objectives through no fault of the teacher. For example, if a student fails to develop needed soccer skills because that student was excessively absent during the soccer unit, the teacher should not be blamed for such failure.

Besides being accountable for student achievement and performance, teachers should attempt to measure their own effectiveness as teachers. The use of a scientific

approach to teaching and the use of a competency-based curriculum format are two ways in which physical educators can determine their effectiveness as teachers. They can also serve as effective means of assessing student performance and achievement. The values of a scientific basis for teaching physical education are discussed in later portions of this chapter, and the competency-based curriculum approach is discussed elsewhere.[5] Marsh states that the basic idea behind "competency-based instruction" is to list specific learning outcomes that are to be achieved at a given level and ascertain if these outcomes are being achieved.[6] This type of approach provides a structure for teaching, the outcomes of which can be objectively measured. It should be mentioned that one of the major objections to competency-based curriculums is the failure to achieve humanistic values.[7]

Other strategies that the teacher can use to ensure proper accountability include:

1. Evaluating students at the beginning and at the end of a unit. Students should be evaluated in all domains—cognitive, affective, and psychomotor—and on the degree to which they meet specified performance and instructional objectives.

2. Engaging in teacher self-evaluation and being evaluated by others (peers and students). Teachers should constantly evaluate themselves. This might be accomplished by informally analyzing

---

*Evaluation instruments may include student evaluation forms, peer observation report forms, rating scales, and the like. See Bucher's Foundations of physical education for a discussion of teacher evaluation.

5 Austin, D. A., Coordinator: Competency based education: its implications for physical education, Journal of Physical Education and Recreation 49:43-54, November-December 1978.

6. Marsh, D. B.: Competency based curriculum: an answer for accountability in physical education, Journal of Physical Education and Recreation 49:45, November-December 1978.

7. Austin, D. A.: Introduction: competency based education: its implications for physical education, Journal of Physical Education and recreation 49:44, November-December 1978.

what happens in physical education classes. A more formal method of evaluation involves videotaping some classes and using "descriptive-analytic" systems for analyzing student-teacher behaviors. Peer observation reports also may be used to provide useful information about teacher effectiveness. Finally, valid evaluation instruments may be used by students to assess teacher effectiveness.

It must be recognized that no one method of evaluating teacher effectiveness and student performance is perfect. It must also be understood that methods of evaluation for teacher accountability are a means to an end rather than ends in themselves. With these warnings in mind, the preceding evaluation strategies can prove very useful to teachers in matters of accountability. They can provide evidence of teacher effectiveness. They can also indicate those areas in which the ineffective teacher can become more effective in influencing student achievement.

SELECTED CHARACTERISTICS OF THE TEACHING-LEARNING PROCESS AND ACCOUNTABILITY

In their quest to improve the teaching-learning process and to objectively deal with the "accountability" question, educators have used many different techniques and approaches in examining this process. One approach has been to identify characteristics of "effective" teachers. There is some debate concerning characteristics of a "good" or "effective" teacher. In fact, there are questions regarding the definition of a *good* teacher. Hamachek[8] presents an overview of the differing viewpoints on this topic, and, based on

research evidence, argues that there are qualities that distinguish "good" and "poor" teachers. He states that effective teachers are more "human" in the fullest sense of the word; they have a sense of humor, are fairly empathetic, more democratic than autocratic, and apparently are more able to relate easily and naturally to students on either a one-to-one or group basis than are poor teachers.

Just as important as the identification of common characteristics of "effective" teachers is an understanding of the characteristics of an "effective" teaching-learning process. Several characteristic behaviors of effective teachers were delineated by Vanek.[9] In presenting these teacher behaviors, Vanek organized the teaching process into the following divisions: *organization, communication, motivation,* and *human relations skills.* She also examined some of the underlying assumptions concerning the teacher-learner process. A summary of Vanek's report follows.

SELECTED CHARACTERISTICS OF THE TEACHING PROCESS
Organization skills

An effective teacher:
1. Establishes a learning climate (rapport between the teacher and students) to heighten students' interest in class activities.
2. Establishes appropriate frame of reference or point of view concerning instruction (summarizes, relates to prior or subsequent instruction, relates to objectives of instruction, and so on).
3. States the purpose of instruction.
4. Sequences material and concepts in a logical and systematic order.
5. Selects, adapts, evaluates, and integrates teaching strategies and materials in view of long-range goals.

8. Hamachek, D.: Characteristics of good teachers and implications for teacher education. In Palardy, J. M., editor: Teaching today: tasks and challenges, New York, 1975, Macmillan Inc., pp. 33-42.

9. Vanek, E. P.: Selected characteristics of the teaching process, Document # Ed 150 123, Washington, D.C., U.S. Department of Health, Education and Welfare, National Institute of Education.

6. Shows evidence of effective and thorough planning.
7. Achieves closure: pulls together major concepts of the instruction to form a cohesive link between past knowledge and understanding and new knowledge and understanding.

Communication skills

An effective teacher:

1. Uses media (blackboard, slides, transparencies, and the like) in an appropriate manner.
2. Gives clear and concise instruction/explanations.
3. Uses models and analogies to simplify and clarify explanations.
4. Uses terminology that is appropriate to the level of the learner or defines technical terms that the student may not know.
5. Uses nonverbal communication (makes eye contact, nods, smiles, touches, and so on).
6. Uses adequate voice projection techniques (speaks loud enough to be heard, varies pitch and loudness for effect, is animated).
7. Adjusts speed of delivery depending on the kind of learning activity and student ability.
8. Models the kind of behavior that reflects: (a) interest in the subject, (b) enjoyment of teaching and learning, and (c) receptivity to others' needs and interests.
9. Uses a variety of questioning techniques.
   a. Asks higher order questions (What is your opinion? How is ___ related to ___? How? Why?) as well as recall questions (When? What?).
   b. Uses questions to achieve inductive or deductive reasoning.
   c. Gets the students to volunteer answers or summarize by pausing so that students know that an answer is expected and can formulate a more complete answer, by building questions out of a student's response, and so on.
10. Provides feedback to the students on their performances.
11. Acts as a receiver of information. Seeks suggestions and makes changes when necessary. Shows an awareness of students' questions and is free to answer them, to say that he or she does not know the answer, or to say that they will be answered later. The teacher also perceives and interprets visual cues given by the class.

Motivation skills

An effective teacher:

1. Provides a mechanism for student input in planning and evaluation.
2. Points out subject matter relevance to the student.
3. Uses a variety of teaching techniques to stimulate interest and participation (problem solving, guided discovery, command teaching, large and small group, and individual discussion and participation sessions).

Human relations skills

An effective teacher:

1. Exhibits a spirit of cooperation and a working rapport with students, faculty, and administrators.
2. Displays a sense of humor in the classroom and gymnasium to liven presentations and relieve tension.
3. Meets class commitments by being prepared and prompt.
4. Is adaptable and flexible.
5. Acknowledges own errors.

The foregoing behaviors characterize techniques used by effective teachers and are qualities to look for when evaluating teacher accountability. Teachers should also analyze their own classes with a view toward exhibiting these teaching behaviors.

THE ART AND THE SCIENCE OF TEACHING

Nathaniel Gage, Director of the Program on Teaching Effectiveness at the Center for Educational Research at Stanford University, and a recognized authority on teaching, presented characteristics of both the art and the science of teaching. He views teaching as "a useful, or practical art rather than one dedicated to the creation of beauty and evocation of aesthetic pleasures as ends in themselves."[10] Gage further elaborates on the art of teaching by saying:

As a practical art, teaching must be recognized as a process that calls for intuition, creativity, improvisation, and expressiveness—a process that leaves room for departures from what is implied by the rules, formulas, and algorithms [of a science of teaching].[10]

In essence, the art of teaching is characterized by a teacher who personalizes teaching by using a personal style, creativity, intuition, sensitivity, and judgment to promote learning. The teacher who advocates the art of teaching recognizes the many variables that interact in the teaching-learning process and believes that no scientific process can control these variables so that the teacher can predict learning outcomes with any degree of certainty.

The science of teaching, according to Gage, ". . . implies that good teaching will some day be attainable by closely following rigorous laws that yield high predictability and control."[10(p. 17)] The example of a chemist using available knowledge of chemistry and other scientific subjects to obtain almost completely predictable results was used by Gage to illustrate a scientific endeavor. He said, however, that when scientists are conducting research, they are themselves practicing an art. He concluded by saying that the idea that a science of teaching exists is erroneous, since teachers are not able to predict with a high degree of certainty the outcome of learning.

Siedentop characterizes the science of teaching as a process in which teaching is amenable to systematic evaluation and capable of being broken down into a series of tasks that can be mastered.[11] The science of teaching involves an understanding of human behavior, behavior modification, and instructional design, delivery, and management. Furthermore, the science of teaching involves the strict adherence to principles of learning such as readiness, motivation, practice, feedback, and progression and sequence.

Siedentop states that another characteristic of the science of teaching is the possibility of examining teaching from a theoretical-scientific perspective.[11(p. 4)] He believes that teaching can and should be studied from the theoretical-scientific perspective to develop a theory of teaching. Although Siedentop states that we are a long way from having such a theory in physical education, we should be moving in that direction in our attempt to understand the teaching process.

Based on the characteristics of a science of teaching given by both Gage and Siedentop, there is a lack of a science of teaching in physical education. Although Gage only speaks of the inability of teachers to produce the outcomes sought in a science of teaching and Siedentop approaches the teaching of skills as if there were a science of teaching, other educators state there is no science of teaching physical education. For example, Pease indicates that "until there becomes a scientific body of knowledge about teaching, or as long as teaching remains an art and not a science, then the behavior of teachers will be subject to the behavioral reinforcers operating at any given time."[12]

DEVELOPING A SCIENTIFIC BASIS FOR TEACHING PHYSICAL EDUCATION

Physical education does not have the necessary theoretical-scientific framework on which to develop a science of teaching. How-

10. Gage, N. L.: The scientific basis of the art of teaching, New York, 1978, Teachers College Press, p. 15.
11. Siedentop, D.: Developing teaching skills in physical education, Boston, 1976, Houghton Mifflin Co., p. 3.
12. Pease, D. A.: Physical education: accountability for the future. In Welsh, R., editor: Physical education: a view toward the future, St. Louis, 1977, The C. V. Mosby Co., p. 153.

Tom Morton.

Identifying the elements of the teaching-learning process.

Hunter[13] has classified the elements of the teaching-learning process in three basic categories: (1) what is to be learned, (2) what the learner is doing to achieve that learning, and (3) what the teacher is doing to facilitate (or interfere with) that achievement.

What is to be learned. Identification of the learning task is the beginning focal point in the teaching process. The type of task that is to be learned will help to determine appropriate student and teacher behavior to be discussed in the next two sections. Learner and teacher behavior will vary considerably, for example, depending on whether the task is easy or difficult, interesting or uninteresting, simple or complex.

The learning task may be any activity that is selected to meet the objectives of the program. Executing a kip in gymnastics, officiating a soccer or volleyball game, explaining and demonstrating the "spot" method of bowling, and creating a dance routine are all possible learning tasks in physical education. The selection of the learning task will be partially dictated by such factors as available facilities and equipment, needs and interests of students, and expertise of the teacher. Learning tasks may be chosen by the teacher, the student, or both.

What the learner is doing to achieve that learning. The learner should exhibit those behaviors and engage in those activities that will lead to the accomplishment of the selected task. Such behaviors and activities must be effective for this particular learner. Suppose, for example, that the learning task is the execution of a kip in gymnastics. Some learners may view a film or watch a demon-

ever, physical educators can and should teach physical education much more scientifically than they currently do. This can be accomplished by: (1) making specific and meaningful selections from a varied set of variables, and (2) by increasing the predictability of learning outcomes by hypothesizing about and testing cause-effect relationships.

Making specific and meaningful selections from a diverse set of variables

By using a more scientific approach, the physical educator will be able to make meaningful selections from a diverse set of variables by identifying the elements of the teaching-learning process and by categorizing these elements into the two phases of the teaching act.

13. Hunter, M.: The science of the art of teaching. In Allen, D. W., and Hecht, J. C., editors: Controversies in education, Philadelphia, 1974, W. B. Saunders Co., pp. 347-348.

stration by others and practice the skill to achieve the learning task. Other learners may accomplish the task more efficiently and effectively if they read a description of how to execute the kip and then practice the skill. As many different methods and techniques as needed should be used by the learner to successfully complete a learning task.

What the teacher is doing to facilitate (or interfere with) that achievement. Although the teacher may on occasion interfere with the achievement of a learning task, the aim of the teacher is to facilitate learning. The teacher's behavior should depend on the task to be accomplished, including the difficulty of the task and its relationship to previously learned tasks. For example, suppose the learning task is to create a routine in synchronized swimming. The teacher's contribution to help students accomplish this movement task may be to provide a stimulating facility with appropriate equipment and supplies for learning and to structure the group (large group, small group, individual) for optimal learning. For this learning task, the teacher may simply act as a guide and lead students to the discovery of the learning task. On the other hand, for a task such as learning to tackle in field hockey, the teacher may take a more direct role and explain and demonstrate the skill, arrange practice conditions, offer appropriate cues, and provide feedback to the learners about their performance.

Categorizing the elements of the teaching-learning process into the two phases of the teaching act. Once the elements of the teaching-learning process have been identified, the next logical step is to categorize these elements into the two phases of the teaching act. The first phase is the *preinstructional phase* and includes those actions that occur before teaching begins; the second phase includes those actions that occur during actual

teaching and is referred to as the *instructional phase*.

Preinstructional phase of the teaching-learning process. The preinstructional phase of the teaching-learning process includes the following elements (which may be classified as lesson planning):

1. Establishing objectives
2. Determining teaching methods and motivational techniques
3. Developing instructional materials
4. Determining equipment and facilities needed
5. Designing evaluation procedures

All the planning in the above phase should be carried out with the students in mind— their present abilities, motivation, age level, and other characteristics. The teacher must plan for the foregoing elements in an objective manner. Using information from the science of educational psychology, including learning theory and characteristics and development of children, can aid in the scientific basis for the art of teaching. For example, based on learning theory, it is known that individuals learn at different rates. It is also known that each individual is a unique being with special interests and abilities. Therefore, the teacher should not attempt to use only one teaching method for teaching a class. The selection of teaching methods should be based on the material to be taught, the students to be instructed, and so on.

Instructional phase of the teaching-learning process. Variables that are important during the instructional phase of the teaching act are those dealing with the actual use of teaching methods and interaction of students and teacher. These behaviors include the manner in which students and teachers think, feel, talk, move, and relate to one another. Ongoing evaluation of learning outcomes and constant feedback should also be a part of the instructional phase of the teaching-learning process.

Increasing the predictability of learning outcomes

To increase the predictability of learning outcomes, teachers of physical education should: (1) identify variables that affect learning, (2) formulate and test hypotheses regarding cause-effect relationships between variables, and (3) follow a scientifically developed and systematic instructional plan or model.

Identification of variables in the teaching-learning process. Important variables that affect the teaching-learning process have been systematically identified and categorized by leaders in the field of education. For example, the variables identified by Dunkin and Biddle[14] are probably the most widely recognized today. They have classified variables that affect the teaching-learning process in a time sequence—those that occur before, during, and after instruction. (This is consistent with our identification of events that occur during the two phases of the teaching act.)

Presage and context variables. The first important group of variables relates to teacher characteristics such as age, sex, social class background, and training experiences and are called *presage* variables. Dunkin and Biddle also indicate that certain *context* variables such as grade level, subject matter, size of class, and type of community are also important to the teaching-learning process. Variables related to the students—their age, needs and interests, what they already know, and so on—are also context variables.

A knowledge of the cause effect relationships between combinations of these two classes of variables becomes very important when determining the types of learning experiences (or tasks) to plan for students. One example of the importance of using information regarding cause-effect between presage and context variables in determining learn-

14. Dunkin, M. J., and Biddle, B. J.: The study of teaching, New York, 1974, Holt, Rinehart and Winston, Inc.

ing tasks is that of class size and selection of task. For instance, a skill such as learning to play a team sport that requires a large number of players should not be selected for a class of six students. Rather, learning tasks of a dual and individual nature should be introduced to small classes. Another example relates to the cause-effect relationship between grade level and learning task. A teacher should not, for example, teach tackle football to third-grade students because of their physical and developmental level.

Process variables. Process variables are those variables associated with the teaching act itself. These variables include the teaching methods that the teacher uses and those aspects of the teaching act that indicate the ways in which students and teachers interact—the way they talk, move, feel, and relate to one another.

Product or outcome variables. Finally, there are the *product* or *outcome* variables—those variables that denote the amount of learning or achievement of educational objectives. How well did the students learn modern dance? How well did they learn to swim? What were the attitudes of the students toward physical education? Did the students develop leadership qualities during certain activities? These questions, and many others, relate to the outcomes of the presage and process variables operating in a given context.

Formulating and testing hypotheses regarding cause-effect relationships between variables. Four types of variables were identified in the last section. With these four types of variables, there are six possible kinds of relationships between pairs of variables of these types: context-process, context-product, presage-process, presage-product, context-presage, and process-product.

A knowledge of each of these six kinds of relationships among the four kinds of variables is important. However, people who want to improve teaching, especially those who are interested in a scientific basis for teaching, are primarily concerned with process-product relationships. As Gage puts it, "they want to know whether the teacher's thinking, behaving, acting—in short, teaching—in one way is demonstrably better in terms of some values or purposes than teaching in another way."[10(p. 23)] In physical education, some pertinent questions relative to process-product relationships are: Did the students learn to play tennis faster through a team teaching format than with a single teacher? Were distributed practice sessions more conducive to learning a motor skill than massed practice sessions? Which should be stressed in the initial teaching of a motor skill, speed or accuracy? An understanding of the cause-effect relationships between variables such as these and their application in the teaching situation are important components of a scientific basis for teaching.

Establishing cause-effect relationships between variables associated with the teaching-learning process makes learning outcomes more predictable and controllable. According to Hunter,[13(pp. 348-350)] the cause-effect relationships in the teaching-learning process can be grouped under two generalizations: (1) learning is incremental and proceeds in sequence, and (2) the use of validated principles of learning contributes significantly to successful learning.

Learning is incremental and proceeds in sequence. There are both dependent and independent sequences in learning tasks. In a dependent sequence, the mastery of one learning stage is essential to the accomplishment of the next learning series. For example, learners must understand how to grip a racquet before being taught the forehand stroke in tennis. In an independent sequence, any one of the learnings can occur before another. Using the tennis example again, the serve may be taught before the forehand stroke or vice versa in this independent learning sequence.

The cause-effect relationship of this generalization is critical to the success of the teaching act. It means that a teacher must analyze the teaching-learning process carefully to determine what the learner already knows, and prescribe learning strategies based on the results of such information. For example, the teacher should not have students continue to practice a skill that has already been mastered. The next skill in the sequence should be introduced once the prerequisite skill has been learned. The teaching progression recommended for golf by the National Golf Foundation is used as a specific illustration of the application of the generalization relating to the incremental and sequential nature of learning. The National Golf Foundation recommends the following sequence for teaching golf: grip, address routine (including the stance), swing (backswing, downswing, and follow-through), approach (short-range accuracy shots such as the "pitch and run" and "chip" shot), and putt.[15]

By disregarding the generalization of the incremental and sequential nature of learning, the teacher may contribute to two negative reactions by students. They may become bored because the teacher continues a skill that they have mastered, or they may become frustrated because they have not accomplished the prerequisite skill for the next sequence of the activity. In the golf illustration, for example, the teacher should not continue to teach the grip after the student has completely learned this skill. Conversely, the teacher should not teach the swing before the student has become proficient in both the mechanics of the grip and the address routine.

Application of the generalization that learning is incremental does not mean that there is one "best sequence" for any particular learning success. It does, however,

---

15. National Golf Foundation: Golf lessons, Chicago, 1972, The Foundation.

mean that the sequence should always be logical and sound. For example, in the teaching of golf, the following sequence might also be used: grip, address routine, putt, short approach, and full swing.[16] A systematic diagnosis of the learner's present knowledge and skill level (process variables) is very important as a foundation for prescribing further activity in keeping with the generalizations of incremental and sequential learning.

The use of validated principles of learning contributes significantly to successful learning. Many learning principles have been validated and may be used as aids to successful learning. These principles can provide answers to some of the questions of cause-effect relationships that are required for a scientific basis for teaching. These validated principles have been well developed in other sources[17] and will not be repeated here. However, examples of two principles of practice and the principle of reinforcement will be given to illustrate how they can be incorporated into the teaching act.

PRINCIPLES OF PRACTICE. From the outset, it should be made clear that many of the principles of learning are based on the results of psychological research in the laboratory and cannot always be applied to gross motor physical education activities. Some of the research findings are also contradictory. Consequently, generalizations pertaining to principles of practice are sometimes in conflict. For example, in research dealing with massed versus distributed practice, Singer[18]

offers the generalization that distributed practice is better than massed practice sessions for the immediate learning of a psychomotor skill. On the other hand, Cratty[19] concludes that in most instances massing of practice results in greater learning of physical skills than does distributed practice sessions.

Several methodological and practical difficulties hamper the conduct of experiments dealing with massed versus distributed practice. Some of the more crucial ones are the definition of massed and distributed practice, the many possible combinations of massing and/or spacing of practices, the failure to differentiate between learning and performance, and the type of skill introduced as the dependent variable (fine or gross motor skill, verbal skill, and the like). The foregoing problems are partially responsible for the disparate findings regarding massed and distributed practice.

The following two generalizations proposed by Cratty seem to be reasonable guides for physical educators to follow in arranging practice sessions: (1) the amount of spacing of practice is related to the type of task and to the stage of learning reached, and (2) initial massing of practice is the most desirable means of acquiring a basis from which to proceed in learning a motor skill.[19(p. 371)] As an illustration, suppose the learning task is basketball and the learners are beginners. The teacher should begin with practice sessions of 30 minutes to 1 hour and note the students' motivation and skill development. Subsequent practice sessions should be adjusted (distributed) according to the interest, skill level, and retention of the basketball skills being taught.

It is generally agreed that "whole" practice results in quicker learning than "part" prac-

16. National Golf Foundation: Golf instructor's guide, Chicago, 1972, The Foundation., p. 5.
17. Hunter, M.: Motivation theory for teachers, 1967; Retention theory for teachers, 1967; Reinforcement theory for teachers, 1967; Teach more—faster!, 1969; and Teach for transfer, 1971, TIP Publications, P.O. Box 514, El Segundo, Calif., 90245.
18. Singer, R. N.: Motor learning and human performance: an application in physical education skills, New York, 1975, Macmillan Inc.

19. Cratty, B. J.: Movement behavior and motor learning, Philadelphia, 1973, Lea & Febiger.

tice if the learner is capable of grasping the "whole" skill.[19(p. 380)] This means that physical education skills such as bowling, swimming, and archery are complete, integrated skills in themselves and should be taught in their entirety. However, in a complex sport such as field hockey, which consists of such skills as dribbling, tackling, fielding, and dodging, each of the skills is an integrated whole and should be taught separately.

THE PRINCIPLE OF REINFORCEMENT. Reinforcement is one of the most fundamental principles of learning. In a general sense, positively reinforced responses tend to be repeated in given situations and negatively reinforced responses tend to be discontinued. In other words, actions followed by pleasurable responses will be repeated and those followed by discomfort will not consciously be repeated. For best results, the reinforcement (reward) should be introduced immediately after the desired response. The reinforcement might range from a "pat on the back" or informing the learner "that was a good try," to giving a tangible reward (medal, badge, money, and so on) for a successful performance.

Since the results of a successful performance are also a form of positive reinforcement, teachers should provide many opportunities for success on the part of students. This will result in a satisfaction and will act as a form of intrinsic reinforcement or reward. Negative reinforcement, in which students might be criticized or punished, is not recommended because it could lead to a poor self-image in students.

These are just three of the many principles of learning that can be used to guide instructional decisions to make learning more predictable and successful. Teachers who use the scientific basis for teaching should constantly monitor the process of teaching and learning to ascertain the cause-effect relationships between variables and should use validated principles of learning to make the teaching-learning process more predictable and successful.

Following a systematic instructional plan or model. After identifying relevant variables that affect learning and establishing cause-effect relationships between variables, the teacher must then use a systematic and logical plan to carry out the teaching act. The approach suggested here is to base the teaching model on a scientifically developed learning model. For example, Gentile[20] has developed and substantiated with research a model of motor skill acquisition (Table 4). The model contains seven steps in the learning process, and each step requires specific actions from the learner. Added to the model are key words or phrases that identify possible actions the teacher can take to facilitate learning at each stage of the process. To give the teacher a better understanding of how the teaching-learning model might be used, a step-by-step analysis of the components of the learning act as identified by Gentile, with suggested actions that the teacher could take to enhance student learning, is presented.

The factoring of human learning of motor skills into seven components or stages makes it possible for teachers to teach one sequence at a time, rather than attend to the total teaching act at once. By helping students to focus on a series of sequentially relevant learning activities, the teacher will be able to facilitate student learning. The teacher will also be able to determine at which stage in the process the student failed to learn. Consequently, intelligent decisions can be made concerning remediation of a particular learning module and/or future learning decisions.

Stage 1: Provide model of goal and motivate learner. The teacher must make sure

20. Gentile, A. M.: A working model of skill acquisition with application to teaching, Quest **17**:3-23, January 1972.

Table 4. Model of skill acquisition
with teacher actions

Learner actions	Teacher actions
Perceives what is to be learned and desires to try	Provides model of goal and motivates learner
Identifies the relevant stimuli in the environment	Provides teaching cues
Formulates a motor plan	Assists learner with motor plan formulation
Emits a response	Provides opportunity for learner to execute movement
Attends to the results	Provides appropriate feedback
Revises the motor plan	Helps learner adjust the motor plan based on feedback information
Emits another response (and repeats steps 5, 6, and 7)	Provides additional chance for execution of movement, gives additional feedback, and helps to revise motor plan until successful

that the learner has a clear concept of the skill to be learned and must create a motivational situation to foster learning of the task. How best can these objectives be accomplished? Should a movie or videotape of the skill be shown? Should the students be instructed to watch the varsity team perform the game that encompasses the skill involved? Or should the teacher introduce the skill to be learned by permitting the students to play the entire game to create increased motivation to learn the component parts of the game? All of these questions are relevant to the solution of the first learning stage of the skill acquisition model. A teacher who

uses the scientific basis for teaching will be guided by research on learning theory, validated principles of learning, specific principles of motor learning, and research in motor learning to help answer these and other questions pertaining to motor skill acquisition.

Stage 2: Provide teaching cues. Once the learner gets a clear picture or model of the goal to be accomplished, the next step is to identify those stimuli (factors) in the environment that are conducive to optimal learning. Those factors that are irrelevant to the acquisition of the motor skill should be disregarded. The teacher can play an important part in learning at this point by identifying the relevant stimuli in the form of "teaching cues," thereby facilitating learning. The objective of teaching cues at this stage is to help clarify the model for the learner.

The teacher may help the learner to focus on relevant stimuli by emphasizing them, either verbally or visually, or both. The learner will probably need more help in selecting and paying attention to relevant stimuli in open skills* in which environmental conditions are subject to change. For example, in touch football, which is an open skill, the learner who is learning to catch a football in an open field must monitor many environmental factors, several of which are subject to change from one attempt to the next. The speed and direction of the ball, the position of the defensive player, and the terrain of the field must all be considered when learning to catch a football while moving. On the other

---

*In open skills, the learner must be concerned with changing environmental conditions as well as the actions of others. The actions of others are not easily predictable and may, in fact, be designed to deceive the performer, such as a pitcher throwing a change-up pitch in baseball. Closed skills are those in which the environment is fixed and environmental factors have little influence on performers. In closed skills, the learner is concerned only with his or her own movements, the results of which are fairly predictable.

hand, when performing a closed skill, such as a routine in gymnastics, the learner is concerned only with executing the various aspects of the routine. Another closed skill is bowling, in which the learner's only consideration is knocking down the pins, which are stationary. In the latter two skills, the learner has fewer stimuli about which he or she must be concerned, thus the teacher will probably be required to provide fewer teaching cues.

There is no one *best* method for helping learners monitor only relevant stimuli in the environment. The teacher should let the learner proceed on his or her own as much as possible in monitoring the environment for relevant stimuli before offering help. The teacher should also refrain from presenting too many teaching cues, which will often cause confusion rather than facilitate learning of the skill. The teacher should combine several specific teaching cues into one general concept and present one or two concepts to clarify a skill. For example, teaching cues for catching a football might be "keep eyes on ball until caught" "catch ball in fingers of both hands," "give when ball makes contact."

Stage 3: Assist learner with motor plan formulation. Formulating an accurate motor plan is probably the most critical step in the process of skill acquisition after the initial motivation to learn has been established. Since the development of a motor plan is conceptualized in an internal manner by the learner, it is difficult for the teacher to determine whether or not an adequate plan is being made. Therefore, the teacher's job at this stage becomes somewhat difficult.

Perhaps the teacher's ability to direct the learner's attention to the relevant factors associated with the skill to be acquired, including a viable model of the skill, is the best aid in helping the learner to formulate a motor plan. Surely a learner will be better able to

formulate an adequate motor plan when there are less distracting environmental factors and a clear perception of the model of the skill to be learned.

Stage 4: Provide opportunity for learner to execute movement. Once the motor plan has been formulated, the learner is ready to practice the skill. Questions relating to massed versus distributed practice, whole versus part, speed versus accuracy, and the value of mental practice must be answered in structuring the environment for meaningful practice sessions. The type and difficulty of the skill and the skill background of the learner will also influence the type of practice environment that is provided.

How the teacher structures the environment is very important in determining whether practice will be meaningful to learners. Based on a combination of theoretical information from a number of scholars and available research evidence, Arnold[21] offered four suggestions related to the teacher's role in facilitating the organization of movement by the learner to match characteristics of the environment. Two of the suggestions that pertain to practice conditions are:

1. The environmental conditions under which a learner practices a motor skill must be similar to the actual environmental constraints that govern performance. This means that closed skills must be practiced under stable, consistent environmental conditions. In contrast, open skills must be practiced under variable, changing, environmental conditions. The teacher's task is to simplify the complex open environment for skills such as softball, field hockey, and tennis, while still maintaining the necessary "openness" of practice condi-

21. Arnold, R. K.: Optimizing skill learning: moving to match the environment, Journal of Physical Education and Recreation **49**:84-86, November-December 1978.

tions. According to Arnold, "Mini-game situations involving two players and a limited number of environmental situations and response options may serve to provide such a simplified, yet open practice environment."[21(p. 85)]

2. The performer of open skills must develop a repertoire of movement patterns, and therefore, the teacher must also provide for systematic variation in the characteristics of the performance context. The open skill performer must learn the probability of occurrence of events in the environment so that he or she can plan ahead, predict, and rapidly select a response from his or her movement repertoire. Therefore, practice sessions should be structured so that students are placed into the actual game situation very early in the instructional sequence. Game-related practice on specific skills can then follow as the need for the skill arises from game play. Also, teachers should help students "learn how to learn" by structuring a learning situation that will facilitate an active process of seeking successful solutions to relevant motor problems by matching movements to the characteristics of the environment.

Teachers should be very attentive to the students during the practice of the skill being taught. The ability to analyze skill learning and make meaningful suggestions is also critical to skill acquisition. The teacher should be able to determine the reason(s) for failure to carry out the motor plan and help the learner to make the necessary adjustments. The most effective way to do this is to teach the learner how to monitor his or her own feedback and change aspects of the movement pattern as needed. In other words, the teacher should teach the learner how to learn.

Although the teacher might provide feedback during the performance of the skill, most of the feedback should be given after the skill has been completed. This is especially true for learners who are at the initial stages of learning a skill. Providing learning cues at this stage will usually suffice. In teaching the serve in badminton, for instance, the learner might be told to "keep your eyes on the bird as contact is made" or "follow through" if these aspects of the skills are executed poorly.

Stage 5: Provide appropriate feedback. Full attention should be given to critiquing the performance and providing feedback about the results. The learner can get some indication of the degree of success of the skill by the performance, but this type of feedback is not always desirable. In fact, in some cases it might be detrimental to the learner. For example, the learner might hit the tennis ball on the wood portion of the racquet but still get the ball over the net. The fact that the result was successful should not preclude feedback about the motor characteristics of the learner that caused the poor hit. Why did the learner fail to hit the ball with the face of the racquet? The teacher should help the learner answer this question.

Feedback may be visual, verbal, tactile, or a combination of these. Feedback may also be intrinsic (information available to the learner as a result of performance) or augmented (information made available to the learner in addition to intrinsic feedback). Teachers should help performers develop internal feedback mechanisms related to kinesthetic senses for them to get the "feel" of the movement. In some cases, however, augmented feedback is needed. For example, if a teacher sees that a performer is taking off too close to a hurdle (in track and field) causing him or her to jump over the hurdle, some feedback to the performer would be necessary. However, the question regarding the type of feedback that should be provided would still need an answer. Should it be verbal ("Mary, you should start your hurdle 2 feet earlier.") or should it be visual feedback (showing a videotape of the performance)? A utilization of research findings in the area of feedback with regard to the skill in question might provide some of the answers to these questions.*

Stage 6: Help learner adjust the motor plan based on feedback information. Based on the results of feedback information, the learner is encouraged to make the necessary changes in the motor plan and/or execution and try again. Indeed, it might be necessary to change the entire goal sought, focus on different stimuli, or execute the motor plan the same way if the previous result was efficient and successful. The major objective is to eliminate whatever impediments there are to successful performance of the skill. Meaningful and successful attention to the results of feedback on the part of the learner will ensure the reduction of extraneous stimuli, improvement in concentration on relevant skill factors and, subsequently, a more predictably successful skill performance.

Stage 7: Provide for additional practice and feedback. The teacher should use additional practice and feedback to improve motor plan.

This teaching-learning model provides a logical and systematic series of stages that comprise the teaching-learning process. Not only should teachers follow the steps in the model, but they should also base their instructional decisions at each step on validated principles of learning, findings of sound research studies regarding a particular instruc-

tional decision,* knowledge of variables that affect learning and their cause-effect relationships, and the individuality of each learner.

A SEQUENTIAL OUTLINE OF TEACHER DECISIONS BASED ON A SCIENTIFIC ANALYSIS OF THE TEACHING-LEARNING PROCESS

The teaching model just described deals with events directly related to the teaching act. As was pointed out previously, instructional decisions and interacting variables that occur before and after the teaching act are just as important as those that take place during the teaching act itself. Teachers should have a systematic and logical method for making decisions throughout the teaching-learning process that will make student learning more predictable and successful.

Hunter[13(pp. 350-352)] identified eleven components or decision areas in which the teacher must act to deliberately exert a productive influence on students' learning. These eleven sequential decisions are based on a scientific analysis of the teaching-learning process. The sequence of decisions in the teaching-learning process is:

1. Deliberate and scientific separation of genuine educational constraints or variables from the typical ethnic, financial, intellectual excuses that constitute reasons for failing to promote student learning. Descriptive-analytical research systems (for example, see the CAFIAS [Cheffers Adaptation of

---

*See the article by Rothstein and Arnold in which they applied the findings of research studies on the use of videotape feedback in the teaching of motor skills. They also presented an illustration of the use of research findings related to the teaching of bowling.

*Nixon and Locke have reviewed research studies dealing with relevant instructional techniques (examples: distribution of practice, feedback, learning strategies) at each stage of the teaching model as well as preactive (before class) decisions such as class size, ability grouping, and schedules and postactive (after class) events such as analysis of teaching. It must be pointed out that their review was completed almost a decade ago. Persons interested in using research findings as a basis for teaching should also review more recent research studies.

the Flanders Interaction Analysis System] as described by Cheffers and Mancini)[22] may be used to determine those variables that influence student learning.

2. Determination of what students have already achieved and what they are ready to learn in terms of degree of difficulty (sequence) and complexity (in affective, cognitive, or psychomotor domain).

3. Identification of productive learning behavior for achievement of the learning task and for each learner.

4. Determination of an instructional objective with specificity in content and perceivability in terms of learner behavior. Instructional objectives must be specific enough for learners to understand what they are expected to accomplish. An examination of the source by Mager[23] will be of great help in developing instructional objectives.

5. Identification of principles of learning that are relevant to the accomplishment of each instructional objective.

6. Adaptation of those principles to the particular situation and to each learner. For example, the principle of whole-part learning indicates that skills must be taught as a whole for best learning. However, extremely difficult skills should be broken down into their component parts and taught in a progressive manner.

7. Incorporation of the teacher's own personality attributes and competence in the specific learning area to enhance the learner's probability of successful accomplishment. This is the only decision area in the teaching-learning process in which, except for "knowing oneself," science has little to offer at present. In this instance, the teacher uses the knowledge of intuition to enhance the teaching-learning process.

8. Synthesis of decisions 1 through 7 in the deliberate design or blueprint for a teaching-learning episode. To maximize successful learning, all the previous decisions must be consciously made before the teacher-learner interaction in the next step occurs.

9. The actual teaching-learning interaction begins. The teaching model previously described and the descriptive-analytical systems for describing teacher-learner interactions may be used to aid the teacher in making decisions at this point.

10. Evaluation is an integral and continuous aspect of the teaching-learning process, not merely a terminal function. Constant monitoring of the learner's progress yields essential current information that may modify the teaching-learning process.

11. On the basis of these evaluative data collected during the teaching-learning process, the determination is made to: (a) reteach, (b) practice and extend the time for mastery, (c) move on, or (d) "abandon ship" because, for some reason, the objective is not attainable by the learner at this time.

These eleven components have been outlined to establish the significance of scientific analysis of the teaching-learning process.[13(p. 351)] As a result of this kind of analysis, successful teaching becomes explainable and predictable. Unsuccessful teaching, that

22. Cheffers, J. T. F., and Mancini, V. H.: Teacher-student interaction. In Anderson, W. G., and Barrette, G. T., editors: What's going on in gym: descriptive studies of physical education classes, Motor Skills: Theory into Practice, Monograph 1, 1978.

23. Mager, R. F.: Preparing instructional objectives, Belmont, Calif., 1962, Fearon Publishers.

is, when students have not learned, is also explainable since it is possible to identify with accuracy where something went wrong. Consequently, the teacher can intervene and provide needed remediation at the proper time without loss of time or energy.

THE USE OF DESCRIPTIVE SYSTEMS FOR ANALYZING THE TEACHING-LEARNING PROCESS

Descriptive-analytical systems are another means of objectively explaining important characteristics of the teaching-learning process. Descriptive-analytical systems are techniques that allow for the systematic observation, recording, and analysis of events (specifically, student and teacher behavior) in the classroom, gymnasium, swimming pool, and on the athletic fields.

Several "descriptive techniques" have been reported in the literature. Probably one of the most popular is the Flanders Interaction Analysis System (FIAS).[24] The system was designed to indicate the prevailing climate in the classroom by determining the pattern of teacher behavior in terms of directness versus indirectness.

Although Flanders' system of interaction analysis is a valid method for analyzing the verbal behavior and interaction between student and teacher, it is not appropriate for measuring nonverbal activity. Since much of the behavior of students and teachers in physical education classes consists of nonverbal behavior, modifications in the FIAS were needed before it could be appropriately used in physical education classes. Some of the descriptive systems that have been adapted from FIAS for observing and recording various aspects of student and teacher behavior in physical education settings and other descriptive systems have been thoroughly discussed by Anderson and Barrette.[25] These systems permit observers to record and describe both verbal and nonverbal behavior.

Information from various descriptive systems for analyzing behavior of students and teachers in the classroom and gymnasium, research and authoritative writing on classroom interaction, and his own research on teaching physical education have been used by Anderson in his book on analyzing teaching physical education.[26] This text contains twenty "clinical tasks" that, when completed properly,* will enable observers to systematically analyze a variety of events in various physical education settings. According to Anderson, methods of analysis should be used that:

1. *Focus on different targets:* Student behavior, teacher behavior, teacher-student interaction, student learning.
2. *Use different observers/evaluators:* The teacher, a colleague, a supervisor, students.
3. *Involve various techniques for collecting data:* Informal notes, descriptive coding of events, criterion-referenced writings, subjective/narrative reports, test scores.
4. *Record different dimensions of teaching:* Student involvement in activities, roles, teacher's method of communication, lesson content, the manner of teacher-student interaction, and several others.[26(p. 3)]

By completing the various clinical tasks, a person can develop skill in the foregoing methods that will enable him or her to logically and objectively analyze actual events as

24. Flanders, N. A.: Analyzing teaching behavior, Reading, Mass., 1970, Addison-Wesley Publishing Co., Inc.

25. Anderson, W. G., and Barrette, G. T., editors: What's going on in gym: Descriptive studies of physical education classes, Motor Skills: Theory into Practice, Monograph 1, 1978.
26. Anderson, W. G.: Analysis of teaching physical education, St. Louis, 1980, The C. V. Mosby Co.
*Anderson presents explicit instructions for coding behavior, including operational definitions of terms and special ground rules for using a particular analytical system.

they happen in a physical education class. For example, one will be able to ascertain the amount of time students spend actively engaged in movement activities or how much time they spend "waiting their turn" or "receiving information" from the teacher. In addition to determining how much time teachers spend talking (instructing, giving explanations, and so on), one can also determine other teacher behaviors and interactions with students. Does the teacher use the "direct" or "indirect" method of teaching, or a combination of methods? How does the teacher interact with students, both individually and in groups? How does the teacher measure student improvement? All these questions and many more may be answered by carefully completing the clinical tasks developed by Anderson.

The ultimate objectives or purposes of analyzing the teaching-learning process should be to improve teaching and increase student learning. The skillful use of methods of analyzing teaching in physical education through the clinical tasks presented by Anderson is one means of helping teachers to realize these objectives.

CONCLUDING STATEMENT

Teachers who develop a scientific basis for teaching physical education will be able to: (1) make specific and meaningful selections from a varied set of options and (2) increase the predictability of learning outcomes by hypothesizing about and testing cause-effect relationships. These actions will be possible because teachers will be able to make use of validated principles of learning, descriptive-analytical research models, teaching models, and an understanding and use of behavior modification, instructional design, delivery, and management in structuring the teaching-learning process. The results of such a scientific approach to teaching will be a more predictable and successful series of learning outcomes.

DISCUSSION QUESTIONS AND EXERCISES

1. List and discuss the characteristics of a scientific basis for teaching. Indicate how this differs from a science of teaching and discuss the difference between the science of teaching and the art of teaching.
2. Compare and contrast the different viewpoints of a science of teaching as expressed by Gage and Siedentop.
3. Explain to a PTA group three reasons why physical education teachers are important.
4. Prepare a presentation on "Accountability of Physical Educators" to be delivered before a meeting of professional physical educators.
5. List and discuss the characteristics of an "effective" teacher and an "effective" teaching-learning process.
6. List and discuss the two general means by which physical educators can develop a scientific basis for teaching physical education. Explain to your supervisor each step of the process.
7. List and discuss the elements of the preinstructional phase of the teaching-learning process and indicate their importance in the realization of effective teaching.
8. Identify and discuss the four types of variables in the teaching-learning process. Indicate which variables you think are most important and tell why.
9. There are six possible kinds of relationships between pairs of the four types of variables. Give two examples of cause-effect relationships for these pairs of variables. Indicate the two pairs of variables about which educators should be most anxious to know the cause-effect relationships.
10. Define a dependent and an independent learning task and give two examples of each.
11. Apply the research findings on mass and distributed practice and reinforcement to the teaching of swimming to beginning swimmers.
12. Using Gentile's model of skill acquisition, teach a handball lesson to a twelfth-grade co-educational physical education class.
13. Define "open" and "closed" skills. Explain why different teaching strategies would be needed to teach these two kinds of skills.
14. Follow Hunter's eleven decision areas in

teaching a skill in physical education. Indicate whether this systematic process has helped you to improve your teaching.

15. Explain the concept of "descriptive-analytical" techniques for evaluating the teaching-learning process. Apply Anderson's twenty clinical tasks to the analysis of one of your physical education classes that has been videotaped.

SELECTED REFERENCES

Anderson, W. G.: Analysis of teaching physical education, St. Louis, 1980, The C. V. Mosby Co.

Anderson, W. G., and Barrette, G. T., editors: What's going on in gym: descriptive studies of physical education classes, Motor Skills: Theory into Practice, Monograph 1, 1978.

Bucher, C. A.: Administration of physical education and athletic programs, ed. 7, St. Louis, 1979, The C. V. Mosby Co.

Bucher, C. A.: Foundations of physical education, ed. 8, St. Louis, 1979, The C. V. Mosby Co.

Bucher, C. A., and Thaxton, N. A.: Physical education for children: movement foundations and experiences, New York, 1979, Macmillan Inc.

Bucher, C. A., and Koenig, C. R.: Methods and materials for secondary school physical education, ed. 5, St. Louis, 1978, The C. V. Mosby Co.

Bloom, B. S., editor: Taxonomy of educational objectives. Handbook 1: cognitive domain, New York, 1956, David McKay Co., Inc.

Bugelski, B. R.: The psychology of learning applied to teaching, New York, 1971, The Bobbs-Merrill Co., Inc.

Cheffers, J. T. F., Amidon, E. J., and Rodgers, K. D.: Interaction analysis: an application to nonverbal activity, Minneapolis, 1974, Association for Productive Teaching.

Decco, J. P., and Crawford, W. R.: The psychology of learning and instruction, Englewood Cliffs, N.J., 1974, Prentice-Hall, Inc.

Dunkin, M. J., and Biddle, B. J.: The study of teaching, New York, 1974, Rinehart and Winston, Inc.

Flanders, N. A.: Analyzing teaching behavior, Reading, Mass., 1970, Addison-Wesley Publishing Co., Inc.

Flanders, N. A.: Teacher influence in the classroom. In Amidon, E. J., and Hough, J. B., editors: Interaction analysis: theory, research and application, Reading, Mass., 1967, Addison-Wesley Publishing Co., Inc.

Gage, N. L.: The scientific basis of the art of teaching, New York, 1978, Teachers College Press.

Gentile, A. M.: A working model of skill acquisition, Quest 17:3-23, January 1972.

Hunter, M.: The science of the art of teaching. In Allen, D. W., and Hecht, J. C., editors: Controversies in education, Philadelphia, 1974, W. B. Saunders Co.

Hunter, M.: The teaching process and the learning process. In Seifman, E., and Allen, D. W., editors: Handbook for teachers, Glenview, Ill., 1971, Scott Foresman and Co.

Krathwohl, D. R., and others: Taxonomy of educational objectives. Handbook II: affective domain, New York, 1964, David McKay Co., Inc.

Mager, R. F.: Preparing instructional objectives, Belmont, Calif., 1962, Fearon Publishers.

Nixon, J. E., and Locke, L. W.: Research on teaching physical education. In Travers, R. M. W., editor: Second handbook of research on teaching, Chicago, 1973, Rand McNally & Co.

Rosenshine, B., and Furst, N. A.: The use of direct observation to study teaching. In Travers, R. M. W., editor: Second handbook of research on teaching, Chicago, 1973, Rand McNally & Co.

Rothstein, A. L., and Arnold, R. K.: Bridging the gap: application of research on videotape feedback and bowling, Motor Skills: Theory into Practice 1:35-62, Fall 1976.

Shockley, J. M.: Needed: behavioral objectives in physical education, Journal of Health, Physical Education, and Recreation 44:47-49, April 1973.

Simpson, E. J.: The classification of educational objectives: psychomotor domain, Illinois Teacher of Home Economics 10:110-144, Winter, 1966-1967.

8 □ Using a systems approach for program development

Courtesy Springfield College, Springfield, Mass.

As a result of the tight job market for physical education teachers, there is an increased emphasis on exposing students majoring in physical education to alternative career possibilities.[1,2,3] Some of these career alternatives include positions as directors and teach-

1. Clayton, R. D., and Clayton, J.: Concepts and careers in physical education, Minneapolis, 1977, Burgess Publishing Co.
2. Groves, R.: Helping students find positions in a tight job market, Journal of Physical Education and Recreation **47**:43, May 1976.
3. Lepley, P. M., and others: Alternative careers for physical educators, Journal of Physical Education and Recreation **48**:29, January 1977.

ers at health spas, industrial fitness centers, correctional institutions, centers for the aged, and the like. In each of these positions, the physical educator is likely to be required to develop a program of physical education or assist in the formation of a program.

In too many traditional physical education programs the curriculums have been developed in a haphazard manner. There has often been little philosophical direction, and professional objectives have not been clearly thought through to guide program development. Furthermore, the selection of activities in such programs is often based on the type and nature of facilities as well as the special interests and competence of teachers, rather than on the needs, interests, and developmental levels of the students. Also, activities that are selected are taught from year-to-year, with little or no variety or progression.

A more systematic and logical approach to program development in physical education is needed. The program must be determined by the developmental needs of the consumer and based on clearly developed objectives. The systems approach is one method that can be used to develop a systematic and logically organized program for physical education.

THE SYSTEMS APPROACH

The systems approach to program development described here is a logical and systematic method aimed at producing desirable educational outcomes; that is, skills, attitudes, and knowledge. In addition to its needs-based emphasis, this model stresses ongoing program evaluation and modification based on the results achieved. The systems model used here is adapted from that developed by Tankard.[4] The elements of this model consist of:

1. Indicating the goals and objectives for the clientele.
2. Assessing the present status of the clientele relative to the goals and objectives.
3. Determining the needs (differences between present status and goals and objectives) of the clientele.
4. Choosing those needs that are to be met immediately and those that are long-term needs.
5. Planning a program to meet the identified needs.

---

4. Tankard, G. G., Jr.: Curriculum improvement: an administrator's guide, Englewood Cliffs, N.J., 1974, Parker Publishing Co., pp. 37-39 and Chapter 10.

6. Indicating the necessary personnel, facilities, equipment, and other resources to implement the program.
7. Evaluating the program to determine the extent to which the program has met its goals and objectives.
8. Revising and/or modifying the program as indicated by the evaluation results.

Illustrations of the use of the systems approach model

The systems model outlined above will be used to develop two physical education programs, one for students in schools and one for people in industry.

Example of the development of a school program in physical education using a systems model. This example is limited to the elementary school and more specifically to the intermediate grades (4-6). To develop such a program, the following steps are carried out.

Step 1. Indicating goals and objectives. Beginning teachers as well as students majoring in physical education might be wondering how one goes about selecting goals and objectives for a physical education program when there are so many different statements of objectives. Identification and statement of goals and objectives is achieved through a logical analysis of the developmental levels, needs, and interests of students, study of the professional literature, and a reflection on personal philosophy and experience and educational philosophy and practice.

In the final analysis, the individual teacher will have to make decisions about which objectives to choose for the program. A sound philosophy of physical education will provide direction and guidance in selecting worthwhile purposes and objectives. (Refer to Chapter 6 for a more complete discussion on this topic.)

The following goal and objectives were

Courtesy Springfield College, Springfield, Mass.

selected for elementary school children in the intermediate grades (4-6):

Goal: To develop each student to his or her optimal potential—physically, mentally, socially, and emotionally—through physical education.

Objectives:

1. To develop the physical foundations for movement.
2. To develop the student's movement skills.
3. To develop the student's cognitive abilities, including an understanding of the structure of movement.
4. To develop for the student a meaningful social experience and a positive attitude toward and appreciation for efficient and effective movement.

In addition to the four professional objectives, instructional objectives and performance or behavioral objectives must also be stated for each of the three domains (motor-skill, cognitive, and affective-social). These instructional and performance objectives for specific activities would not normally be stated until after the needs of the students have been assessed and the activities for the program have been selected. However, they will be stated here for the affective-social domain to illustrate the procedure.

Instructional objectives:

1. To demonstrate a positive attitude toward and appreciation for efficient and effective movement through participation in gymnastics.
2. To demonstrate positive social traits, such as good sportsmanship, respect for the rights of others, and the ability to get along with others, through gymnastics.

Performance objectives: After exposure to a unit on gymnastics, the student will be able to:

1. Demonstrate a positive attitude toward gymnastics by enthusiastically participating in the class during the gymnastics unit.
2. Demonstrate an appreciation for gym-

Courtesy Springfield College, Springfield, Mass.

nastics by participating during out-of-school hours.

3. Demonstrate good sportsmanship by not making excuses when he or she loses, even if he or she believes that the judging was poor.

4. Respect the decisions of the judges by not disputing or arguing with them after they render a score.

5. Demonstrate leadership qualities by helping those students with less skill in gymnastics than himself or herself.

6. Demonstrate leadership qualities by acting as a squad leader.

7. Demonstrate emotional stability by not displaying temper tantrums or other unacceptable means to vent anger and frustration.

8. Demonstrate good social qualities by working well in a squad.

Step 2. Assessing present status of students. The second step, after identifying and stating the goal and objectives of the physical education program, is to assess the present status of the students in the fifth grade. This assessment should include the areas of skills, knowledge, and attitudes and appreciations.

Probably the most difficult of the domains to evaluate is the affective-social domain. However, there are means of assessing the status of students in these areas. For example, self-concept can be assessed by using the Martinek-Zaichokowsky Self-Concept Scale or the Piers-Harris Children's Self-Concept Scale. Also, there are other less formal means of evaluating children in the areas of affective and social learnings. Such techniques as personal observations, interviews, questionnaires, and anecdotal records may be used to assess attitudes and appreciations in physical education. Bucher and Thaxton[5] provide a thorough coverage of evaluating the affective-social domain.

5. Bucher, C. A., and Thaxton, N. A.: Physical education for children: movement foundations and experiences, New York, 1979, Macmillan Inc., Chapter 22.

Step 3. Determining needs to be met. The needs to be met are determined by comparing the difference between the present status of the students and the goals and objectives that are identified. In the affective area, for example, the teacher might discover during the "assessment" stage that some students exhibit poor sportsmanship. Therefore, that teacher would include methods and activities in the program to meet this demonstrated need. The same determination of needs would be made for each of the objectives in all three domains. The teacher should be cognizant of the individual differences of students and determine needs on an individual basis.

Step 4. Choosing short-term and long-term needs. Once needs have been determined, the next step is to determine which needs are to be met immediately and which are the long-term needs. The grade level and/or age of the students and the nature of the need will largely determine whether it is classified as a short-term or long-term need. The need to develop a positive self-concept and the need to develop good sportsmanship qualities will be used to illustrate how one determines the appropriateness of classifying needs. For example, if students in the fifth grade cannot get along with their classmates, they need to develop sportsmanship. The urgency of meeting this need is obvious since the inability of students to get along with their peers will militate against the teaching of group activities such as team games. On the other hand, the development of a positive self-concept might be established as a long-term goal for fifth grade students.

Another consideration in carrying out this step of the model is the operational definition of *short-term* and *long-term* with respect to time. For instance, the development of good sportsmanship (such as the ability to get along with others) might be allotted a 4-week unit. However, if there is a need to control antisocial behavior such as using abusive language or striking another student, the short-term goal to meet such a need might be more immediate (within 1 week, for instance). The long-term goal to develop a positive self-concept in fifth grade students might be within the school year. If these kinds of needs were evident in high school students, however, the target time for meeting such needs might be even shorter. Each teacher will have to decide which needs are to be met immediately and which are long-term needs. The teacher must also indicate an approximate time-frame for meeting such needs.

Step 5. Planning a program to meet the identified needs. The program of physical education for elementary school students at the intermediate level (grades 4-6) includes: (1) the content of activities and experiences and the sequence and progression used to present the content, (2) the teaching methods to be used, and (3) the evaluation to be conducted and the evaluation instruments to be used.

Physical education content for intermediate level students includes movement awareness experiences and such activities as gymnastics and tumbling, self-testing activities, games of low organization and relays, team games, individual and dual games, and fundamental movements related to rhythms and dance. A complete yearly activities plan for fifth grade boys and girls is presented elsewhere.[5(p. 130)]

In the activities plan for fifth grade students, basic movement skills are incorporated into specialized movement activities such as gymnastics and tumbling, volleyball, and rhythms and dance. It was determined during the assessment of student needs that they had achieved the necessary competencies in basic foundations of movement in the primary grades.

In addition to the activities for the motor-skill domain, the students would also be provided activities and experiences to meet objectives for the cognitive and affective-social domains. Having students write short papers on the history of the sport that they are learning is one way to develop cognitive understandings. Other examples of activities to develop objectives in the cognitive domain include having students explain concepts related to movement activities, such as "player rotation" in volleyball or "levers" in throwing a ball. An example of fostering social learning is to have students interact within a group by participating in team games. Acting as student leaders should help students develop qualities of leadership. Providing opportunities for students to achieve success would be one means of developing a positive self-concept in students.

A combination of methods would be used to present the content of physical education activities and experiences to students. The problem-solving method, for example, could be used to teach general skills such as running, jumping, throwing, and kicking. The more traditional method of explanation, demonstration, and allowance for practice, for example, could be used to teach some specialized sport skills such as baton passing in relay racing and the crawl stroke in swimming.

The inclusion of plans for evaluation of the process and the program outcomes is vital at this stage of the systems process. Both the evaluation process and instruments for evaluation should be related to the performance objectives and instructional strategies that are used in the program. For instance, the performance objective: "The student will demonstrate a positive attitude toward physical education by the end of the year," might be evaluated by using a checklist and observing the degree of enthusiasm with which students participate in class activities. Some other instrument such as a questionnaire might also be used. The type of evaluation

process selected will determine the evaluation instrument that is needed. It is advisable to plan for the use of several evaluation strategies.

Step 6. Indicating the resources needed to implement the program. When a lack of equipment, facilities, or even teaching expertise precludes the inclusion of certain activities deemed vital to the success of the program, additional resources might be requested. For example, suppose that swimming were assessed as an important need for students in the upper elementary school grades. Suppose further that no pool is available at the school. One solution to this problem would be the use of a community-owned pool or to urge children to develop swimming skills on their own. When teachers do not have the expertise to teach certain activities, they might be required to take inservice or graduate courses or attend workshops, clinics, or seminars to gain the necessary competence. Another strategy is to hire a qualified specialist on a part-time basis to teach selected activities.

The involvement and support of the administration should be sought before attempting any program development. Administrative support is critical at this stage. In implementing the plan to use community resources, for example, the approval of the school principal would be necessary. Furthermore, administrative approval and assistance would be necessary for students to be transported between school and the community facility.

Step 7. Evaluating the program. The overall goal of the physical education program is to develop each student to his or her optimal level in the physical, mental, social, and emotional domains. Both formative and summative evaluation should be conducted in conjunction with the development of such a program. According to Bloom and his coworkers, "formative evaluation" is used during the construction and use of a new curriculum or program, and "summative evaluation" is the assessment that occurs at the end of the program.[6]

Since the program of physical education should constantly be revised and/or modified to meet the needs of the students, formative evaluation is emphasized. There should be an ongoing evaluation of the process of developing the program, and there should also be an assessment of the degree to which students achieve program objectives. An example of formative evaluation in the affective-social domain is the observation of students by the teacher to determine whether they participate enthusiastically in class. Another example is the observation of students to note whether they exhibit leadership qualities by such acts as peer teaching or being a squad leader. Specific tests, such as Coopersmith's Self-Esteem Inventory to measure self-concept or a sociogram to evaluate social status of students within the class, might also be used to assess progress toward meeting objectives in the affective-social domain.

The preceding examples might also be used to illustrate how formative evaluation can be used to evaluate the process of program development. For example, it might be discovered through an examination of formative evaluation data that some students failed to develop certain leadership qualities because the program was not designed to provide them with enough opportunities to encourage initiative and leadership. Specifically, the traditional method of teaching was used instead of a problem-solving approach, no student aides were used, and peer teaching was discouraged. Changes should be made in stages of the systems model when evaluation data reveal weaknesses.

Summative evaluation is useful in determining the degree to which the total program meets the overall goal. This type of evaluation should be conducted at least once at the end of the school year. However, intermediate summative evaluation might be conducted at the conclusion of certain units of instruction. An illustration of summative evaluation is the use of the LaPorte Score Card[7] or some other evaluation instrument to assess program effectiveness. This type of evaluation would be conducted at the end of the year and is referred to as *long-term evaluation.* An example of intermediate summative evaluation is the use of an attitude rating scale to ascertain the attitudes of students toward tennis at the conclusion of a unit on tennis.

Step 8. Responding to evaluation results. Aspects of the program would be revised according to the results of both formative and summative evaluation data. Formative evaluation results seem to be most critical since these data are secured on a continuous basis during the operation of the program. For example, if a significant number of students continually fail to demonstrate qualities of leadership in a program in which the traditional method of teaching is used, a problem-solving technique could be used. Also, if formative evaluation results indicate that goals and objectives require some alterations, such changes could be made. If students could not meet the objectives of badminton during a 4-week unit, for instance, either the length of the unit might be increased or the objectives might be modified.

---

6. Bloom, B. S., Hastings, J. T., and Madaus, G. F.: Handbook on formative and summative evaluation of student learning, New York, 1971, McGraw-Hill Book Co., p. 6.

7. LaPorte, W. R.: The physical education curriculum, Los Angeles, 1968, College Book Store. (Revised by John M. Cooper, Indiana University.) The score card contains standards for a national program of physical education for schools and colleges. It is also intended to be an evaluation instrument for assessing the physical education program and the general health, recreation, and safety programs in elementary and secondary schools.

An overall assessment of the program would be determined through summative evaluation techniques, and changes and/or modifications could be made accordingly. For example, suppose the results of program evaluation indicate that physical education is offered only twice per week. Suppose further that the classroom teacher rather than a specialist in physical education was the teacher of physical education. If a significantly large number of students failed to meet program objectives in such a program, those aspects outlined above could be changed to help determine if they were the reasons for student failure.

Example of the use of a systems approach to develop a physical fitness program for people in industry

Step 1. Indicating goals and objectives

Goal: To design a fitness program that will serve as a preventive medical measure (particularly for cardiovascular heart disease) for selected employees of an industrial operation.

Objectives*:

1. To have the program supervised by a person with a doctorate degree in physical education and a specialization in exercise physiology. One or more aides (depending on the size of the program) would also be needed.
2. To conduct the program in conjunction with the medical department at the company and to have a medical doctor as a part of the fitness program staff.
3. To provide individualized prescription exercises for each participant in the program.
4. To provide an education component to the program in which information will be discussed, such as proper diet, ef-

fects of exercise on the body, stress in daily life, and other health-related topics.
5. To provide equipment that will monitor and display the physiological responses of the body to the exercise regimen.
6. To provide an attractive facility and to conduct activities that are interesting but effective, thereby attracting employees into the program with wide levels of fitness needs.
7. To provide for periodic evaluation of the program with a view toward improving it.
8. To develop in the participants a positive attitude toward exercise and an appreciation of exercise as a viable means of keeping fit.

Step 2. Assessing current status of participants. A thorough medical evaluation of each person in the fitness program is the means by which current status is checked. The medical evaluation would include a complete medical history, physical examination, hematology and blood chemistry, including red blood cell count, hematocrit, serum cholesterol, triglycerides, and glucose and uric acid level measurements. These tests would be conducted by the medical staff.

A resting electrocardiogram and an exercise stress test should also be a part of the medical evaluation. Conducted by the fitness staff, the exercise stress test is a continuous, graded test designed to stress the individual up to 85% of age-predicted maximum heart rate.[8] Heart rate, blood pressure, and ECG readings are monitored during the stress test.

Other aspects of the testing program include evaluation of:
1. *Body composition anthropometric measurements.* Skinfold calipers are used to determine the percentage of body fat. Height and weight measurements and

---

*These are general (or professional) objectives. Specific instructional and performance objectives should also be specified. These objectives would be based on the prescribed program of activities for each individual in the program.

8. Ellestad, M. H.: Stress testing principles and practice, Philadelphia, 1975, F. A. Davis Co.

measurements of circumferences of the chest, upper arm, and thigh are also recorded.[9]

2. *Physical fitness components.* Muscular strength and endurance and joint flexibility will be evaluated. A battery of tests to assess the strength and endurance of the major muscle groups of the body includes the bench press; 30-second, bent-legged sit-ups; pull-ups for males; flexed-arm hang for females; and push-ups. Flexibility of the lower back is important in a fitness program, therefore, a test, such as the sit and reach test, should be included to evaluate flexibility in this body area.[9,10]

3. *Cardiovascular-respiratory endurance.* The Tecumseh Submaximal Exercise Test[11] and/or the Cooper 12-Minute Run Test[12,13] should be used to assess cardiovascular-respiratory fitness.

Step 3. Determining needs to be met. The needs to be met by the individuals in the exercise program are determined by comparing the difference between their present status (determined in the previous step) and the specific goals and objectives that have been prescribed for each individual in the program. For example, an objective for a female under 30 years of age is "To be able to run 1.65 miles in 12 minutes." Suppose the test results obtained in the last step indicate that one female ran 1 mile in 12 minutes. The

need for this person is to run an additional 0.65 miles in 12 minutes. Needs for other objectives are assessed in the same manner.

Step 4. Choosing short-term and long-term needs. The director of the program and his or her aides would have to determine which needs require immediate attention and which needs are long-range needs. Immediate needs include any situation or condition that would prohibit or make it difficult for an individual to safely and successfully benefit from the fitness program. Minimal muscular strength and endurance, for instance, is needed in the legs for a person to successfully engage in a jogging program. Because the fitness program might include jogging, the development of minimal levels of muscular strength and endurance in the legs would be a short-term need. Another short-term need is the necessary equipment and facilities for the fitness program. A long-term need is one that would be planned for some time during the program, for example, attaining an acceptable level of cardiovascular fitness. For some individuals, the goal of developing cardiovascular fitness might take 8 weeks; for others, it might take 4 months; and for some, it might take longer to accomplish.

Step 5. Planning a program to meet the identified needs. An individualized fitness program is to be designed for employees of a business establishment. The program design consists of staff selection, facilities planning, equipment selection, and actual planning of program activities. A part of the program design will also include a method for evaluation and prescription of individualized exercise programs.

STAFF SELECTION. The first step in planning a physical fitness program is to select a staff. A licensed physician should be hired to act as the medical director of the program. This person should assume the leadership role in the interpretation of medical information. The physician should work closely with the program director in determining the

9. Larson, L. A., editor: Fitness, health, and work capacity: international standards for assessment, New York, 1974, Macmillan Inc.

10. Digennaro, J.: Individualized exercise and optimal physical fitness, Philadelphia, 1974, Lea & Febiger.

11. Montoye, H. J., Willis, P. W., III, and Cunningham, D. A.: Heart rate response to submaximal exercise: relation to age and sex, Journal of Gerontology 23:127, April 1968.

12. Cooper, K. H.: The new aerobics, New York, 1970, Bantam Books, Inc.

13. Cooper, M., and Cooper, K. H.: Aerobics for women, New York, 1972, Bantam Books, Inc.

health status of each person being tested and in helping to disseminate this information to each of the participants. Consistent with previously stated needs and objectives, the director of the program should have a doctorate degree in physical education with a specialization in exercise physiology. Staff assistants must also be hired. They must be well-trained in exercise physiology and capable of leading an exercise program.

FACILITIES. Elaborate facilities are not necessary to conduct a fitness program for people in industry. An exercise room large enough to accommodate the number of participants and shower, locker, and changing areas are the minimal required facilities. When no facilities are available at the company site, employees may be permitted to participate in programs that are conducted by other agencies (Y's, commercial fitness centers, and the like).

The facility for this program will consist of a fitness area for ten different exercise stations with two equipment set-ups at each station, a general recreation area for volleyball, badminton, and handball, an area for structured fitness classes, and a running track. Locker, shower, and dressing facilities will be provided to accommodate the anticipated number of participants in the program.

EQUIPMENT. Like facilities, a fitness program for people in industry does not require a large quantity of expensive equipment. A dozen jump ropes, some weights, and a few stopwatches are sufficient for a basic program. However, more sophisticated equipment may be used. A general inventory of equipment for the proposed program includes treadmills, bicycle ergometers, weight machines (those by Universal or Nautilus are recommended), rowing machines, stereo system, wall mirrors, wall clocks (with second hand timers), weight scales, barbells and dumbbells, slant boards, and jump ropes.

THE FITNESS PROGRAM. The basic core of

the program will be a circuit/interval regimen. There will be ten stations, with two sets of equipment at each station. There will be a general warm-up before beginning the circuit of exercises and a cool-down built into the last two stations of the circuit.

There will be a thorough evaluation of each person who wishes to participate in the fitness program. All evaluation procedures were discussed in step 2 of the model.

The program of exercises will be from 15 to 60 minutes, a minimum of 3 times a week, at a level of intensity that is between 60% and 90% of the predicted maximum heart rate of the individual.[14] The specific prescription of exercises for an individual depends on his or her present needs. The program prescription will initially be developmental and progress to a maintenance regimen.

There will be ten stations in the circuit/interval exercise regimen. A pacing device will be used to time, pace, and score the exercise. The pacing device will be the kind described by Yarvote and co-workers:

The device measures performance and displays simultaneously the time and effort in relation to each exerciser's individualized goal. It paces the rate of exercise at the required level and provides a final percentage reading of the amount of exercise accomplished.[15]

With slight modifications, the stations that were described by Yarvote and co-workers for the Exxon facility in New York City will be used for this program:

1. Medicine ball throw—A medicine ball (9 pounds for men, 5 pounds for women) is thrown against a sensor pad mounted on the wall above head level. This builds up the extensor muscles of

14. American College of Sports Medicine: Guidelines for graded exercise testing and prescription, Philadelphia, 1976, Lea & Febiger.
15. Yarvote, P. M., and others: Organization and evaluation of a physical fitness program in industry, Journal of Occupational Medicine 16:589-601, September 1974.

the arm and upper back and the flexors of the shoulder girdle as well as acting as a warm-up for the next station.

2. Rope jump (first cardiovascular stress)—The participant skips rope on a sensor pad.

3. Wall-pulley weights—This exercise improves muscular strength, endurance, and flexibility of the upper extremities, trunk, legs, and upper back.

4. Rowing machine (second cardiovascular stress)—In addition to the desired effect on the heart, the extensors and flexors of the legs, shoulder girdle, extensors of the back, and abdominal musculature are exercised.

5. Knee-thigh weights—The quadriceps and hamstrings of the legs are strengthened. This station is also a warm-up for the next station.

6. Stationary bicycle ergometer (third cardiovascular stress)—The leg extensors are exercised, particularly the quadriceps.

7. Sit-ups on a slant board with knees bent—This exercise develops the strength and endurance of the abdominal musculature and aids in the maintenance of good posture and the prevention of back problems.

8. Treadmill (fourth cardiovascular stress)—This exercise produces the greatest stress on the cardiovascular system as the participant runs on the treadmill at a designated speed and grade over a set distance.

9. Dumbbells (cooling-down station)— This exercise improves the strength of the biceps and shoulder girdle.

10. Wall volley (cooling-down station)— This exercise develops eye-hand coordination and strength in the arm extensors. It also develops the wrist and fingers.*

---

* Station 10 is different from the one used at Exxon.

A part of the development of the fitness program will be plans for evaluating the process and the outcomes in terms of goals and objectives of the program. The actual evaluation of the program, however, will not be conducted until later in the systems process.

Step 6. Indicating resources needed to implement the program. At this point, the program director should indicate the resources that are needed to implement the program. There must be adequate facilities, equipment, and personnel to conduct the program, or parts of the program will have to be modified if such resources are not available. For example, if bicycle ergometers are not available when the program is to begin, some other stress exercise (such as running in place) would have to be substituted for this station. In some cases, there might be a permanent limitation of resources, which will cause a restriction in program offerings. One such limitation is the size of the fitness facility. If the facility is small, the total number of participants will have to be limited. The program must be organized and conducted in accordance with available resources.

Step 7. Evaluating the program. Being scientifically designed and conducted, the program will be evaluated in specific terms. For example, target heart rates, blood pressure, and work levels will be established and measured. At specified intervals (about every 6 months) during the program, anthropometric measurements, ECG readings, and percentage of body fat for each participant will be recorded. These measurements will enable the staff to evaluate the degree to which participants are meeting the objectives that were initially established. The effect of the various exercise stations in producing the desired changes in program participants will also be evaluated.

Step 8. Responding to evaluation results. The process of development as well as aspects of the program will be modified in accordance with the results of program evaluation data. For example, if it were revealed that a certain exercise is not as effective as originally thought to be, a new exercise would be used. Evaluation and subsequent modification and/or substitution in aspects of the process or product will be continuous. The final goal is to conduct a program that will enable all participants to realize the objectives set for them.

The use of a systems approach to solve problems in physical education

Systems approach models can be used to solve specific problems in physical education programs as well as to develop programs. The systems model described by Hyman[16] was used to solve a specific problem in physical education. This model contains the following eight steps:

1. Identification of the problem
2. Analysis of the environment
   a. Resources
   b. Constraints
   c. Needs
3. Specification of goals and objectives
4. Generation of alternative solutions
5. Selection of a solution
6. Design of the system (program)
7. Evaluation of the system (program)
8. Assessment, revision, and recycling of steps in the program as needed

Step 1. Identification of problem. The problem was to revise a physical education and athletics program so that the department of dance, health, physical education, and recreation would be in compliance with Title IX of the Education Amendments of 1972.* The following subproblems were also identified:

1. Study the specific mandates of Title IX
2. Document the number of courses of-

fered separately for males and females and the number that were coeducational
3. Examine the athletic program to determine the number of sports offered for males and the number offered for females
4. Examine the athletic program to determine the number of hours that men and women use the facilities for practice, respectively

An ad hoc committee on curriculum was formed to devise means of solving the various problems. The chairperson of this committee met with the members of the committee and discussed the ramifications of Title IX in detail.

Step 2. Analysis of the environment. The various problems related directly to certain aspects of the physical education and athletics program. Therefore, the committee members had to examine the organizational structure, curriculum offerings, personnel, and facilities and equipment of the entire program of physical education.

An analysis of the physical education program revealed the following constraints: (1) limited facilities and equipment, (2) state certification requirements, (3) limited budget, and (4) separate men's and women's divisions with separate course offerings for each sex.

The needs were identified by noting the discrepancy between the present program and the mandates of Title IX, with particular attention to the constraints within the department and the college. The greatest overall need was to reorganize all separate courses for men and women and make them coeducational courses. In some cases, this required submitting curriculum proposals to the department for approval and subsequently to the college committee on curriculum for its approval.

Step 3. Specification of goals and objectives. The overall goal was to equalize opportunities for males and females in physical ed-

---

16. Hyman, J. L.: The systems approach and education, The Educational Forum 38:493-501, May 1974.

*Title IX is designed to prohibit sex discrimination in any program or activity receiving financial assistance from the federal government.

Courtesy Woodlands High School, Hartsdale, N.Y.

ucation classes and athletic programs. Specific objectives were:

1. To offer enough sections of courses so that no student would be barred on the basis of sex
2. To equalize intercollegiate athletic teams for men and women
3. To equalize the intramural program for men and women
4. To reorganize the physical education program from separate men's and women's programs into one coeducational program
5. To equalize teaching assignments, coaching assignments, and released time for men and women faculty

Step 4. Generation of alternative solutions. Two possible solutions were proposed with regards to the reorganization of the physical education program. One proposed solution was to have a single coordinator of physical education for one program comprising both men and women. The other proposal was to have a single program of physical education for both men and women but to have co-directors, one male and one female.

Two possible solutions were also offered for the problem of equalizing class offerings. One was to offer only coeducational sections of courses that did not involve contact sports and to offer separate courses in those classes

in which contact sports such as wrestling and football were taught. The other option was to offer three sections for each course: one for men, one for women, and one for both sexes.

Step 5. Selection of a solution. The solution to the problem of program reorganization was to merge the men's and women's programs into one coeducational program, with a single coordinator of physical education. The coordinator was to be elected by the members of that program. The physical education program was one of four programs (dance, health, and recreation are the others) in the department. There was a chairperson for the department.

The option of offering three sections of each course in which there was a contact sport being taught and coeducational courses in all other classes was recommended.

Step 6. Design of the program. Since there was already a program of physical education within the Department of Dance, Health, Physical Education, and Recreation, a restructuring of the program was all that was necessary. In the restructured program of physical education, all aspects were coeducational. There was one coordinator who was chosen on the basis of competence rather than sex. Office space in the reorganized physical education program was based on personal and professional preferences rather than sex.

Classes were revised so that they were co-educational rather than designated by sex. As mentioned previously, however, there were three sections of classes in which contact sports were taught. These sections allowed for male students, female students, or students of both sexes to register for each of the classes.

Step 7. Evaluation of the program. The design of the program allowed for constant evaluation. For instance, although coordinators and other administrative personnel in the department were elected for 3 years, a provision was made for changes to be made at the end of each year. Changes in some aspects of the program could be made at any time if those aspects of the program were not working. For example, changes had to be made in office assignments for the co-supervisors of the major program because of personality conflicts.

Classes were evaluated through student evaluation reports and teacher observation reports. Particular attention was paid to those courses that were changed from one sex only to coeducational courses.

Aspects of program administration were evaluated largely on the basis of the degree to which program objectives were achieved. In the first few months of operation, the revised program was functioning in an efficient and productive manner. Classes were scheduled with dispatch. Teachers were happy with their program assignments. Students expressed satisfaction because they could register for the courses of their choice without being restricted from some classes because of their sex.

Step 8. Assessment, revision, and recycling of steps in the program. At each step in the process of redesigning the program, the results of formative evaluation were analyzed to determine if revisions and/or recycling of

steps were necessary. In some cases, revision of a step was necessary. For example, the final solution to the problem regarding class offerings was changed as a result of additional information.

The revised system has not been in operation long enough to determine whether the total program needs to be revised in light of summative evaluation results. The final objective is to provide physical education experiences for students in a nondiscriminatory manner and to provide a quality education as defined by behavioral objectives. Several documents[17-19] can be used to evaluate the degree to which a school complies with the provisions of Title IX.

CONCLUDING STATEMENT

Because of a tightening job market for teachers as well as other reasons, physical educators are exploring alternative career opportunities. In the many types of job situations in which they find themselves, physical education teachers are likely to be asked to develop a new program, revise an existing program, or solve one or more of the problems related to a physical education program. A systematic, logical, and scientific method of carrying out any one of these tasks is needed. The two systems approach models discussed in this chapter are recommended for pro-

17. U.S. Department of Health, Education and Welfare, Office for Civil Rights: Final Title IX regulation implementing education amendments of 1972—prohibiting sex discrimination in education, Washington, D.C., July 21, 1975, Government Printing Office.
18. U.S. Department of Health, Education and Welfare, Office for Civil Rights: Memorandum to chief state school officers, superintendents of local educational agencies and college and university presidents. Subject: Elimination of sex discrimination in athletic programs, Washington, D.C., September 1975, Government Printing Office.
19. Lopiano, D. A.: A fact-finding model for conducting a Title IX self-evaluation study in athletic programs, Journal of Physical Education and Recreation 47:26-30, May 1976.

gram development, program revision, and problem-solving in physical education.

DISCUSSION QUESTIONS AND EXERCISES

1. Using the systems approach model adapted from Tankard's model, develop a physical education program for elderly persons.
2. Explain to your classmates the essential difference between the systems models developed by Tankard and Hyman.
3. Explain the difference between formative and summative evaluation regarding the evaluation of a college physical education program.
4. Discuss the roles of a physician and an exercise physiologist in the organization and conduct of a fitness program for people in industry.
5. Develop an alternate exercise for each of the ten stations of the program described in this chapter. Explain the function(s) of each exercise.
6. Evaluate the physical education program (in terms of its compliance with Title IX) at the school in which you student teach. Use one of the references indicated in this chapter for this task.
7. Present a written critique of the systems approach as a means of program development and/or revision. Indicate the strengths and weaknesses of the model you critique.
8. Explain the differences between instructional and performance objectives. Write five instructional objectives and ten performance objectives for the cognitive domain for a fifth grade class in badminton.

SELECTED REFERENCES

American College of Sports Medicine: Guidelines for graded exercise testing and exercise prescription, Philadelphia, 1976, Lea & Febiger.

Bucher, C. A.: Administration of physical education and athletic programs, ed. 7, 1979, The C. V. Mosby Co.

Bucher, C. A.: Foundations of physical education, ed. 8, St. Louis, 1979, The C. V. Mosby Co.

Bucher, C. A., and Koenig, C. R.: Methods and materials for secondary school physical education, ed. 5, St. Louis, 1978, The C. V. Mosby Co.

Bucher, C. A., and Thaxton, N. A.: Physical education for children: movement foundations and experiences, New York, 1979, Macmillan Inc.

Churchman, C. W.: The systems approach, New York, 1968, Dell Publishing Co., Inc.

Feyereisen, K., Fiorins, A. J., and Nowak, A. T.: Supervision and curriculum renewal: a systems approach, New York, 1970, Appleton-Century-Crofts.

Hyman, J. L.: The systems approach and education, The Educational Forum 38:493-501, May 1974.

Jacobs, J.: A model for program development and evaluation, Theory into Practice 13:15-21, February 1974.

Kaufman, R. A.: Educational system planning, Englewood Cliffs, N.J., 1972, Prentice-Hall, Inc.

Larson, L. A.: Curriculum foundations and standards for physical education, Englewood Cliffs, N.J., 1970, Prentice-Hall, Inc.

Mager, R. F.: Preparing instructional objectives, Belmont, Calif., 1962, Fearon Publishers.

Swerkes, B. S.: A systems model for the development of physical education curriculum, unpublished doctoral dissertation, Los Angeles, 1972, University of Southern California.

Tankard, G. G., Jr.: Curriculum improvement: an administrator's guide, New York, 1974, Parker Publishing Co.

9 □ Closing the gap between research and practice

Courtesy Springfield College, Springfield, Mass.

Let there be therefore (and may it be for the benefit of both) two streams and two dispensations of knowledge; and in like manner two tribes or kindreds of students in philosophy—tribes not hostile or alien to each other, but bound together by mutual services—let there in short be one method for the cultivation, and another for the invention, of knowledge.[1]

---

1. Bacon, F.: Preface to the Novum Organum. In Eliot, C. W., editor: Prefaces and prologues, New York, 1938, P. F. Collier and Son Corp., p. 146.

The previous statement is from Francis Bacon's preface to his famous *Novum Organum*, which was written in 1620. In the present debate regarding the problems and prospects of researchers and practitioners closing the gap between theory and practice, both groups need to be reminded of Bacon's words.

Although no actual figures have been recorded, there have been considerable discussions and proposals concerning the disparity between research findings and educational application. There is discussion by people representing both groups—the practitioner and the researcher. The scenario goes like this:

PRACTITIONER: Researchers think that they are pious, intellectual visionaries who are too preoccupied with logic, reason, and theoretical abstractions to be concerned with giving us workers in the field some suggestions as to the possible applications of their research findings. They should understand that their high and mighty theories are of no value to us. We do not understand their esoteric language and statistical notations. Unless researchers help to translate their findings and indicate possible applications for them, they will be worthless because no use will be made of them. I know you think that we are just talking out of frustration, but listen to what one of your colleagues had to say: "More than one basic laboratory behaviorist stands aloof from the mundane efforts of those who attempt to improve methods of training the mentally retarded or of teaching history."[2]

The researcher had a look of puzzlement on his face as the practitioner demonstrated pride in his performance. The dialogue continued.

RESEARCHER: How can the people who need to make use of our research findings expect us to be engaged in both research and development. We cannot spend our time on limited, individual questions. We must focus our attention on broad issues; we must seek to develop theories that will offer broad generalizations. Our energies must not be wasted on work that will divert us from our main focus. Furthermore, it is the responsibility of the persons who wish to consume the knowledge that is provided by pure researchers to prepare themselves for that task. They must spend some time becoming conversant with the research literature. They must develop the conceptual and research skills necessary to understand research and apply the results of research to their professional jobs. I should like to also remind you that my colleague of whom you spoke did not stop with the statement you quoted. He also said ". . . many an applied educational investigator ignores the ivory-housed theorists, or half-digests as profound truth what was offered as provisional guess."[2] So you see that you cannot put the blame on us for failing to make use of our findings.

There appeared to be a stand-off. But the researcher of whom both spoke was speaking with the true researcher's objectivity; therefore, he was chosen to act as arbitrator.

ARBITRATOR: I think there is an answer to this problem. Why not have a third party perform the development function of indicating specific implications of research findings? Both educator and scientist are working hard enough. Their efforts simply are not coordinated; they are out of touch with one another. Cronbach, a former president of the American Educational Research Association, has stated that ". . . institutions outside the university should be developed to carry the main burden of demonstration, dissemination, and educational development."[3]

The persons who would perform the task of coordinating the research findings of pure researchers and apply them to the individuals on the job would need to have knowledge of both research and educational processes and a dedication to both.[4] People such as this might be thought of as "translators" of research, "intermediaries" as de-

2. Gilbert, T. F.: A structure for a coordinated research and development laboratory. In Glasser, R., editor: Training research and education, New York, 1962, John Wiley & Sons, Inc., p. 560.

3. Cronbach, L. J.: The role of the university in improving education, Phi Delta Kappan 47:544, June 1966.
4. Locke, L. F.: Research in physical education, New York, 1969, Teachers College Press.

Courtesy Jackson State University, Jackson, Miss.

scribed by Travers,[5] or "educational engineers" as suggested by Hamreus.[6] Regardless of the name given to these individuals, their functions are most important. They would provide the needed job of developing and disseminating research findings for use by practitioners. And this job must be done on a large scale if research findings are to be put to use without the normal "research lag."

The preceding dialogue captures the essence of perceived problems of practitioners and researchers regarding the discovery and use of research findings in physical education as in education in general. An extensive examination of the literature revealed that there actually is a significant time lag between the time that research in physical education is conducted and the utilization of relevant findings in the gymnasium and on the playing fields.

This chapter will present an objective appraisal of the current thinking regarding the

disparity between theory generated by research and educational practice of teachers and coaches. The chapter will also examine the problems that both practitioners and researchers encounter in their respective functions in general. Finally, some proposals, examples, and suggestions will be offered to help close whatever gap exists between research and practice in physical education programs.

THE DISPARITY BETWEEN RESEARCH AND EDUCATIONAL PRACTICE

Current evidence indicates that there is a gap between what is known through theory and research and what is practiced in the local school, college, university, agency, corporation or other setting. Although the majority of those authors surveyed indicated that there is indeed a "gap" or "disparity" between research and educational practice (Barnes,[7] Brophy,[8] Guthrie and Seifert,[9] Taylor,[10] and Travers[5(pp. 525-558)]), a well-respected educator (Cronbach[3(pp. 539-545)]) spoke for the opposing viewpoint. A gap was also said to exist between theory and practice in physical education (Locke[4] and Nixon and Locke[11]).

The willingness of authors to quantify the degree of the chasm between research and

5. Travers, R. M. W.: A study of the relationship of psychological research to educational practice. In Glaser, R., editor: Training research and education, New York, 1962, John Wiley & Sons, Inc., p. 556.
6. Hamreus, D. G.: Instructional system development. In Crawford, J., editor: National research training manual, Monmouth, Ore., 1969, Oregon State System of Higher Education.

7. Barnes, F. P.: Research for the practitioner in education, Washington, D.C., 1964, Department of Elementary School Principles, NEA.
8. Brophy, J. E.: Some good five cents cigars, Educational Psychologist 11:46-51, 1974.
9. Guthrie, J. T., and Seifert, M.: Research and education in reading, Journal of Research and Development in Education 11:12-19, Spring 1978.
10. Taylor, C. W., Ghiselin, B., and Wolfer, J. A.: Bridging the gap between basic research and educational practice, National Education Association Journal 51:23-25, January 1962.
11. Nixon, J. E., and Locke, L. F.: Research on teaching physical education. In Travers, R. M. W., editor: Second handbook of research on teaching, Skokie, Ill., 1973, Rand McNally & Co.

practice varied greatly. Consider, for example, the almost insurmountable split that was expressed for reading by Guthrie and Seifert: "The spheres of basic research and the practice of instruction in reading are nearly as separated as the two cultures C. P. Snow described for science and the humanities."[9(p. 12)] Then listen to the unspecified degree of separation in the assertion by Taylor, Ghiselin, and Wolfer that ". . . a great and immediate need exists for speedy action to close the gap between what is known through research and what is applied in educational practice."[10(p. 23)]

Viewpoints expressed by the foregoing authors are exclusively those of researchers and/or college professors. What do teachers in elementary and secondary schools think about the disparity between research and educational practices? Although there is not much information to be found in the professional literature, informal discussions on this topic with practitioners in the schools, speakers at professional conventions, and actual practices in the classrooms and gymnasiums reveal that the "gap" is real. Broderick, who has taught on all levels of the educational spectrum and who is currently a director of physical education in a high school, probably typifies the feeling of many practitioners with his statements on this subject.[12] While not actually specifying the size of the gap between research and practice, Broderick inferred that the disparity was great as evidenced by the many problems that were said to have prevented practitioners from using the results of research. Some of these problems will be discussed later in this chapter. At this point, three examples of the gap between research and practice in physical education are presented.

Examples of the disparity between research and practice in physical education

Although several writers (cited previously) have indicated that there is a gap between research and practice in education and physical education, they have not quantified the degree of the practice nor cited specific research studies. The actual number of schools in which a particular practice is conducted is difficult to ascertain. However, some authors have noted that educational practice is sometimes guided by factors other than research findings. Speaking of coaches, Cratty, for example, said that even those who coach national teams often use naive training strategies and techniques that are at marked odds with a great deal of research.[13] Although written information regarding specific practices in the schools is scarce, specific research studies indicating the desirable practices are prevalent. Following are practices that are considered to be widespread among teachers and coaches in the schools. After stating the practice, research evidence that fails to support that practice is presented.

Teaching methods. The first example of the gap between research and practice in physical education deals with teaching methods, specifically with elementary school programs. The actual practice is the use of only one teaching style or strategy to teach physical education. The traditional or formal method of teaching physical education is the prevailing practice in many schools. This method was described by Nixon and Locke:

The traditional model of the well-taught physical education lesson remains essentially the same everywhere—explanation, demonstration, drill on the basic skills, practice in leadup activities, and game participation—all dispatched with much

---

12. Broderick, R. J.: Research as viewed by the teacher, Paper presented at the AAHPER National Convention, Detroit, 1971.

13. Cratty, B. J.: Psychology in contemporary sport: guidelines for coaches and athletes, Englewood Cliffs, N.J., 1973, Prentice-Hall, p. 31.

concern for organizational efficiency, discipline and a high level of teacher control.[11(p. 1211)]

The practice of using only the traditional method of teaching physical education on the elementary school level is contrary to the results of research. Research indicates that a combination of teaching strategies is the most effective procedure in enhancing student learning in elementary school physical education. For example, Thaxton, Rothstein, and Thaxton,[14] using 67 elementary school students as subjects, compared the effectiveness of the traditional method and the movement exploration method* of teaching physical education. They concluded that a combination of these methods is the most beneficial teaching strategy in teaching selected activities to elementary school girls. In their study, in which two classes were taught by the movement exploration method and two classes were taught by the traditional method, the movement exploration method was significantly better for teaching gymnastic activities and fitness activities. On the other hand, the traditional method was better for teaching basketball skills. The effectiveness of a particular teaching method was based on the degree to which students learned the physical activities taught by the teacher using a particular teaching method during the experimental period.

The results of the research study by Thaxton, Rothstein, and Thaxton were similar to the findings of other studies in which the movement and traditional teaching methods were compared. In their review of literature on studies dealing with teaching methods, they noted that out of ten studies in which elementary school children were used as subjects, the authors of five studies concluded that the movement exploration method was significantly better in teaching selected skills, fitness parameters, motor ability, and running and jumping. For example, a study to determine the effect of a movement education program on the performance of selected skills and the development of certain behavior traits in first grade students was conducted by Vitalone.[15] It was concluded that the movement classes made greater improvement in skill performance and acquired more new skills than the control groups.

Gravlee[16] conducted a study to compare the effectiveness of the movement exploration and the traditional method of teaching in a 4-week unit on selected motor skills to first grade children. At the conclusion of the study, the movement exploration group was significantly better than the traditional group in running and jumping skills but not in batting, throwing, and catching.

In a study involving kindergarten and primary grade students, Leslie[17] compared the relative effectiveness of the movement exploration and the traditional approach in

---

14. Thaxton, A. B., Rothstein, A. L., and Thaxton, N. A.: Comparative effectiveness of two methods of teaching physical education to elementary school girls, Research Quarterly 48:420-427, May 1977.

*Movement exploration is a method of teaching that is characterized by guided discovery and problem solving. Guided discovery is a style of teaching in which the teacher poses problems or questions to guide the student in discovering answers. The problem-solving approach is one in which the teacher designs a program that encourages students to solve problems through experimentation.

15. Vitalone, G. E.: A study of certain behavior traits and the physical performance of a selected group of first grade children participating in a program of movement experiences, unpublished doctoral dissertation, New York, 1964, New York University.

16. Gravlee, G.: A comparison of the effectiveness of two methods of teaching a four week unit on selected motor skills to first grade children, unpublished master's thesis, Greensboro, N.C., 1965, University of North Carolina.

17. Leslie, M. D.: Effects of movement exploration on physical fitness and motor ability in kindergarten and primary grades, Completed Research in HPER 31: 102, 1971.

the development of physical fitness and motor ability. At the end of a 6-month experimental testing period, it was concluded that movement exploration contributed more positively to both physical fitness and motor ability than did the traditional physical education classes.

Structuring practices. Coaches and teachers must structure the environment for the learner to optimize goal attainment of the learning task. In far too many cases, however, students do not spend enough time being actively engaged in meaningful learning activity. For example, Costello and Laubach observed a total of 193 elementary school students in three separate 5-minute segments (a total of 15 minutes per student). He indicated that students spent the largest portion (35.4%) of their time "waiting." It was further stated that "this was generally characterized by waiting in line for a turn to participate in either a practice trial or game."[18] When combining the time that students spent waiting in line and listening to the teacher talk, students in these classes spent almost two thirds (60.8%) of the total time they were observed either waiting or listening to the teacher.

In some schools with limited facilities and equipment and large classes, all students cannot actively engage in practicing the learning task at the same time. However, there are other meaningful learning activities in which they can be engaged. One teaching strategy for situations in which all students cannot be actively engaged in the learning task is to use mental practice.

Mental practice. Mental practice is defined as the symbolic rehearsal of a physical skill activity in the absence of any gross muscular movements. A bowler mentally rehearsing the next roll of the ball down the lane and a diver sitting motionless and imagining himself or herself going through the motions of a swan dive are examples of mental practice. Research has indicated that mental practice, when combined with actual physical practice, improves performance. In a thorough review of the research literature on mental practice in physical education, Richardson[19] analyzed 21 studies that were deemed suitable for analysis. He concluded that statistically significant positive findings were obtained in 11 studies, seven studies showed a positive trend in favor of the mental practice technique, and three studies reported negative findings.

A wide variety of activities was used in the studies reviewed by Richardson, including card sorting, mirror drawing, dart throwing, basketball shooting, juggling, ring tossing, and hitting a tennis ball. In addition to the general conclusion that mental practice together with physical practice improves performance in a variety of activities, a few other useful conclusions were revealed. For instance, it was pointed out that the degree of familiarity with the physical performance of a task is related to the efficiency of mental practice relative to physical practice. It was concluded that there is a trend that suggests that when mental practice and physical practice trials are alternated during the acquisition of a skill, the improvement in performance will be as good or better than physical practice trials only. These conclusions indicate that teachers will need to experiment with various means of using mental practice for optimal use of this technique.

Lay[20] offered a practical suggestion for

18. Costello, J., and Laubach, S. A.: Student behavior. In Anderson, W. G., and Barrette, G. T., editors: What's going on in gym: descriptive studies of physical education classes, Motor Skills: Theory into Practice, Monograph 1, 1978.

19. Richardson, A.: Mental practice: a review and discussion, Research Quarterly 38:95-107, March 1967.
20. Lay, N.: Practical application of selected motor learning research, Journal of Physical Education and Recreation 50:78-79, September 1979.

using the results of research on mental practice to help students improve their performance of motor skills. Instead of having students waiting to "shoot a basket" or "hit a tennis ball," she suggests that teachers might have a station with loop films, posters, or written handouts from the teacher. Along with the study of these materials, students would be urged to think through the skill that they are attempting to learn. Admittedly audiovisual aids add an additional teaching modality. However, using mental practice in conjunction with physical practice should prove especially valuable in large classes with inadequate facilities and equipment in which a limited number of students will be actively engaged in physical practice.

Speed versus accuracy. The third example of practices in physical education and athletics that are at variance with the findings of sound research involves the topic of speed versus accuracy. This is a critical motor learning concept to understand when structuring practice conditions that are conducive to optimal learning. Should coaches and teachers emphasize accuracy in presenting those skills that require both speed and accuracy? Or should they emphasize speed? Woods[21] indicated that in spite of research findings to the contrary, recent publications dealing with instruction for specific sport skills have stressed the desirability of instruction with initial emphasis on body form and control and the slowing of speed of body movement until the rudiments of the skill are learned.

To bring some evidence to bear on this question, Woods conducted a research study involving 21 male, high school students who had never played tennis or received instruction in tennis. Woods sought to determine the effect that a varied instructional emphasis on speed and accuracy would have on the acquisition of a forehand tennis stroke. Each of the 21 subjects was assigned to one of three experimental groups: speed-accuracy group, accuracy-speed group, and equal emphasis group. Each subject underwent 60 trials (forehand tennis stroke) during each practice session (instruction lasted 24 days), which resulted in 1440 trials during the study. The speed-accuracy group and the accuracy-speed group received instruction and practice that concentrated on speed and accuracy, respectively. At the termination of a midtest period on the twelfth day of the study, the emphasis for each group was changed (the speed-accuracy group emphasized accuracy and the accuracy-speed group emphasized speed).

Limiting his conclusions to a tennis skill that requires ball velocity and ball placement (speed and accuracy) simultaneously, Woods indicated that: (1) the most desirable results were obtained by equal and simultaneous emphasis on both speed and accuracy, (2) the second most desirable results were obtained by beginning with speed and terminating with accuracy, and (3) the least desirable results were obtained by initial emphasis on accuracy followed by speed.

The findings by Woods are in agreement with the results of earlier studies by Fulton[22,23] and Solley,[24] and more recent studies by Hornak[25] and Sage and Hornak.[26] The re-

21. Woods, J. B.: The effect of varied instructional emphasis upon the development of a motor skill, Research Quarterly 38:132-142, March 1967.

22. Fulton, R. E.: Speed and accuracy in learning a ballistic movement, Research Quarterly 13:30-36, 1942.
23. Fulton, R. E.: Speed and accuracy in learning movements, Archives in Psychology 300:1-53, June 1945.
24. Solley, W. H.: The effects of verbal instruction of speed and accuracy upon the learning of a motor skill, Research Quarterly 23:231-240, 1952.
25. Hornak, J. E.: The effects of three methods of teaching on the learning of a motor skill, unpublished doctoral dissertation, Greeley, Colo., 1971, University of Northern Colorado.
26. Sage, G. H., and Hornak, J. E.: Progressive speed practice in learning a continuous motor skill, Research Quarterly 49:190-196, May 1978.

sults of Fulton's studies were surprising because they were contrary to popular practice
at the time. The popular notion was to practice at slower speeds at the beginning of a
learning task and increase the speed once accuracy is obtained. This practice was supported by a basic theory on motor learning
formulated and presented in 1928 by Poppelreuter[27] in Germany. Contrary to Poppelreuter's theory, Fulton reasoned that
when a person practices at a high speed and
then strives for accuracy, the movement of
the act does not have to be changed, but a
new movement is required when transfer-
ring from low-speed practice to high speed.
Fulton concluded that in discrete motor
tasks, such as golf and tennis, effective performance would be retarded if early emphasis were placed on accuracy at the expense of
speed.

In summary, research supports the notion
that early emphasis on speed is more beneficial if speed is the prevailing factor in the final performance, but if both speed and accuracy are equally important, an early emphasis
on both is more effective. Those teachers and
coaches who continue to slow down speed
and favor accuracy in all teaching situations
are helping to create the gap between research and practice in this area of motor
learning.

REASONS FOR THE GAP BETWEEN RESEARCH FINDINGS AND THEIR APPLICATION TO TEACHING IN PHYSICAL EDUCATION

Although the factors considered to be responsible for the gap between research and
the practice of physical education are listed
and discussed as "Problems of practitioners"
and "Problems of researchers," they are very

much interrelated. Actually these factors are
inseparable because actions by one group
affect the factors listed as problems of the
other group. The present organizational arrangement is used to facilitate a logical presentation of the material, rather than to at-
tribute the problems to one group or the
other.

It should also be mentioned that there are
many problems that prohibit the development and dissemination of research findings.
Information regarding these problems and
proposed solutions to them have been thoroughly discussed in other sources
(Locke,[4(pp. 25-26,33-38)] Rothstein,[28] and Stadulis[29]). Emphasis is placed on the fact that the
development and dissemination of research
findings are two of the most important considerations in any attempt to close the gap
between research findings and educational
practice. Responsible people and organizations in the profession must deal with these
problems. The present discussion focuses on
the various "problems" of practitioners and
researchers.

Problems of practitioners

Several authors (Broderick,[12] Kroll,[30]
Locke,[4(pp. 1-50)] Rothstein,[28(pp. 56-60)] and
Stadulis[29(pp. 47-53)]) have cited one or more of
the following four problems as contributing
factors to the gap between research and
practice in physical education: (1) inadequate
knowledge of research, (2) negative attitude
toward research as a means of shaping educational practice, (3) lack of time and resources to apply research findings to the
teaching situation, and (4) limited availability of the results of research findings.

27. Poppelreuter, A.: Analyse der erziehung zur exak-
theitsarbeit nach experimental-psychologischer meth-
ode, Zeitschrift fur Angewandte Psychologie, Band 29,
1-40, 1928.

28. Rothstein, A. L.: Practitioners and the scholarly
enterprise, Quest **20**:59-60, June 1973.
29. Stadulis, R. E.: Bridging the gap: a lifetime of waiting and doing, Quest **20**:48-53, June 1973.
30. Kroll, W.: Perspectives in physical education, New
York, 1971, Academic Press, Inc.

Inadequate knowledge of research. The inadequate preparation in research skills and conceptual knowledge mentioned by the educators listed in the preceding paragraph is a basic factor contributing to the gap between research and practice in physical education. In the absence of the necessary preparation to understand and interpret research reports, it is not unusual that practitioners do not use the results of research.

Rothstein places the problem of acquiring technical and conceptual skills needed for consumption of research with the quality of research preparation provided for teachers at both the undergraduate and graduate levels.[28(p. 56)] The technical terminology of the research specialist that is unfamiliar to the ordinary teacher was mentioned by Locke as a factor that stifles communication between researcher and practitioner. "The ordinary teacher, unfamiliar with basic terms and subtle distinctions in the vocabulary of research, is likely to find the usual research report nearly incomprehensible."[4(p. 24)]

The importance of quality preparation in research methods to subsequent understanding and ultimate use of research by teachers cannot be overemphasized. The quality of the research preparation in undergraduate and graduate school will also affect the degree of communication between researchers and practitioners and the consumption of research reports by practitioners. The rationale is that a teacher or coach who receives a sound background in research and statistics will be better able to read and interpret research reports. Furthermore, that person will be better equipped to communicate with the researcher who conducted the study. An examination of *Research Quarterly* reveals the need for special training to understand the special terminology that is used by researchers. For example, studies in the October 1979 *Research Quarterly* contain topics such as multivariate analysis of variance, analysis of covariance, factor analysis,

Type I errors, and alpha level. These are technical topics in research and statistics that require special training to understand.

Negative attitude toward research. The negative attitude that some teachers have about research also deters them from using information revealed through research. Several reasons have been suggested to account for this negative attitude, including the view that research is irrelevant and impractical to the concerns of practitioners (Barnes,[7(pp. 3-4)] Rothstein,[28] and Stadulis,[29(pp. 48-49)]), an inadequate understanding of research (Broderick[12(p. 4)] and Locke[4]), and the failure of research to answer specific questions teachers ask about the teaching-learning process (Barnes[7]). Whatever the reasons for this negative attitude, it militates against the effective use of research findings that may be useful in optimizing learning.

The relationship between negative attitudes toward research and failure to use research findings by teachers was expressed by Stadulis. He said that "the low priority which teachers give research in designing and evaluating educational decisions seems to confirm Locke's assertion that teachers generally lack any substantial motive to read research reports."[29(p. 48)] One might expect graduate faculty members of professional preparation institutions to help prospective physical educators to develop positive attitudes toward research as a means of improving educational practice. However, as Stadulis states: "It is a simple fact of common experience that many graduate faculty members also have confused or negative attitudes toward research."[29(p. 49)]

Lack of time and resources to apply research findings to the teaching situation. It is often heard that teachers are too busy to deal with theoretical matters; they must concentrate on daily tasks. According to Broderick,[12(pp. 2-3)] the large classes, the coaching, and the "extra duties" such as patrolling the hall, monitoring at the bus stop, and acting as a nurse's assistant, inhibit the utilization and implementation of research by the teacher. Although not talking about research, Turner[31] listed some of the extra duties that teachers at the precollege level perform. He indicated that the following extra duties reenlightened the college teachers at Appalachian State University who participated in the faculty internship: bus duty, homeroom duty, lunchroom duty, locker room duty, daily and hourly attendance reports, lining fields, planning for pep rallies, cleaning gym area, and other routine school matters.

Even with this additional mention of the many duties of teachers, a study was conducted to determine if teachers do believe that they are too busy to apply the findings of research to the teaching of physical education and coaching. Results from more than 30 randomly sampled junior and senior high school teachers and coaches confirmed Broderick's position.

The lack of facilities and equipment with which to implement many of the research findings exacerbates the problems indicated above. For example, many schools may not possess skinfold calipers, bicycle ergometers, treadmills, or all the other equipment and facilities that are necessary to conduct a program in cardiovascular fitness. Special equipment is needed to implement some other research findings as well. Without such equipment, teachers who are willing and able to use research findings will encounter difficulty.

Some researchers contend that very little facilities and equipment are needed to implement research findings. For instance, they believe that a jogging program could be used instead of bicycle ergometers and treadmills to improve cardiovascular fitness (indicated as an important component of total fitness by physiological research[32]). Regardless of the logical arguments that might be presented, practitioners are not likely to use the results of research if they perceive facilities and equipment to be inadequate for such applications.

Limited availability of the results of research findings. Researchers most often attempt to publish the results of their studies in prestigious professional journals. In writing of the problem of poor communication between researcher and practitioner, Locke noted that ". . . physical educators are faced with a growing problem of the unavailability of relevant research."[4(p. 24)] Providing a possible clue to this condition, he indicated that ". . . as more and more of our best researchers are drawn into funded projects, they seem inclined to publish in prestigious technical and scholarly journals ordinarily not available to physical education teachers."[4(p. 24)]

Broderick, a former physical education professor and now a practitioner on the secondary school level, made a special plea for researchers to publish their studies in journals that teachers and coaches read:

Researchers should understand that the average teacher spends most of his professional reading time with J.O.H.P.E.R. [formerly the Journal of Health, Physical Education, and Recreation and now the Journal of Physical Education and Recreation—JOPER] and the coaching magazines—Scholastic Coach, Athletic Journal, and Coaching Clinic. The Physical Educator magazine and the Physical Education Newsletter

31. Turner, E. T.: Sending the college professor back to high school, Journal of Physical Education and Recreation **47**:38, May 1976.

32. American College of Sports Medicine; Position statement on The recommended quantity and quality of exercise for developing and maintaining fitness in healthy adults, Medicine and Science in Sports **10**: vii-x, 1978.

are two other primary sources of reading. The Research Quarterly seems to be the most preferred technical journal read, although the increase in price of late has greatly reduced its use in my own Eastern area.[12(p. 13)]

Indirectly, Broderick is asking for researchers to publish some of their studies in the magazines and journals that practitioners read. He also noted that it is financially impossible for the average teacher to afford all the journals, papers, and newsletters that are published each month.

Another source of research information that teachers and coaches could use, but that is also largely inaccessible to them, is theses and dissertations. They are usually kept in the libraries at the colleges and universities at which the studies were conducted. Some unpublished theses and dissertations are printed on microcards, microfilms, and more recently on microfiche, all of which are sold commercially and are contained in various college libraries. Theses and dissertations that are not located in a particular library may be secured through the interlibrary loan service provided by many libraries. To use this source, one must consider the time and effort it would take. Many practitioners do not have the time or the inclination to use the interlibrary loan procedure to get unpublished research studies of importance to them.

Problems of researchers

In addition to the problems of practitioners, a few factors related to the activity of researchers were also stated as reasons for the gap between research and practice in physical education (and education in general). These problems are: (1) poor quality of research (Locke[4(pp. 19-22,27-38)]), (2) unwillingness of researchers to be concerned with the application of their findings (Rothstein[28(p. 57)]), and (3) relatively few conclusive research findings (Barnes,[7(p. 16)] Har-

rison and Jones,[33] and Heath and Nielson[34]).

Poor quality of research. Locke asserts that ". . . educational research has suffered from serious problems of quality."[4(p. 19)] To help support his claim, he quotes from Bloom: ". . . about 1 out of 1,000 reported studies seem to me to be significant, approximately 3 studies per year."[4(p. 20)] In physical education, Locke further notes: ". . . research that is poorly designed, inadequately reported, and seriously misleading, constitutes a major impediment to the intelligent guidance of physical education."[4(p. 20)]

Authors of recent studies are beginning to note the inadequacies of previous research studies, especially with regard to methodological concerns. One of these authors is Dubois[35] who conducted a comparative study of sports and occupational attainment. Dubois cited two examples of studies that failed to use a comparison group and one study in which no controls were used on variables known to have important effects on attainment. He also mentioned one study that used control variables as well as a comparison group, but that had a low return rate (38%) for the questionnaires. Sage and Hornak,[26] examining background literature for their research on progressive speed practice in learning a continuous motor skill, cited six studies in this type of research with methodological shortcomings. The major weakness of the other studies, according to Sage and Hornak, is that practice speed for each group has been held constant through-

33. Harrison, P., and Jones, B. J.: Research and women in sports: closing the gap, The Physical Educator **32:** 84-87, May 1975.

34. Heath, R. W., and Nielson, M. A.: The research basis for performance-based teacher education, Review of Educational Research **44:**479, Fall 1974.

35. Dubois, P. E.: Participation in sports and occupational attainment: a comparative study, Research Quarterly **49:**28-37, March 1978.

out the pretransfer practice. They state: "Research designs employing one constant speed of practice for each treatment group seem inappropriate if one wishes to make application for motor skill acquisition."[26](p. 191) Sage and Hornak, as well as other authors who noted weaknesses in previous research studies, avoided these weaknesses in their own research.

Unwillingness of researchers to be concerned with the application of their findings. Much of the significant research affecting educational practice in the last 50 years is the result of basic research.* The failure of investigators engaged in basic research to be concerned with the application of their findings might be a cause of such a lag in some cases. Complicated theoretical propositions that are sometimes advanced by researchers engaged in pure or basic research without some explanation of their practical uses are of little value to teachers and coaches.

Rothstein presented a rationale to account for the unwillingness of researchers to concern themselves with the application of research findings:

. . . This may be due to the limited scope of such research activity [applied research]. A specific answer to a specific problematic question (which often will be tied to a single set of unique situational variables) has only limited utility. It is preferable, from the researcher's viewpoint, to explore the underlying basic components within any area of inquiry, the supposition always being that when sufficient information has been gathered and understanding of relationships between components achieved, both generalization and, ultimately, application will be possible.[28](p. 57)

Research has its own technical language, and consumers must become familiar with this language. Individuals engaged in basic research also need time to concentrate on the construction of broad theories. However, if

the significant information provided by basic researchers is to be useful, in view of the admitted lack of conceptual knowledge and technical skills in research by teachers and coaches, investigators engaged in basic research should devote a portion of their time to development and dissemination functions.

Relatively few conclusive research findings. The fact that different researchers reach disparate conclusions regarding the same research topic makes these studies less useful to practitioners. Examples of research in two different areas are presented to illustrate the conflicting and/or nonsignificant findings of such research. The first example of conflicting research results is in the area of physiology of muscular activity and deals with the effect of warming-up prior to performance on subsequent athletic performance. Busuttil and Ruhling[36] cited eight studies that found that warm-up is essential for optimal skill execution and seven studies in which the conclusion was that warm-up produced no significant favorable effects on performance in a given activity. They concluded, on the basis of their review of the literature, ". . . that the warm-up controversy still remains highly unsolved."[36](p. 69) In an earlier study, Singer and Beaver[37] also noted the conflicting results of research studies pertaining to warming-up before a performance. They mentioned four studies that supported warm-ups and four that did not support warm-ups.

In the study by Busuttil and Ruhling, in which 16 male, Caucasian volunteers served as subjects, the effect of warm-up on selected physiological parameters (heart rate, blood pressure, deep body core temperature, and

---

*Pure or basic research is concerned with the development of theories or broad generalizations.

36. Busuttil, C. P., and Ruhling, R. O.: Warm-up and circulo-respiratory adaptations, Journal of Sports Medicine and Physical Fitness 17:69-74, 1977.
37. Singer, R. N., and Beaver, R.: Bowling and the warm-up effect, Research Quarterly 40:372-375, May 1966.

the like) was measured. The results of the study indicated that there were no significant differences between the experimental and the control groups on the parameters being studied.[36(p. 72)]

The conflicting results of research studies pertaining to warm-up were attributed to the variety of sports activities used as the criterion variable, different types, durations, and intensities of exercise during the warm-up, and studies in which investigations had been poorly designed and data collection procedures were often inaccurate and unreliable.[36(p. 69)] Moreover, the type of warm-up differed in some studies. There are two types of warming-up: active and passive. The first type is typically used in studies and is subdivided into two subtypes: formal and informal (also referred to as related and nonrelated).[38] Formal warming-up involves practicing the specific movement and skills that will be used in the subsequent activity (some persons also refer to this as specific warm-up). Shooting basketballs, hitting tennis balls, and taking a few laps around the track before a race are examples of formal or specific warm-up. Informal or general warm-up usually involves exercising the large muscles of the body through such activities as calisthenics.

Another illustration of research yielding no significant differences is in the area of motor learning and involves "level of difficulty" of material studies. In summarizing studies in this area, Nixon and Locke report that "nearly all of the studies in which initial practice on an easy motor skill is contrasted with initial practice on a more difficult version of the same task yield nonsignificant results."[11(p. 1217)] For example, Singer, studying the transfer effects and ultimate success in

archery resulting from the degree of difficulty of the initial learning, observed no significant difference in the transfer effects from practice on an easier task as compared with the transfer effects of a more difficult task in comparison to precise distance practice.[39]

The subjects for Singer's study were 58 students enrolled in three archery service classes at Ohio State University. The investigator was the instructor. The students were assigned to three different classes: Class A (N = 20), Class B (N = 18), and Class C (N = 20). Class B was the control group and remained at the 25-yard line. Class A was tested at the 20- and then the 25-yard line, while Class C shot from the 30- and the 25-yard lines. One of the conclusions drawn from this study was that "there is no significant difference in specific yard stripe accuracy as a result of the previous number of practice days and prior shooting at varying distances from the target."[39(p. 538)]

The examples illustrate the inconclusive results and conflicting conclusions reached by some investigators who conduct research on the same topic and how these studies present problems for practitioners who attempt to use the results of such research to guide their educational practice. The nature of such nonsignificant results and disparate conclusions renders single studies ineffective as a means of providing intelligent guidance for teaching. However, useful, practical, and applicable information may be revealed by integrating the research findings of several studies and testing the significance of the combined results, even when some of the studies show nonsignificant findings.

Different methods of analyzing research findings. Several procedures for combining the sometimes disparate results of research

38. Karpovich, P. V., and Sinning, W. E.: Physiology of muscular activity, Philadelphia, 1971, W. B. Saunders Co., p. 30.

39. Singer, R. N.: Transfer effects and ultimate success in archery due to degree of difficulty of the initial learning, Research Quarterly 37:532, December 1966.

have been presented by Gage.[40] The review of these procedures for combining and synthesizing results of research studies was focused on research in education. Rothstein[41] has proposed some of these techniques as possibilities for application of research in various areas of physical education. These procedures, each of which is a form of "meta-analysis," (some of the meta-analysis procedures attributed by Rothstein[41(p. 63)] to Glass), seem to be particularly useful for physical education research. The term *meta-analysis of research* describes a specific procedure that is used to combine the results of different studies.[42] Using the meta-analysis concept, Rothstein and Arnold[43] have applied the chi-square statistic to the analysis of data for identified "critical factors or variables" in studies that used some form of videotape replay in providing feedback to students. The purpose of this technique, which is a form of meta-analysis that they labeled the "Critical Factors Approach," is to determine which factors differentiate among the various studies examined.*

PARADIGMS FOR "BRIDGING THE GAP" BETWEEN RESEARCH AND EDUCATIONAL PRACTICE

A resolution of the problems of researchers will aid in closing the gap between research and practice in physical education.

---

40. Gage, N. L.: The scientific basis of the art of teaching, New York, 1978, Teachers College Press, pp. 27-31.
41. Rothstein, A. L.: Future possibilities in research application, Journal of Physical Education and Recreation **51**:63-64, February 1980.
42. Glass, G. V.: Primary, secondary, and meta-analysis of research, Educational Researcher **10**:3-8, 1976.
43. Rothstein, A. L., and Arnold, R. K.: Bridging the gap: application of research on videotape feedback and bowling, Motor Skills: Theory into Practice **1**:35-62, Fall 1976.
*An example that presents a summary of the procedure and conclusions reached through the use of the critical factors approach is presented later in this chapter.

These points will not be expanded on here. However, some proposals for practitioners are discussed, which may serve to help close the gap between research findings and actual practice of physical education.

Proposals for practitioners

The following three proposals for the physical educator are discussed: (1) get a thorough background in research, (2) become involved in the conduct of some research, and (3) apply the findings of sound research to educational and other practices.

Get a thorough background in research. Physical educators must receive a comprehensive education in research, including an understanding of statistics, if they are to bridge the gap between research and the practice of physical education in educational and other settings. A thorough background in research and statistics will enable the physical educator to develop a knowledge of the following competencies:

1. Research and statistical theory and terminology
2. Where to find research reports
3. How to evaluate research studies and interpret research findings

The need for a knowledge of research and statistics. An understanding of research is basic to developing the other competencies listed above. This knowledge of research should include an understanding of research and statistical theory and a familiarity with the basic terminology in research and statistics. To illustrate the need for a knowledge of research and statistics, suppose a coach were interested in information regarding the effects of warming-up on athletic performance. Suppose further that the coach, in examining the literature, locates the following study: "Effects of warm-up on the heart rate during exercise." An understanding of this study would require a knowledge of such research concepts as samples and populations, dependent and independent variables, research design, and the like. A knowledge of statistical concepts such as correlation coefficient and levels of significance is also necessary.

A perusal of the abstract of the study on warm-up will further illustrate and emphasize the need for research and statistical knowledge:

Eight track athletes were studied to determine the effects of a warm-up and a lack of a warm-up on the heart rate during specified exercise routines. The variables of anticipatory increase in heart rate, maximum heart rate, and recovery decrease in heart rate were studied. The difference between these variables was not significant at the .05 level of confidence. The same variables were correlated with the Harvard Step Test scores for the subjects. High correlations were found between the variables of maximum heart rate and recovery decreases in heart rate, and the step test scores.[44]

Some of the specific questions regarding this study would be: Is the sample of eight track athletes representative of the population to which the results are to be applied? Are the measured variables of heart rate and anticipatory heart rate appropriate for this study? Is the product-moment correlation technique appropriate for the analysis of data for such a small number of subjects? A thorough understanding of research and statistics is needed to answer these questions.

The need for a knowledge of where to find research reports. The need to be able to locate research reports might seem like an obvious statement. However, it is emphasized here because so many times people become frustrated when they are unable to find relevant literature on a particular topic. They consequently abandon their search, in many cases, as a result of such frustration.

Information on literature searching should be a part of a research course if students are deficient in this skill. Haag[45] has suggested a strategy for searching the literature in which one works from a substantive source (encyclopedias, dictionaries, and yearbooks) to a location source (card catalogue and bibliographies). By using this strategy, ". . . one can first acquire a general overview of the broad subject under consideration as well as a familiarity with the vocabulary used professionally in that subject area."[45(p. 54)] Haag recognizes the need for a researcher/scholar to move back and forth on the continuum between substantive and location information sources as the research topic dictates.

An example of a person searching for information on ergogenic aids in athletics is used to illustrate each step of the procedure recommended by Haag. Using a bibliographic research guide to the literature, the person would first become acquainted with titles of reference sources on ergogenic aids. A search of encyclopedias, dictionaries, and yearbooks would then be made to get information pertinent to ergogenic aids. For example, ergogenic aid was defined in the *Dictionary of Education* as "a special foodstuff, drug, or other aid which may or may not improve performance or hasten recovery."[46] The *Encyclopedia of Educational Research* and the *Encyclopedia of Sport Sciences and Medicine* would be examined for information on this topic.

Appropriate reviews of research would be examined after all sources in the previous step have been exhausted. *Exercise and Sport Science* is one bibliographic review of research that might be useful. The *Annual*

44. Howard, G. E., Blyth, C. S., and Thornton, W. E.: Effects of warm-up on the heart rate during exercise, Research Quarterly 37:360, October 1966.

45. Haag, E.: Literature searching in physical education, Journal of Physical Education and Recreation 50: 54-58, January 1979.
46. Good, C. V., editor: Dictionary of education, New York, 1973, McGraw-Hill Book Co., p. 23.

Review of Physiology would also be examined.

Abstracts of research in physical education, health, and recreation would be examined for specific research pertaining to ergogenic aids in athletics. Probably the best source in physical education containing abstracted research reports is *Completed Research in Health, Physical Education and Recreation Including International Sources.* Another source that would be examined is the University of Oregon's Health, Physical Education and Recreation Microfilm Publications, which is a microfiche collection of unpublished research materials such as doctoral dissertations, master's theses, and some scholarly books and journals.

At this point in the literature search, with a good idea of the key sources that are needed, the person would consult one of the citation indexes. The *Science Citation Index* would be checked for sources on ergogenic aids or athletics in general. For instance, by examining the "permuterm subject index" for 1975, two studies were found on anabolic steroids (which are ergogenic aids) under the topic of athletes. By then referring to the "source index" with the name of the lead author of the article, the complete reference information was found. The "citation index" section would be used to look up all key sources to locate the names of the sources and the persons who made the citations.

Periodical indexes such as the *Readers' Guide to Periodical Literature* and the *New York Times Index* would be checked to find current articles in magazines and journals. The Physical Fitness-Sports Medicine Index might also be checked for specific information on ergogenic aids. In addition to these indexes, ERIC's Current Index to Journals in Education (CIJE), and Resources in Education (RIE) would be used. Bibliographies such as the *Bibliography of Research Studies in Education* and *Master's Theses in Educa-*

tion would also be examined for information on ergogenic aids in athletics.

The card catalogue would be checked to ascertain if the research and other material on ergogenic aids is in the library. The card catalogue would be consulted when searching for specific titles or an author's work. In addition to telling whether the particular source is in the library, the card catalogue would also indicate the location of the source in the library.*

Generally when reviewing the literature on a particular topic, it is advisable to locate the more recent sources. An examination of the bibliography of these sources will often contain valuable source citations of previous works. By following such a procedure, the researcher/scholar can quickly become familiar with the literature on a given subject.

The need for a knowledge of how to evaluate research studies and interpret research findings. Once research studies are located, they must be evaluated to determine their value. The person reviewing the study must have an adequate knowledge of research, including statistics, to ascertain whether the research is quality material. For example, is the research methodology acceptable (that is, selection of subjects, research design, analysis of the data, and so on)? Accurate interpretation of the results would also be necessary to determine the utility of such research in guiding educational practice.

The completion of courses in research and statistics, reading of research reports, and being involved in research studies, if possible, will aid in the understanding of research. Such a knowledge will equip the person with the necessary information to evaluate research reports and interpret the findings.

---

*Refer to the study by Haag [45(pp. 54-58)] for a complete discussion of the topic of "Literature searching in physical education." This author has included a comprehensive listing of sources to which one would go when searching the literature.

CHECKLIST FOR CRITIQUING RESEARCH STUDIES

Author:
Title and source of article:

Statement of problem	*Concise*	*Not clear*	*Too broad*	*Other*	*Comments*
Hypothesis to be tested	*Concise*	*None stated*	*Implied but not stated*	*Other*	*Comments*
Level of significance selected	*.05 level*	*.01 level*	*Other level*	*Reason for level*	*Comments*
Data collection	*Size of sample*	*Type of sample*	*Reason for choice*	*Instrument(s) used*	*Comments*
Data analysis	*Design*	*Statistical tests used*	*Reason for choice(s)*	*Results of analysis*	*Comments*
Conclusions reached	*Consistent with data analysis* Yes No		*Conclusions are untenable* Yes No		*Comments*

Checklist for critiquing research studies.

A checklist for critiquing research reports is presented to aid the student and physical educator in evaluating research and interpreting the results of research. We have also used the checklist to critique an actual study in physical education. A summary of that critique is included as an example of how the checklist can be used (p. 156).

The checklist contains the essential facets of a research study, that is, a statement of the problem, hypothesis to be tested, levels of significance chosen, data collection, date analysis (including sample, instrumentation, and design), and conclusions reached. The study chosen for review is "The development of aerobic capacity: a comparison of continuous and interval training." This study was chosen because it represents a timely topic of interest to a variety of different groups (people in educational institutions, people in industry, older adults, and so on) and because it will help clarify one means of evaluating and interpreting a research study.[47]

STATEMENT OF THE PROBLEM. The problem was to ". . . determine the relative effectiveness of continuous and interval training in developing CR [cardiorespiratory] endurance through the comparison of exercise programs suitable for use by college-age males.[47(p. 200)] This is a rather straightforward, concise statement of the problem. The definition of the two terms, *continuous training*

47. Gregory, L. W.: The development of aerobic capacity: a comparison of continuous and interval training, Research Quarterly 50:199-206, May 1979.

```
                    CHECKLIST FOR CRITIQUING RESEARCH STUDIES

Author:  Gregory, L. W.
Title and source of article:  "The development of aerobic capacity:  a comparison of continuous and interval training,"
  Res. Q. 50:2, 1979.
```

	Concise	*Not clear*	*Too broad*	*Other*	*Comments*
Statement of problem	X				Comparison of effectiveness of continuous and interval training in developing CR endurance of sedentary college-age students.

	Concise	*None stated*	*Implied but not stated*	*Other*	*Comments*
Hypothesis to be tested			X		Null hypothesis of "no significant mean differences between groups" is assumed, but experimental hypothesis as well as null hypothesis should be stated by the researcher.

	.05 level	*.01 level*	*Other level*	*Reason for level*	*Comments*
Level of significance selected	X			None given	No reason needed since .05 and .01 levels of significance are commonly accepted as appropriate for research with no unusual risks involved.

	Size of sample	*Type and selection of sample*	*Reason for choice*	*Instrument(s) used*	*Comments*
Data collection	28	Incidental sample from captive group	Subjects volunteered for study	Treadmill, gasometer, pulmo-analyzer, physiograph	Subjects should be representative of sedentary college-age male student population. Because of attrition, final sample was reduced to 21 subjects.

	Design	*Statistical tests used*	*Reason for choice(s)*	*Results of analysis*	*Comments*
Data analysis	Simple randomized design	T tests and analysis of covariance	Comparison of three means	Null hypothesis rejected when control group vs. experimental group	The t tests permitted comparison of mean differences between pre- and posttest within group data, and ANCOVA allowed for initial differences among group means. Multiple range test used as post hoc procedure.

	Consistent with data analysis		*Conclusions are untenable*		*Comments*
Conclusions reached	Yes _X_	No ___	Yes ___	No ___	Continuous and interval training methods are equally effective for population of male sedentary college-age students.

Illustrated use of checklist.

(slow-paced running over long distances without rest) and *interval training* (intermittent, fast-paced running over short distances with intervening rest periods), further clarifies the problem.

HYPOTHESIS TO BE TESTED. No hypothesis was stated for this study. Although the null hypothesis is implied in research studies, it should be stated by the investigator. A null hypothesis indicates that there is no significant difference in the mean scores of two groups that come from the same population. The investigator should also state an experimental hypothesis, which is a hunch as to what the results of the experiment will be.

Two alternatives are possible for each of three different analyses: (1) the comparison of the difference between pretest and posttest means for each of the three groups (one control group and two experimental groups), (2) the comparison of the difference between posttest means for the control group and each of the two experimental groups, and (3) the comparison of the difference between the posttest means for the two experimental groups. For example, the investigator might hypothesize that the mean posttest score for the continuous training group will be significantly greater than the mean posttest score for the interval training group, or that the mean posttest score for the interval training group will be significantly greater than the mean posttest score for the continuous training group. The hypothesis that the investigator makes to guide the research study should be based on the results of other studies in the area of aerobic development and a knowledge of the conceptual framework of the two training methods.

LEVEL OF SIGNIFICANCE SELECTED. The .05 level of significance was selected to test the results of the experimental data. This indicates that in 95 out of 100 times that this experiment is conducted, the compared mean scores will result from the introduction of the experimental variable rather than chance caused by sampling error. Stated another way, rejecting the null hypothesis at the 5% level indicates that a difference in means as large as that found between the two groups in question would not likely have resulted by chance more than 5 out of 100 replications of the experiment.

Closely associated with the selection of levels of significance in making decisions regarding null hypotheses is the probability of making an error. There are two types of errors— Type I and Type II errors. A Type I error is the rejection of a null hypothesis when it is actually true. A Type II error is the acceptance of a null hypothesis when it is really false. A discussion of the ramifications of risking each of these errors is beyond the scope of this text. The reader is urged to consult a statistics or research text for information on this topic.

DATA COLLECTION. The subjects for this study were 28 male physical education majors and minors at Oklahoma State University. The subjects represented an incidental sample since they were volunteers for the study and were available to the researcher. Furthermore, the subjects were a sample of a subgroup of sedentary, college-age, male students who had not engaged in any form of regular or systematic training for at least 1 year prior to the study. As a result of attrition, the final test group consisted of 21 subjects; seven subjects, for various reasons, dropped out during the study.

Standard instrumentation for physiological research dealing with oxygen uptake and other cardiorespiratory endurance measures was used in this experiment. Specifically, the Balke treadmill was used to increase heart rate, and a Tissot gasometer was used to collect 30-second volumes of expired air on three occasions during the treadmill test. Gas samples of the final collection were retrieved in rubber aliquots, which were immediately attached to a Godart pulmoanalyzer. The pulmoanalyzer determined the percentage content of oxygen and carbon dioxide. Heart rate was monitored using a physiograph and biotelemetary receiver and transmitted by Narco Biosystems. Bipolar chest electrodes in a CM_5 position were used for monitoring.

DATA ANALYSIS. A simple, randomized design with pretest and posttest protocols was used for this study. Within and among group training changes were analyzed by t tests and analysis of covariance (ANCOVA), respectively, with Duncan's New Multiple Range Test as a post hoc procedure. The need to "correct" the final mean scores for subjects on the dependent variables (body weight, oxygen uptake, and treadmill test) to account for initial differences in scores on these variables justified the use of ANCOVA.

The results of correlated t tests indicated that the experimental groups experienced significant improvements in both measures of cardiorespiratory endurance (oxygen consumption and treadmill test); however, no significant changes in either measure were observed in the control group. These improvements were significant at the .01 level of significance for oxygen consumption and at the .001 level for the treadmill test. No significant body weight changes were observed for either group.

Results of the analysis of covariance revealed that there was a significant difference in adjusted group means for both measures of CR endurance for the continuous and interval training groups when compared with the control group. The difference between groups in oxygen consumption was significant at the .05 level of significance and at the .01 level for the treadmill test. There was no significant difference between the continuous and interval training groups in aerobic capacity as measured by either oxygen consumption or the treadmill test at 180 bpm.

CONCLUSIONS REACHED. The researcher concluded that ". . . continuous and interval training methods are equally effective in developing CR endurance when the same total work is performed."[47(p. 205)] While the results of this study were in agreement with other comparison studies, Gregory indicated that the results of his study were obtained by using exercise programs suitable for a sedentary population. The person seeking to engage in an aerobic training program should consider either a continuous or interval training program. This is contrary to popular belief that a continuous training program is best suited to CR endurance development.[47]

SUMMARY AND CRITIQUE. Each category of the checklist for critiquing research studies (see p. 155) is explained in more detail in the text. The purpose of the checklist is to provide an overview of information from which to further evaluate the study. Spaces for comments are also included for each category so that enough information can be recorded to make the checklist yield more useful explanatory notes. For example, data collection is an important aspect of the "Procedures" section, but only the basic facts can be included in the checklist without comments. However, these data and comments (p. 156) are sufficient to give a general idea of this aspect of the procedure or method used in this study. More detailed information is provided in the text for the evaluation of the study.

Based on a total evaluation of the study, it is rated highly satisfactory. The conceptual framework of the study is sound (Astrand and Rodahl,[48] Cooper,[49] and Fox and Mathews[50]). The procedures or methods (selection of subjects, instrumentation, testing protocol, and so on) and data analysis are consistent with established research concepts and practices (references for research and statistics are included in the "Selected References" section).

The limitations of the study include the small number of subjects (21), the restricted sample (male, physical education major and minor students at one university), and the use of Duncan's New Multiple Range Test as the post hoc testing procedure to analyze pairs of mean differences in the case of significant F-ratios.

There is no absolute number of subjects that can be called an appropriate sample size for all experiments. However, researchers and statisticians (Drew[51] and Winer[52]) consid-

48. Astrand, P.-O., and Rodahl, K.: Textbook of work physiology, New York, 1970, McGraw-Hill Book Co.
49. Cooper, K. H.: The new aerobics, New York, 1970, Bantam Books, Inc.
50. Fox, E. L., and Mathews, D. K.: Interval training: conditioning for sports and general fitness, Philadelphia, 1974, W. B. Saunders Co.
51. Drew, C. J.: Introduction to designing research and evaluation, ed. 2, St. Louis, 1980, The C. V. Mosby Co.
52. Winer, B. J.: Statistical principles in experimental design, New York, 1962, McGraw-Hill Book Co.

er a sample size of less than 30 subjects small. The sample is even smaller than it appears because the 21 subjects were randomly assigned to one of three groups. The largest group contains only nine subjects, considerably below the 30 subjects that is regarded as an adequate sample size. The size of the sample and the manner in which it was selected partially determine whether the subjects were drawn from a normally distributed population. The normality of the population from which samples are drawn is one of the necessary conditions for parametric statistics (refer to Winer[52] for a comprehensive treatment of methods of determining sample size and the assumptions underlying parametric statistics).

The restricted sample size affects the external validity of the study, or the generalizability of the results of the study. In other words, the researcher should be very careful in extrapolating the results of the present study to a larger population for which the sample might not be representative. For example, it should not be inferred from these data (on sedentary, male, physical education major and minor students) that continuous and interval training exercise programs will be effective for female college students or for male history majors in good physical condition. The latter two populations are quite different from the sample population in the study.

Although Duncan's New Multiple Range Test is discussed as one of the multiple comparison tests to be used in determining differences in group means, it is said to be less powerful than other tests (Winer[52]). This and other limitations of the study are minor and do not significantly affect the validity of the results.

Become involved in some research. If possible, the physical educator should become involved in the actual conduct of research during undergraduate studies. There are many settings besides the schools in which research can be conducted, for example, the neighborhood playground, community center, homes for the aged, and industrial fitness centers. Specific examples of research that might be conducted in these settings include studies to determine the physical activity preferences of different ethnic groups attending a community center or playground, examine the leisure interests of a group of older adults, measure the physiological responses of middle-aged men and women to different jogging programs, and compare the work absentee rate of persons in industrial fitness programs with that of persons not in such programs.

For students to become engaged in research at the undergraduate level, faculty members must be willing to assist and guide the students in their research projects. Rothstein offers specific examples of ways to involve more faculty members in research and get more students involved in the process as well:

Send the student interested in swimming to the swimming coach, after fair warning has been given, to discuss his ideas. Perhaps you will end by involving your colleagues in research also. Try to interest your colleagues in having their students participate as subjects. Approach your colleagues directly and attempt to involve them in research—thereby allowing students to become involved as research assistants.[53]

In addition to the suggestions of Rothstein for getting undergraduate students and faculty members involved in research, it is suggested that students enroll in a course in research and measurement as soon as possible. Such a course may be taken prior to, or concurrently with, the conduct of research. The

53. Rothstein, A. L.: Involving undergraduates in research, Journal of Health, Physical Education, and Recreation **44**:71, March 1973.

necessary conceptual information about the research process and the needed understanding of the language of research and statistics should be obtained in a course in research and measurement.

Apply the findings of sound research to educational and other practices. The findings of sound research studies should be used to guide the practice of physical education in educational institutions and other settings. It is not advisable to base important practices regarding the conduct of physical education on the results of a single research study. Previously discussed problems with research, such as nonsignificant findings and inconclusive results, and faulty research methodology in some studies warrant this caveat. The results of several studies that are in agreement relative to their findings should be used to influence the intelligent practice of physical education.

An illustration of the use of findings of several studies to guide teachers, coaches, and others in the conduct of physical education is the recommended quantity and quality of exercise for developing and maintaining fitness in healthy adults by the American College of Sports Medicine. This organization made specific recommendations regarding the frequency, intensity, quantity, and quality of training and expected improvement in maximum oxygen uptake (Vo_2 max). The results of 33 studies were used to make the following recommendations:

1. Frequency of training: 3 to 5 days per week.
2. Intensity of training: 60% to 90% of maximum heart rate reserve or, 50% of maximum oxygen uptake (Vo_2 max).
3. Duration of training: 15 to 60 minutes of continuous aerobic activity. Duration is dependent on the intensity of the activity, thus lower intensity activity should be conducted over a longer period of time. Because of the importance of the "total fitness" effect and the fact

that it is more readily attained in longer duration programs, and because of the potential hazards and compliance problems associated with high intensity activity, lower to moderate intensity activity of longer duration is recommended for the non-athletic adult.
4. Mode of activity: Any activity that uses large muscle groups, that can be maintained continuously, and is rhythmical and aerobic in nature, e.g. running-jogging, walking-hiking, swimming, skating, bicycling, rowing, cross-country skiing, rope skipping, and various endurance games and activities.[32(p. vii)]

The foregoing recommendations contain the guidelines for developing a suitable fitness program for healthy adults. Such a program would be based on the findings of sound research. Although these recommendations were made by professionals in various disciplines concerned with sports medicine, individual practitioners should be guided by such recommendations when organizing a fitness program for adults.

Although the recommendations of the American College of Sports Medicine regarding exercise programs for adults were based on the results of a number of research studies, it is not clear how these research findings were synthesized for use. The beta-analysis technique for integrating the results of several studies was mentioned earlier as a promising procedure for physical education. An example of the use of that procedure (the "Critical factors approach" by Rothstein and Arnold) is presented next.

AN EXAMPLE OF THE "CRITICAL FACTORS APPROACH" IN SYNTHESIZING THE RESULTS OF RESEARCH STUDIES

To demonstrate how the "Critical factors approach" can be applied to practical situations in physical education, Rothstein and Arnold[41] chose to synthesize and analyze studies dealing with the use of videotape feedback in the teaching of motor skills. They chose feedback* because it has been identified by several authors as the single most important variable in the learning and performance of motor skills.

A total of 52 studies were examined to provide answers to the questions that were proposed regarding the use of videotape replay as a source of feedback when teaching motor skills. The following steps were observed in synthesizing and analyzing the studies:

1. Formulate specific, critical questions regarding the implementation of some general concept of learning in physical education
2. Determine the critical factors or variables that are associated with the topic in question
3. Search the literature for the research studies (review of research)
4. Organize and synthesize the data
5. Analyze the data
6. Apply the findings of the research studies to the teaching situation

The process of each of these steps will be explained by summarizing the study by Rothstein and Arnold. The same process could be used to combine and integrate information pertaining to other topics.

Step 1. Formulate specific questions regarding general concept in learning. The general concept is that feedback is important in facilitating the acquisition of motor skill

---

* Feedback is defined by these authors as "information available to the learner regarding performance." There is both intrinsic feedback (information resulting from the learner's own feelings and observations) and augmented feedback (additional information supplied to the learner). Intrinsic feedback may be visual (watching the ball go into the basket, auditory (hearing the "swish" of the racquet), or kinesthetic (getting the "feel" of the movement). Augmented feedback may be visual (flashing of judges' scorecards in gymnastics) or verbal (giving oral corrections). The teacher or coach usually provides augmented feedback to learners in physical education.

learning. Based on a knowledge of the types of feedback and the parameters of the teaching-learning process, it was stated that the teacher should assume as a primary responsibility the provision of augmented feedback information concerning student performance. This statement raised a number of "how" and "what type" questions. For example, Should feedback information be supplied verbally by the teacher or coach? Should feedback be provided through the visual modality by using videotape replay of the performance? Should both techniques be used? Once the modality and general technique for providing feedback have been answered, questions must be answered regarding specific procedures to follow to maximize the beneficial effect of feedback information on learning. These questions may include: What instructions, if any, should be given in conjunction with the use of videotape replay? How many viewings should be provided and at what intervals during practice? Is videotape replay equally effective for different skill levels and for all types of activities?

Step 2. Determine the critical factors associated with the topic in question. The use of videotape replay as a technique for providing feedback to students was chosen as the topic for investigation. Relevant questions were posed in the previous step. Based on previous information, the variables (or factors) chosen to be used in summarizing studies are: age, sex, skill level, treatment condition, length of study, type of test, and result.

Step 3. Search for literature for research studies. At this point, the reviewer is ready to search the literature for research studies on videotape replay as a means of feedback. Rothstein and Arnold consulted two main sources: *Completed Research in Health, Physical Education, and Recreation* and *Dissertation Abstracts*. Completed studies of many of the abstracts could be obtained

Author (yr.)	Sex	Age	Task	Skill level	Treatment conditions	Time	Test	Result
Armstrong, W. (1971)	F	Col	Tennis	Beginner	Lec-Demo	2x/wk	Broer	Sig. imp.
					Lec-Demo VTR each class	10 wk	Miller	
					Lec-Demo VTR 1/wk			

through interlibrary loan or might be found on microcard or microfiche.*

Step 4. Organize and synthesize the data. Studies were initially divided into two groups, based on the significance or nonsignificance of the results of the study. The variables used for the study were organized in the above manner:

Step 5. Analyze the data. When all the information has been organized and synthesized, it must be analyzed so that it can be applied to the solution of the problem in question. Rothstein and Arnold numerically summarized the variables that were organized and presented in tabular form (see example above). The data were numerically summarized according to variables and separated into significant and nonsignificant studies. An example of the summary analysis for the variable "Sex of subject" (Table 5) shows how the data were organized for analysis. A similar table was constructed for each of the variables used in the analysis. The frequency data for each table (a total of seven) was subjected to chi-square analysis.

An analysis of the data resulted in the following conclusions:

1. Advanced beginners benefited more from the use of videotape replay than beginners.
2. Repetitive use of the videotape replay (five or more opportunities over a semester or three or more viewings per session) was necessary for improvement to be significantly greater than control conditions.

---

*See the section on "Literature searching" for more information on possible sources for review.

Table 5. Sex of subject

	Sig.	Non-sig.
Male	6*	14
Female	6	12
Both	3	3
Not given	4	4

*Number of studies.

3. Cues to direct the learner's attention to specific parts of the replay are necessary to successful use of the videotape replay to facilitate learning and performance.[54]

Step 6. Apply the findings of research to the teaching situation. Based on the meta-analysis of the data and from other research on feedback, the following suggestions for applying the findings to the teaching situation were offered by Rothstein:[54(pp. 59-60)]

1. *Use verbal cues during viewing.* Help the learner to focus on relevant information on the screen by verbally indicating what aspect of the videotape replay to watch.

2. *Use videotape replay frequently and repeatedly.* For positive benefits to accrue, the videotape replay should be used a minimum of five separate times, with multiple replays each time. Several viewings are necessary because the player's attention tends to wander during the first and sometimes during the second viewing. Multiple viewings afford the viewer time to focus on all relevant

---

54. Rothstein, A. L.: Effective use of videotape replay in learning motor skills, Journal of Physical Education and Recreation 51:59, February 1980.

aspects of the performance and thus a chance to more fully analyze the performance.

3. *Use the replay with advanced beginners or intermediates.* Advanced beginners or intermediate players will benefit more from videotape replay because they have the necessary knowledge to relate error information noted on the screen to possible performance outcomes. They can also modify their behavior to conform to the feedback provided. The information presented through videotape replay is not precise enough for advanced performers.

4. *Practice following administration of feedback.* The learner should be provided with opportunities to practice the skill or activity immediately following the feedback so that errors can be corrected without great delay. If possible, similar practice environments (before and after the feedback) should be provided for the learner.

5. *Zoom in on particular aspects of performance.* By using a zoom lens on the camera, relevant aspects of the performance may be given attention. It is one means of forcing performers to focus on certain aspects of the skill.

6. *Vary the camera angle.* Many different angles of the learner are necessary if a complete picture of the performance is to be seen. This varying of camera angle is used on television during instant replay and provides additional information from the various angles.

7. *Coincide the use of the videotape replay with the goals of the activity.* Make the view of the performance consistent with the goals of the activity. In taping a soccer film, for example, the focus should be on the movement of the feet as they contact the ball or tackle an opponent. In other activities, gymnastics, for example, the focus of the camera and the cues to viewing should be on the form of the movement itself.

CONCLUDING STATEMENT

The evidence to date indicates that there is a gap between research findings and the practice of physical education. This disparity is a result of many factors: inadequate knowledge of the research process by practitioners, with the resultant inability to evaluate, interpret, and use the results of research; the time constraints placed on teachers during their daily teaching duties and "extra duties"; nonsignificant and inconclusive findings of research studies; unwillingness of some researchers to translate findings of their research into practical suggestions for lay users; and the lack of a mechanism within the profession for the development and dissemination of research information.

This chapter dealt mainly with suggestions for practitioners to better equip themselves to utilize the findings of sound research studies in improving the practice of physical education. Practitioners were urged to (1) get a thorough background in research and statistics, (2) become involved in the conduct of some research during undergraduate school, and (3) apply the findings of sound research to educational and other practices. A discussion of ways in which physical educators can gain these competencies was presented, and examples were given. A promising method for synthesizing the results of several studies so that the combined findings can be used to intelligently guide the practice of physical education was presented.

If both practitioners and researchers seriously consider the proposals in this chapter and if the AAHPERD as well as individual educational institutions provide for the development and dissemination of research findings, the gap between research and the practice of physical education can be reduced.

DISCUSSION QUESTIONS AND EXERCISES

1. Present a rational discussion to support the assertion that there is a gap between research

findings and the practice of physical education.

2. Give an example of a motor learning concept in which practice is contrary to research findings.

3. List and discuss the essential steps in the research process of conducting a research study.

4. List and discuss the four problems associated with practitioners that were included in this chapter. Indicate the proposals for the solution of these problems.

5. List and discuss three problems of researchers. Discuss two means of overcoming the problem of "relatively few conclusive research findings" in using the results of research.

6. Why must a teacher have a knowledge of research and statistics to help bridge the gap between research and the practice of physical education?

7. Outline the procedure you would follow in searching the literature for information on weight training for women. Indicate the sources that you would check in a priority order.

8. In what way(s) can the research finding that "a positive self-concept enhances learning" be used in physical education classes to improve the teaching-learning process?

9. Conduct a survey in two different schools (one elementary and one secondary) to determine the number and kinds of educational decisions made by administrators that were based on research findings.

10. Conduct a survey among physical educators in your school to determine the percentage and kinds of educational practices that are based on research findings and subsequent application to practical teaching situations.

11. Apply the beta-analysis procedure to the synthesis of research studies dealing with whole and part learning.

12. Use the "Guide for Critiquing Research Studies" to evaluate and critique a study in the latest issue of the *Research Quarterly*.

SELECTED REFERENCES

Barnes, F. P.: Research for the practitioner in education, Washington, D.C., 1964, Department of Elementary School Principles, National Education Association.

Best, J. W.: Research in education, Englewood Cliffs, N.J., 1970, Prentice-Hall, Inc.

Bloom, B. S.: Twenty-five years of educational research, American Educational Research Journal 3:211-221, May 1966.

Bucher, C. A.: Physical education: an emerging profession, Journal of Health, Physical Education, and Recreation 39:42-47, September 1968.

Cronbach, L. J.: The role of the university in improving education, Phi Delta Kappan 47:539-545, June 1966.

Clifford, G. J.: A history of the impact of research on teaching. In Travers, R. M. W., editor: Second handbook of research on teaching, Chicago, 1973, Rand McNally & Co.

Haag, E. E.: Literature searching in physical education, Journal of Physical Education and Recreation 50:54-58, January 1979.

Kneer, M. E., editor: Curriculum theory into practice, Journal of Physical Education and Recreation 49:24-37, March 1978.

Locke, L. F.: Research in physical education, New York, 1969, Teachers College Press.

Locke, L. F., editor: The scholarly enterprise, Quest 20:1-114, June 1973.

Locke, L. F.: Research on teaching physical education: new hope for a dismal science, Quest 28:2-16, Summer 1977.

Myers, J. L.: Fundamentals of experimental design, Boston, 1966, Allyn & Bacon, Inc.

Nixon, J. E., and Locke, L. F.: Research on teaching physical education. In Travers, R. M. W., editor: Second handbook of research on teaching, Chicago, 1973, Rand McNally & Co.

Rothstein, A. L., and Arnold, R. K.: Bridging the gap: application of research on videotape feedback and bowling, Motor Skills: Theory into Practice 1:35-62, Fall 1976.

Rothstein, A. L., editor: Puzzling the role of research in practice, Journal of Physical Education and Recreation 51:39-64, February 1980.

Taylor, C. W., Ghislen, B., and Wolfer, J. A.: Bridging the gap between basic research and educational practice, National Education Association Journal 51:23-25, January 1962.

Travers, R. M. W.: A study of the relationship of psychological research to educational practice. In Glaser, R., editor: Training research and education, New York, 1962, John Wiley & Sons, Inc.

Weber, J. C., and Lamb, D. R.: Statistics and research in physical education, St. Louis, 1970, The C. V. Mosby Co.

Winer, B. J.: Statistical principles in experimental design, New York, 1962, McGraw-Hill Book Co.

10 □ Providing physical education and sport for handicapped persons

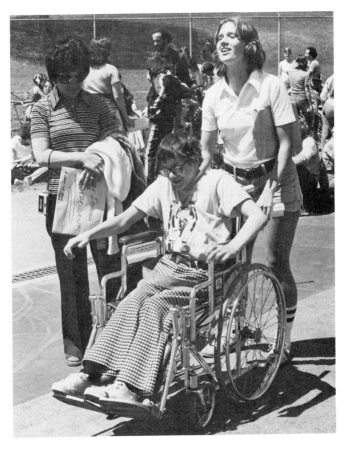

Courtesy Springfield College, Springfield, Mass.

The recognition of the need to improve educational services for handicapped persons was characteristic of the 1970s. It is receiving further attention in the 1980s. This increased attention resulted largely from two factors—the large percentage of handicapped individuals of school age receiving inadequate services and the demands by parents that their handicapped children be properly educated.

There is a considerable variation in statistics relating to the number of handicapped

165

Table 6. Prevalence of handicapped children in the United States

Handicap	Percentage of population	Number of children ages 5 to 18*
Visually impaired (includes blind)	0.1	55,000
Hearing impaired (includes deaf)	0.6 to 0.8	330,000 to 440,000
Speech handicapped	3.5 to 5.0	1,925,000 to 2,750,000
Crippled and other health impaired	0.5	275,000
Emotionally disturbed	2.0 to 3.0	1,100,000 to 1,650,000
Mentally retarded (both educable and trainable)	2.5 to 3.0	1,375,000 to 1,650,000
Learning disabilities	2.5 to 3.0	1,100,000 to 2,200,000
TOTAL	11.2 to 15.4	6,160,000 to 9,020,000

*Number of children based on 1978 population estimates.

school-age children (numbers vary between six and nine million[1,2,3]). Table 6 contains a summary of figures provided by Gearheart and Weishahn.[2(pp. 18-19)] They indicate that these figures were derived from a composite of federal reports and other generally accepted published estimates. The table indicates the lowest percent usually reported as the minimum of this range and a median figure as the upper limit.

Gearheart and Weishahn also presented data indicating the number and percentage of children receiving services and those in need but not receiving services. Viewed in total, more than half of the handicapped children in the United States do not receive appropriate educational services. In terms of categories, the emotionally disturbed (85%), the crippled and other health impaired (80%), and the hearing impaired (75%) were in greatest need of educational services.[2(p. 19)]

1. U.S. Department of Health, Education and Welfare: Services for crippled children, Public Health Service Publication No. 2137, Washington, D.C., 1971, U.S. Government Printing Office, pp. 11-12.
2. Gearheart, B. R., and Weishahn, M. W.: The handicapped child in the regular classroom, ed. 2, St. Louis, 1980, The C. V. Mosby Co., p. 18.
3. Arnheim, D. D., Auxter, D., and Crowe, W. C.: Principles and methods of adapted physical education and recreation, ed. 3, St. Louis, 1977, The C. V. Mosby Co., pp. 14-15.

LEGISLATION TO ENSURE EQUALITY OF EDUCATIONAL OPPORTUNITY FOR HANDICAPPED PERSONS

There have been many court decisions and laws passed to ensure equality of educational opportunity for handicapped individuals.

Public Law 94-142

Because of the specific mention of physical education in the final regulations implementing P.L. 94-142 (Education of All Handicapped Children Act of 1975), it is discussed in some detail. First, there is an overview of what the law means for all handicapped individuals. Next, some specific aspects of the law as they relate to physical education are discussed.[4]

Overview of the law. The final regulations of P.L. 94-142 spell out the federal government's commitment to providing all handicapped children with a free and appropriate education. Specifically, full educational services must be provided for: (1) handicapped children not currently receiving a free and appropriate education and (2) severely handicapped youngsters receiving inadequate assistance.

4. Technical information related to P.L. 94-142 is taken from the Physical Education Newsletter, Number 87, November, 1977. By permission.

Courtesy Springfield College, Springfield, Mass.

Handicapped children, as defined in P.L. 94-142, are those who require some type of special education and related services. The law further defines special education as "... specifically designed instruction, at no cost to parents or guardians, to meet the unique needs of a handicapped child including classroom instruction [adapted physical education instruction is a part of this], and instruction in hospitals and institutions." Also, related services, under the act, are defined as "transportation and developmental, corrective, and other supportive services, including occupational therapy, recreation, and medical and counseling services. . . ." Although gifted children might need special education and related services, they are not covered under the law.

Other specific stipulations of P.L. 94-142 require:

1. State and local educational agencies to initiate policies to ensure all handicapped boys and girls the right to a free and appropriate education.
2. Planning of individualized educational programs, with conferences among parents, teachers, representatives of local educational agencies, and, where appropriate, children themselves. These conferences must be held at least once a year.
3. Due process for parents and children, to ensure that their rights are not abrogated.
4. A per pupil expenditure which is at least equal to the amount spent on nonhandicapped children in the state or local school district.
5. The state and local agency shall carry out the

Courtesy Springfield College, Springfield, Mass.

mandates of the law according to specific time-tables provided therein.

6. The development of a comprehensive system of personnel training, including preservice and inservice training for teachers.
7. That handicapped students will be educated in the "least restrictive environment." This means that they will be mainstreamed into the regular class whenever possible. [4(p. 2)]

Aspects of P.L. 94-142 related to physical education. Section 121a.307 of the regulations of P.L. 94-142, which spells out the requirements for physical education, follows.

121a.307 Physical Education

(a) *General.* Physical education services, specially designed if necessary, must be made available to every handicapped child receiving a free appropriate public education.

(b) *Regular physical education.* Each handicapped child must be afforded the opportunity to participate in the regular physical education program available to nonhandicapped children unless:

(1) The child is enrolled full time in a separate facility; or
(2) The child needs specially designed physical education, as prescribed in the child's individualized education program.

(c) *Special physical education.* If specially designed physical education is prescribed in a child's individualized education program, the public agency responsible for the education of that child shall provide the services directly, or make arrangements for it to be provided through other public or private programs.

(d) *Education in separate facilities.* The public agency responsible for the education of a handicapped child who is enrolled in a separate facility

Courtesy Springfield College, Springfield, Mass.

shall insure that the child receives appropriate physical education services in compliance with paragraphs (a) and (c) of this section.

The House of Representatives, in a special report, made the following reference to physical education:

The committee expects the Commissioner of Education to take whatever action is necessary to assure that physical education services are available to all handicapped children, and has specifically included physical education within the definition of special education, to make clear that the Committee expects such services, specially designed where necessary, to be provided as an integral part of the educational program of every handicapped child.[4(p. 3)]

Apparently the Committee recognized that appropriate physical education instruction might not be provided for handicapped children on the same basis as their nonhandi-

capped peers. Therefore, the special report was included to ensure that such physical education programs be instituted for handicapped children.

The physical education program for handicapped students must be individualized according to the needs of each handicapped individual. Students should be included in the regular program whenever possible and special adapted programs established as needed. Students should not be mainstreamed into the regular physical education program when their handicap(s) prevents them from receiving an adequate educational experience. Conversely, they should not be placed in a special class and left there. Handicapped youngsters should be scheduled in and out of regular classes, depending on their ability to cope with the specific activity being taught at a particular time. The final consideration is to provide the handicapped child with the "least restrictive environment" or one that permits the child to achieve his or her maximum potential.

Other legislation

Other legislative acts relating to handicapped persons and affecting physical education programs are Section 504 of the Rehabilitation Act of 1973 (P.L. 33-112) and the Education Amendment Act of 1974 (P.L. 93-380). The final rules and regulations for Section 504 were signed by the Secretary of the Department of Health, Education and Welfare in 1977. The provisions of this statute guarantee the rights of handicapped persons in programs for which schools and other sponsoring groups receive federal funds. P.L. 93-380 is designed to ensure that handicapped individuals be placed in the least restrictive alternative environment for educational purposes. Part VIB of the law specifically states that

. . . to the maximum extent appropriate, handicapped children should be educated with children who are not handicapped, and that special classes, separate schooling or other means of removal of handicapped children from the regular educational environment, occurs only when the nature or severity of the handicap is such that education in regular classes with the use of supplementary aids and services cannot be achieved satisfactorily.

THE HANDICAPPED: CATEGORIES AND DEFINITIONS

Many terms have been used to classify and define handicapped individuals. These terms vary from publication to publication. Categories of children designated by the United States Congress in relation to legislation for handicapped persons will be the primary classifications used in this text. These categories include the mentally retarded, hard-of-hearing, deaf, speech impaired, visually handicapped, seriously emotionally disturbed, crippled, and other health impaired

or learning disabled children who may require educational services out of the ordinary. These handicapping conditions are defined here.

mentally retarded—Persons characterized by a level of mental development impaired to the extent that the individual is unable to benefit from the standard school program and requires special services. This includes such subcategories as slow learners, educable mentally retarded, and trainable mentally retarded.

hard-of-hearing—Persons in whom the sense of hearing, although defective, is functional with or without a hearing aid. The hearing loss is generally of such a nature and severity as to require one or more special educational services.

deaf—Persons in whom the sense of hearing is nonfunctional for the ordinary purposes of life (inability to hear connected language with or without the use of amplification). This general group is made up of the congenitally deaf and the adventitiously deaf.

speech impaired—Persons experiencing pronounced organic or functional speech disorders that cause interference in oral communication. This includes persons exhibiting language disorders resulting from such specific handicaps as stuttering, cleft palate, speech, or voice problems.

visually handicapped—Persons who have such severe visual loss as to require special educational services. This includes subcategories such as blind, legally blind, partially sighted, and visually impaired.

seriously emotionally disturbed—Persons having psychiatric disturbance without clearly defined physical cause of structural damage to the brain, which limits the ability of the individual to govern his own behavior. These are of such a nature and severity as to require one or more special services, particularly with reference to their education.

crippled—Persons with orthopedic impairments that might restrict normal opportunity for education or self-support. This is generally considered to include individuals having congenital impairments, for example, clubfoot or absence of some body member, impairments caused by some disease, for example, poliomyelitis, bone tuberculosis, and encephalitis, neurological involvements that may result in conditions such as cerebral palsy, and impairments caused by accidents, for example, fractures or burns that cause contractures.

other health impaired—Persons having health handicaps not covered in other categories, of such a nature and severity as to require one or more special services, particularly with reference to their education. These could include asthma; rheumatic fever; conditions of less than the usual amount of strength, energy, or endurance; conditions resulting from chronic illness or environmental causes; epilepsy; diabetes; or cardiac disease.

learning disabled—Persons with learning dysfunctions that prevent them from learning or functioning in a regular educational program. These individuals exhibit a disorder in one or more of the basic psychological processes involved in understanding or in using spoken or written language. These may be manifested in disorders of listening, thinking, talking, reading, writing, spelling, or arithmetic. They include conditions that have been referred to as perceptual handicaps, brain injury, minimal brain dysfunction, dyslexia, developmental aphasia, etc. They do not include learning problems that are a consequence primarily of visual, hearing, or motor handicaps; mental retardation; emotional disturbances; or environmental disadvantages.[5]

In addition to those terms already defined, certain other terms used in relation to programs for handicapped persons must also be defined. These terms are *impaired, disabled, handicapped, exceptional person*, and *adapted physical education*. The concept of mainstreaming is discussed in the next section and, therefore, will not be defined here.

impaired—This refers to an identifiable organic or functional condition; some part of the body is actually missing, a portion of an anatomical structure is gone, or one or more parts of the body do not function properly or adequately.

disabled—This refers to a limitation or restriction of an individual, because of impairments, in executing some skills, doing specific jobs or tasks, or performing certain activities.

handicapped—Handicapped individuals, because of impairment or disability, are adversely affected psychologically, emotionally, or socially, or in a combination of ways.[6]

exceptional person—The exceptional person is one who, because of some physical, mental, emotional, or behavioral deviation, may require a modification of school practices or an addition of some special service in order to develop to his or her maximum potential.[3(pp. 14-15)]

adapted physical education—The Committee on Adapted Physical Education defines adapted physical education as ". . . a diversified program of developmental activities, games, sports, and rhythms suited to the interests, capacities, and limitations of students with disabilities who may not safely or successfully engage in unrestricted participation in the vigorous activities of the general physical education program."[6(p. 63)]

THE QUESTION OF MAINSTREAMING

Mainstreaming is one of the most talked about aspects of special education today. The traditional definition of mainstreaming is to take handicapped students from a special class and have them become a part of the regular class with nonhandicapped students. In recent years, this definition has lost favor among some special educators and other teachers who believe that students are frequently placed into the regular class without any support services or modification of regular class instructional procedures. A new concept of mainstreaming that is being favored by more educators today is that of providing

5. U.S. Department of Health, Education and Welfare: Better education for handicapped children, annual report, fiscal year 1969, Washington, D.C., 1970, U.S. Government Printing Office.

6. Stein, J. U.: A clarification of terms, Journal of Health, Physical Education, and Recreation 42:63, September 1971.

Courtesy Springfield College, Springfield, Mass.

educational services for handicapped students in the "least restrictive environment." In essence, this means that a handicapped child is placed in a special class or a regular class or is moved between the two environments as dictated by his or her abilities and capabilities. Furthermore, the school assumes the responsibility of providing the necessary adjunct services to ensure that handicapped students perform to their optimum capacity, whether integrated into the regular program or left in a special class.

Pros and cons of mainstreaming

The reasons usually given in support of mainstreaming are:

1. Handicapped students will not feel alienated and different because they are in the same environment with normal people.
2. The self-image of handicapped individuals will be improved; they will develop a negative self-image in a special class.
3. Performance of handicapped students will be better because they will use normal students as models for achievement.
4. A more conducive environment for social development will be provided.
5. It will be more economical since less special classes and schools will be required.
6. The teacher and nonhandicapped students will learn more about the nature, needs, and special problems of handicapped students in an integrated environment.

Those persons who oppose the concept of mainstreaming contend that the positive features indicated by adherents are grossly exaggerated and that there is an absence of hard data to support the practice of mainstreaming. For example, Macy and Carter note that "although there is philosophical and emotional support for mainstreaming, there have been few reports of empirical research regarding its effectiveness."[7] Those persons who oppose mainstreaming cite the following negative results of the practice:

1. Class size will become unmanageably large with the addition of handicapped students.
2. There will be a decline in performance of middle and high achievers.
3. Handicapped students will become frustrated and will be more inclined to fail because of their placement in classes with students who are much more advanced than they.
4. The educational process will be hampered because teachers will be required to spend more time with handicapped students.
5. The teacher's job will be much harder since the classroom teacher is not as well equipped or prepared to handle the handicapped as is the special education teacher.
6. Many of the normal children will not accept children with handicapping conditions; the normal child will ridicule the handicapped child.
7. Handicapped students will become frustrated because of the lack of understanding of their handicapping condition(s) by peers and teachers.

According to many educators, mainstreaming can be successful if certain basic practices are adhered to before and during the process of mainstreaming. The handicapped person should be placed in the educational environment that produces optimal growth and development, that is, the "least restrictive environment." Stein, consultant to the American Alliance for Health, Physical Edu-

cation, Recreation, and Dance, states "the idea behind mainstreaming is that if an individual can safely, successfully, and with personal satisfaction take part in a regular program or in unrestricted activities, no special program is necessary."[8] However, this should be viewed as the ideal. It must be realized that some handicapped students must be educated in special self-contained classrooms. Other handicapped individuals might be able to benefit from some services in a regular class and some activities in the special class.

The developmental concept applied to program planning

The use of the developmental approach to programming for handicapped persons will help to promote the positive and successful mainstreaming that is sought. In this approach, there is individual planning of educational programs. This developmental concept of education rejects the notion of rigid categories that result in people being stigmatized. Rather, it advances the notion that there is a hierarchy of developmental tasks through which each individual must progress. In other words, each person grows and develops in a sequential pattern in all domains—physically, mentally, emotionally, and socially. By observing behavior manifestations in each of these developmental areas, and on an individual basis, instructional programs can be planned. Arnheim, Auxter, and Crowe[3] have provided a thorough presentation of the application of the developmental concept.

Klein, Director of Educational Services in the Department of Health, Education and Welfare's Head Start Bureau, has offered some suggestions relevant to this discussion.

7. Macy, D. J., and Carter, J. L.: Comparison of mainstream and self-contained special education programs, The Journal of Special Education 12:303, Fall 1978.

8. Stein, J. U.: Sense and nonsense about mainstreaming, Journal of Physical Education and Recreation 47:43, January 1976.

Get to know the individual child's problems, reactions, strengths and weaknesses. If you see him or her as a child first—rather than as a stutterer or an epileptic—you will realize that most behavior is not related to the disability. If a child is acting especially shy or having tantrums, it may not be related to cerebral palsy or deafness, but may be a normal developmental stage.

Get to know all you can about the specific disability. Chances are your group will have one or two handicapped children. Find out the ways that a cleft palate or a visual problem can affect a child. It is important that you get all the information possible and then trust your own judgement and your knowledge of children.

Listen to parents; they're experts about their child. Talk to them at a prearranged time—not in front of the child. Encourage the parents to come to the classroom to observe and to offer suggestions based on their experiences. Make it a two-way exchange: you will learn from them.*

Introduce the special child to the class gradually. Ask the parents to bring the child in some day after school. Let the child explore the classroom and begin to feel comfortable with it. In phasing a special child into the class, take your cues from the other children: note when they feel comfortable, scared, belligerent or enthusiastic.

Capitalize on the special child's strong points. Set up situations where the child can do well in the group. A mentally retarded boy might have some playground skills the others appreciate; a deaf girl may do well in the dress-up corner or in building with blocks.

Know what comes within the range of normal behavior for the age group you work with. Know the problems of normal children in the age group and their typical reactions.

Know your own level of frustration, how much you can take. Don't consider yourself a failure if you need to ask for help or send a child home occasionally. Some handicapped children have more difficulty than others in groups. Remember that in any classroom situation there are days when things

don't go as smoothly as you'd like—when you wonder if you really picked the right profession.[9]

SUGGESTED ORGANIZATIONAL STRUCTURES FOR HANDICAPPED PERSONS

Various organizational structures have been proposed to provide educational experiences for handicapped persons. Some of these organizational options are also used for nonhandicapped students in regular classes. However, the organizational plans outlined by Puthoff[10] and Arnheim, Auxter, and Crowe[3(pp. 438-440)] are included here because they provide viable options for physical educators faced with the task of planning activity programs for handicapped individuals.

The four organizational structures suggested by Puthoff are:

1. *Integrated or combined class*—Handicapped students are placed in regular classes that are modified as needed with respect to goals, activities, and methodology. The students' needs, interests, present status, and goals would provide the basis for individualizing instruction. Individual activities such as track and field and gymnastics and self-testing activities such as sit-ups and flexed-arm hangs are suggested since performance in these types of activities does not affect the success or failure of other students, as would be the case with a team sport such as soccer or volleyball.

2. *Dual class structure*—Handicapped

---

*We do not recommend having parents help with their own children. They will be much more effective in working with other children with the same handicap as their child.

9. Klein, J.: Mainstreaming handicapped children: tips for teachers. Cited in the National School Public Relations Association: Educating all the handicapped, Arlington, Va. Reprinted by permission from Education U.S.A., Copyright 1980, National School Public Relations Association.

10. Puthoff, M.: Instructional strategies for mainstreaming, Mainstreaming physical education, National Association for Physical Education for College Women and The National College Physical Education Association for Men, Briefings 4, 1976.

students are placed in an integrated class setting part of the time and in a special class the rest of the time. The decision to place the student in a particular setting would be based on the principle of the "least restrictive environment." Students would be placed in special classes only for those special needs that cannot be met in an integrated class.

3. *Separate class* — Handicapped students are placed in a class separate from the regular physical education class when the students are not yet ready for the regular class setting or their handicap is too severe to permit them to participate with nonhandicapped students. Those handicapped students who require placement in special classes would still be in the regular school setting and would have opportunities to interact with nonhandicapped students during noninstructional hours. For example, all students should be allowed to have the same recess periods so that they can interact on a social basis.

4. *Flexible model plan* — Handicapped students are placed in regular classes when they can safely and successfully participate in the activities provided and in a separate class when more individualized instruction is needed because of their handicap. For example, students with severe physical handicaps might be placed in a special class for instruction in team activities. These students, however, might be placed in a regular class for individual and self-testing activities. In other words, the activities and the handicapping condition become the basis for participation, whether it is with a regular or a separate class.

The organizational structures suggested by Arnheim, Auxter, and Crowe are related specifically to class organization. These options are:

1. *Formal class organization* — All the students perform the same activity at the same time under the direction of the teacher or student leader. This type of class organization permits the teacher to observe the performance of all students more adequately than if each student was participating in a different activity. A disadvantage of this structure is the lack of opportunity to give individually assigned activities to students with special needs.

2. *Informal class organization* — Each student has an individual physical education program. This method is difficult with students who are immature and irresponsible since a great deal of self-initiative is required on the part of students. This method is used most frequently at the college or upper grade levels of the secondary school, but, according to Arnheim, Auxter, and Crowe, it can be used successfully with mature boys and girls of junior high school age. The major advantage of this method is that it provides for the needs of students on an individual basis. The major disadvantage is the lack of teacher control of the class. Another disadvantage is the time necessary for the teacher to prepare individual activity programs.

3. *Group organization* — Students are organized into groups based on similarities in the type of disability or the activity program needed. All students with scoliosis might be grouped together to perform the same corrective exercises, another group with upper limb impairment might be placed together for a game of modified soccer, and another group with the same disability might be placed together for some special activity. Students in such an organizational plan may remain in the same groups throughout the class period or they may be changed to allow for more flexibility in their programs. This method combines the advantage of group work with that of individuality of assignment. Student aides can be used very effectively in this type of homogeneous grouping.

Courtesy Springfield College, Springfield, Mass.

4. *Combined method*—Students are grouped according to a combination of the preceding types of class organization plans. This method attempts to capitalize on the advantages of each of the methods of organization; that is, to provide for individualization of instruction, to provide for some small group activity, and to use formal activity sessions during which the teacher is in more direct control of the work that students perform. The following is an example of this plan:

5 minutes—Formal warm-up consists of all students doing the same exercises under the leadership and direction of the teacher or a student leader.

5 minutes—Students are divided into homogeneous groups according to their needs and perform three activities or exercises with the members of their group under the direction of a student leader.

10 minutes—Each student performs five exercises or activities specifically assigned to him (her), doing the number of repetitions assigned and recording his (her) progress on his (her) exercise card. (Activities using special equipment can be assigned here, since students are able to take turns in the use of special pieces of apparatus.)

5 to 10 minutes—Games, relays, and contests are

organized and led by the teacher, finishing with formal dismissal of the class, if desired.[3(p. 440)]

GUIDELINES AND PROGRAM PLANNING FOR STUDENTS WITH SPECIFIC HANDICAPS

Types of handicaps to be discussed include physical handicaps, emotional disturbances, mental retardation, and learning disabilities. (Multiple handicaps will be discussed briefly.) These particular handicaps will be discussed because of their prevalence among students and the difficulties they might present for physical educators. The causes, consequences, and general guidelines for program planning for each handicap will be given. More information about the various handicaps may be obtained from sources listed at the end of this chapter.

Physical handicaps

Physically handicapped persons, as discussed in this text, include those with visual and auditory handicaps, cerebral palsy, low degree of fitness, poor coordination, and such orthopedic handicaps as loss of a limb or scoliosis.

Causes and consequences. Physical handicaps may result from a number of factors, including disease, congenital disorders, trauma, growth and developmental disorders, or accidents. Some physical disabilities or impairments may be hereditary. Whatever the cause for the specific physical handicap, the program must be adapted to meet the needs of students with such handicaps. Generally, a person with a physical handicap will attempt to compensate for it in some manner, for example, by acting in socially unacceptable ways.

The consequences of a particular handicap depend on its extent and duration. Some handicaps are very minor and are operative for only a short period, such as a sprained ankle or low fitness levels. More serious handicaps of a longer duration include loss of limbs, blindness, deafness, and musuclar dystrophy. Obviously the kind and amount of activity provided in the physical education program for students with physical handicaps should be determined by the severity and duration of the handicap.

Guidelines for program planning.[11] The nature and extent of physical handicaps differ widely, resulting in many different functional levels and capacities. Therefore, physical activities should be modified according to the person's functional ability, for example, persons who have prosthetic devices or persons who use canes or crutches.

The basic instructional and program strategies for any sound physical education program should be observed when teaching handicapped students. However, certain other guidelines may be helpful when teaching students with physical handicaps.*

1. Obtain medical approval for the planned program.

2. If the person with the physical handicap is receiving physical therapy, the program of physical education should be planned to complement the therapeutic exercises.

3. Plan an individualized program of exercises and activities to meet the special needs of each student.

4. Be aware of the dangers of twisting, bending, falling, and lifting motions for those persons with spinal cord impairments such as spina bifida (a congenital abnormality characterized by a developmental defect in one or more vertebral arches through which the contents of the spinal canal

---

11. Adapted from Geddes, D.: Physical activities for individuals with handicapping conditions, ed. 2, St. Louis, 1978, The C. V. Mosby Co., pp. 105-106.

*Most books on adapted physical education contain information specifically related to the organization of programs and teaching strategies for physically handicapped students. For example, see Geddes; Arnheim, Auxter, and Crowe; and Fait.

may protrude[12]). Because of a lack of motor dexterity and the increased possibilities for further injury, including paralysis, the teacher should be extremely careful of the types of physical activities included in a physical education program for persons with spina bifida.

5. In activities in which there is an impairment or disability of the lower extremities, substitute sitting or lying positions for standing positions. When the person is fitted with a prosthetic device, wears braces, or is able to ambulate with a cane or crutches, physical activities may be modified whereby the handicapped person can participate while standing.

6. Provide frequent periods of rest and less vigorous games and activities for those with limited endurance.

7. Use the maximum number of sensory modalities that are appropriate for a specific physical impairment or disability. For example, visual communication would not be used for students with visual handicaps, but kinesthetic stimuli (guiding the body parts through the desired movement), tactile stimuli (use of touch to relate to the person which body part is to be used), and verbal stimuli (oral instructions) would be emphasized.

8. Teach the person with an orthopedic handicap to fall correctly from crutches, wheelchairs, or unsupported positions.

9. Have the nonhandicapped students simulate the handicap to gain a better insight into the problems and difficulties handicapped students face in performing physical activities. For example, require students to use only one hand for some activities in classes in which there are some students with only one hand.

10. Promote self-acceptance and help to instill confidence in handicapped students by providing opportunities whereby they can achieve success.

11. Help the students develop skills and talents that compensate for a physical disability or impairment. The person who has paralysis of the lower limbs and is confined to a wheelchair, for instance, might be taught and encouraged to develop the upper body through weight training. Such a person might also be taught track and field skills that require only the use of the upper body, such as the discus and javeline throw.

12. Help alleviate a student's fears about dressing and showering with others if that student has an obvious deformity or loss of limb. This objective might be accomplished by having a talk with the student about the handicap and helping him or her find a solution that is satisfying and realistic. The student should be encouraged to meet the challenges of his or her handicap with humor rather than with fear of ridicule or embarrassment.

13. Provide body awareness activities to compensate for the loss of limb or lack of mobility. Specific activities for body awareness might include the teacher pointing to different parts of the body and asking the students to do the same, the teacher asking students to draw pictures of themselves, the teacher requiring the students to play games such as "Do This, Do That" and "Simon Says," in which they have to point to and move different parts of their bodies on command.

14. Provide exercise programs that increase range of motion, alleviate contractures, and improve postural maintenance, balance, muscular power, endurance, and coordination. For example, exercises such as the gorilla walk (flexibility and coordination), frog stand (balance and arm strength), and wheelbarrow (arm, shoulder, and abdominal strength) might be used.*

15. Pay special attention to the concept of progression for students who have been inactive for a long time. Often these students need a period of relearning; therefore, start with basic movement skills and body mechanics, stressing large muscle activity. Gradually include modified or adapted activities requiring specific fine motor activities.

16. Modify ambulatory or locomotor activities for those students with lower extremity impairments. For example, students in a relay race

---

12. Adams, R.: Program implications for children with orthopedic and related impairments. In AAHPER: Physical education and recreation for impaired, disabled, and handicapped individuals: past, present, and future, Washington, D.C., 1975, The Alliance, p. 125.

*These are three of the suggested exercises for the primary grades for developing physical fitness. These and other exercises suggested for primary through intermediate grades were recommended by the President's Council on Physical Fitness and Sports. See Bucher and Thaxton for a description of these exercises.

might be required to hop instead of run when there are students in the class with only one leg.

Emotional disturbances

It has been estimated that there are approximately 1,300,000 emotionally disturbed children of school age in the United States. Of this number, only 15% are receiving educational services.[2(p. 19)] Emotionally disturbed children exhibit a wide range of behavioral characteristics. Overt behavior might range from hyperactivity to extreme withdrawal. Moran and Kalakian state that, as a group, emotionally disturbed children possess deficiencies in at least one of the following categories:[13]

1. Characteristics associated with interpersonal relationships
   a. Deficient in social skills, inability to conform to group patterns, little social conscience
   b. Demands constant attention or appears antisocial and plays alone
   c. Demonstrates a willingness to follow rather than lead
2. Emotional characteristics
   a. Exhibits emotional responses of unhappiness or depression
   b. Exhibits inconsistencies in responses
   c. Exhibits a rigidity in expectations of everyday living
   d. Demonstrates carelessness, irresponsibility, apathy, and a low capacity to delay gratification
3. Learning characteristics
   a. Demonstrates poor work habits
   b. Demonstrates a lack of motivation
   c. Demonstrates disruptive class behavior
   d. Demonstrates a lack of involvement
   e. Demonstrates an inability to follow directions or seek help

13. Adapted from Moran, J. M., and Kalakian, L. H.: Movement experiences for the mentally retarded or emotionally disturbed child, Minneapolis, 1977, Burgess Publishing Co., p. 6.

   f. Demonstrates a short attention span
4. Physical characteristics
   a. Exhibits poor motor coordination
   b. Experiences difficulty in making space and time assessments
5. Other characteristics
   a. Demonstrates hyperactivity
   b. Demonstrates hostility
   c. Experiences fears or tendencies toward fantasy life
   d. Exhibits a poor self-concept
   e. Experiences unhappiness and insecurity within himself or herself
   f. Exhibits personality traits of depression and withdrawal

In summary, the emotionally disturbed person can be described as one who exhibits poor interpersonal relationships, acts out in class or completely withdraws from activities, is given to periods of depression, shows little motivation, and generally demonstrates poor work habits. Some emotionally disturbed persons also experience deficiencies in perceptual and motor skills that make it difficult for them to perform the more complex activities in which perception and motor control are important.[3(p. 379)] However, physical education is one program in which many emotionally disturbed children can achieve success. Many emotionally disturbed individuals possess exceptional physical skills. The physical education teacher must structure the environment with rules and class routines to facilitate appropriate actions and behavior so that disruptive behavior will not adversely affect participation.

Causes and consequences. There are two schools of thought regarding the cause of emotional disturbances—some authorities believe the cause is organic while others believe that it is environmental. In the past, brain damage or some other neurological disturbance was considered the major cause of emotional disturbances. Recently, however, environmental conditions, such as family disorganization, sibling rivalry, depressing home surroundings, and undue pressure from parents to succeed in school, are considered the major causes of emotional disturbances.

Some of the results of emotional disturbances are the inability to learn at a rate commensurate with intellectual and physical development, poor interpersonal relationships with peers and adults, inappropriate emotional responses, inadequate development of perceptual and motor skills, unhappiness, and low self-esteem.

Guidelines for program planning and teaching[11(pp. 123-128)]

1. Become acquainted with the characteristics of emotionally disturbed persons and keep a record of all pertinent data of children in your classes. Note such behavior as constantly talking during verbal instructions to the class, daydreaming, a student poking a classmate, or students who are completely withdrawn from class activities. Refer students with emotional problems that impair learning and/or disrupt classroom management to the proper school authorities (psychologist or nurse).

2. Be firm with students who display disruptive behavior. Make them responsible for such behavior. For example, prohibit a student from playing in a team game if he or she constantly disrupts such games with arguing, hitting, or the like.

3. Develop a system for "selectively ignoring" students who act out in class; failing to call attention to a minor disruptive act of a student is one means of accomplishing this objective. While the teacher may ignore the student during the class, the teacher should talk to the student in private after class about his or her disruptive behavior. Students often exhibit disruptive behavior to gain attention. If attention is not gained by such behavior, sometimes that is enough to cause the student to discontinue the behavior. Teachers should be very careful in using this strategy. They should not ignore a student who is asking for help. Sound judgment is needed to know when to ignore and when to offer help.

4. Praise those students who demonstrate improvement in their behavior patterns, in both small group and large group situations.

5. Teach students how to relax by providing relaxing activities such as aquatics and rhythms and dance. There are also specific methods of teaching relaxation. Moran and Kalakian, for example, recommend having children assume a comfortable position, preferably on mats, lying on their backs, and having them think about breathing and breathe slowly and deeply. Next, they suggest having students try to make their bodies as "tight" and "hard" as possible, and then having them make their bodies "soft" and "light as a feather." They believe that practice in slow, deep breathing should be alternated with the tightening and relaxing of the muscles. Another method they recommend is to have the children very slowly roll their arms in and out while resting on the mat. Have the students repeat this procedure with the legs. Finally, have them combine slow inward and outward rolling of the arms and legs with slow, deep breathing.[13 (p. 390)]

6. Increase the attention span of students by removing distracting objects. For example, keep all equipment out of sight that is not being used.

7. Plan several games and activities for each class to allow for the short attention span of students.

8. Provide for aquatics in the program. The warm water is relaxing and provides a sedative effect for hyperactive students.

9. Stress program material that aids in the development of social and personal development. Such activities as rhythms and dance, team games such as field hockey and softball, and self-testing activities are recommended.

10. Modify the rules when appropriate for students to achieve success.

11. Organize classes according to a routine or set procedure; however, discourage stereotyped play activities that develop rigid behavioral patterns, such as constantly playing with a ball, jumping rope, and playing hopscotch alone.

12. Establish rapport with students by being firm and consistent in dealing with them, yet letting them know that you care about them as people and want to help them succeed both in school and in life.

13. Plan for behavior control by using the following intervention techniques:
   a. Allow free-play periods and other activities at times when control is not necessary.
   b. Plan activities that allow for success by all. Acting out behavior is sometimes engaged in because of a feeling of frustration and failure.
   c. When necessary, physically restrain students.
   d. Provide both positive and negative reinforcement.
   e. Use humor in the classroom or gymnasium.

14. Use emotionally disturbed students as teacher's aids when possible.

15. Use direct, eye-to-eye contact when dealing with students.

16. Establish a feeling of mutual respect among the children.

17. Protect students from embarrassment and ridicule while behavior is unstable.

The following guidelines and instructional principles were adapted from Arnheim, Auxter, and Crowe,[3 (pp. 338-384)] and Moran and Kalakian.[13 (pp. 338-340)]

1. Use a variety of methods of teaching and a variety of games that will accommodate children who function at different physical, social, and emotional developmental levels. The short attention span of these children makes it necessary to plan for a variety of games so that the interest of the students can be recaptured when initial activity is no longer productive. In many cases, the command method (explanation, demonstration, and allowances for practice) should be used at the initial stages of a class. However, problem-solving methods such as movement exploration and guided discovery should be used to provide opportunities for students to explore and discover on their own. Writing of the benefits of the problem-solving method of teaching emotionally disturbed students, Arnheim, Auxter, and Crowe state that "the element of choice, the availability of a variety of solutions, and the climate of encouragement to seek a new response create motivation to participate in activity that may have been lacking in many emotionally disturbed children."[3 (p. 390)]

2. Use instructions that are direct, specific, and short.

3. Provide a majority of the instruction in a small group or on a one-to-one basis, if possible.

4. Provide immediate reinforcement for desired behavior. Examples include the awarding of inexpensive items such as ribbons and certificates, and sometimes just words of praise such as "That was very good, Johnny."

5. Adhere to the principle of progression in teaching. Use the part-whole method of teaching complicated activities. In teaching the front crawl swimming stroke, for example, the following sequence might be used:
   a. Arm stroke in standing position
   b. Arm stroke, front crawl in standing position with rhythmic breathing
   c. Flutter kick from prone float
   d. Flutter kick and arm movements with rhythmic breathing from prone float

6. Pick the appropriate time to encourage a child to approach, explore, and try a new activity or experience. Arnheim, Auxter, and

Crowe believe that a new experience is often met with resistance by emotionally disturbed children. They believe that teachers must try to build guarantees of success into the new experience. Successful experiences often provide the impetus to try new activities.

7. Provide activities that are within the abilities and levels of development for all students. Successful experiences are satisfying to students and decrease anxiety levels and increase self-esteem and confidence.

8. If necessary, separate children who cause disruption in the class. Stress activities of a group nature with these students to help them develop acceptable social behaviors.

9. Use demonstrations freely in a class with emotionally disturbed children. Also, use kinesthetic methods of teaching, including manual guidance for all students except the hyperactive child. Be sure to gain a rapport with students before attempting to use manual guidance as a teaching technique. The teaching of the forward roll in tumbling is used to illustrate these principles. After an explanation of the skill, the teacher or a student leader would demonstrate the forward roll. The teacher would then have the students practice the forward roll. As the students are attempting to perform the forward roll, the teacher would assist them by holding their heads down with one hand and pushing up and forward with the other hand, keeping the children in a tucked position.

10. Avoid direct confrontations with students over matters of discipline by diverting their attention or changing the activity. When students become overly aggressive, impulsive, and disorganized during a particular activity, change to an activity that you know the students enjoy.

11. Avoid introducing high levels of competition into the program. Highly competitive situations will cause the hyperactive child to become more aggressive, and failure will cause frustration and additional disruptive behavior.

Mental retardation

Like other types of handicapped individuals, mentally retarded persons are being given greater attention by educators, psychologists, physicians, sociologists, and others concerned with this problem. The work of the Joseph P. Kennedy, Jr. Foundation, among others, is largely responsible for the increased focus on mentally retarded persons. This organization provides financial and other support to foster research and education for mentally retarded persons. According to the American Association on Mental Deficiency (AAMD), mental retardation indicates "subaverage general intellectual functioning existing concurrently with deficits in adaptive behavior, and manifested during the developmental period."[14] This means that a person who is mentally retarded has difficulty in learning and is unable to apply what is learned to daily life situations.

Mentally retarded individuals are usually described according to the degree of retardation. Psychologists classify the mentally retarded as follows:

profoundly retarded—IQ under 19. These individuals require custodial care.

severely retarded—IQ of 20 to 35. These individuals can be trained to care for some of their bodily needs, develop some language, and have great difficulty in social and occupational areas.

moderately retarded—IQ of 36 to 51. These individuals usually are unable to perform academic skills with any degree of mastery, can be trained to perform daily routines, and can usually func-

---

14. Grossman, H. J.: Manual on terminology and classification in mental retardation, Baltimore, 1973, Garamond and Pridemarks Press.

tion in a sheltered workshop with close supervision.

mildly retarded—IQ of 52 to 68. These individuals have some degree of educability in terms of reading and writing. They are educable in the areas of social and occupational functioning.

Educators describe mentally retarded persons as totally dependent, trainable, and educable. The totally dependent person would be in the same category as the profoundly retarded. These persons are unable to perform even the most simple self-care requirements. They require complete supervision and care throughout their lives.

The trainable mentally retarded person has an IQ of between 20 and 35 and is able to be trained in a supervised setting to perform the personal requirements for living. While the trainable mentally retarded person will require a sheltered existence, the educable mentally retarded person will be able to maintain an independent living style in the community. The educable mentally retarded person exhibits characteristics similar to those of borderline and mildly retarded persons as classified by psychologists. Although they possess the intellectual capacity (their IQ ranges from 50 to 80 or more), educable mentally retarded persons may be limited in their adaptability because of emotional and behavioral problems.

Mentally retarded persons should be helped to achieve at their optimal level, regardless of the category to which they have been assigned on the basis of intelligence tests. Physical educators can aid in the development of mentally retarded persons by planning and conducting a sound program that provides opportunities for these students to achieve success and personal fulfillment.

Causes and consequences. Mental retardation may be caused by abnormal conditions in the prenatal (before birth), paranatal (during birth), and early postnatal (after birth) environment. Some prenatal factors are inadequate nutrition, toxins, endocrine deficiencies, exposure to x rays or radium, blood-group incompatibility of mother and infant in Rh or other blood factors, and German measles (rubella) in the mother during the first 3 months of pregnancy. Paranatal factors include anoxia (oxygen deficit), cerebral hemorrhage, and mechanical injury of the brain in the process of birth. Common among the many postnatal causes of mental retardation are infective diseases in infancy, most notably encephalitis and meningitis, that may lead to brain inflammation. Some mildly retarded persons are thought to have been so affected because of inadequate stimulation toward growth and development during the formative years.

The questions related to hereditary factors in mental retardation are largely unanswered. However, heredity is now regarded as a less prevalent cause of mental deficiency than previously supposed. Nevertheless, some hereditary factors are thought to cause mental retardation, for example, rare forms of mental deficiency, such as phenylpyruvic amentia and the amaurotic idiocies, have been traced to metabolic disorders arising from single recessive genes. Microcephaly and other such conditions result from defective genes in some cases. However, they may also be produced by prenatal pathogenic factors.

The most serious consequence of mental retardation is the limited contributions these people make to society. It is also costly to provide adequate facilities and care for profoundly mentally retarded persons since they often have to be institutionalized. Furthermore, recent legislation has mandated that every child should be educated, level of functioning notwithstanding.

Physical educators should especially be

aware of the relationship between mental retardation and motor development. Evidence has indicated that proper motor development is a key factor in cognitive maturation. Work by Cratty,[15,16] Kephart,[17] and Strauss and Kephart[18] are notable in this regard. Research by these authors has demonstrated that mentally retarded persons, as a group, are less proficient in physical and motor skill development than normal persons. In many cases, however, physical education is the most beneficial type of education in which these people will engage. Sound, challenging programs of physical education are needed to help close the gap between mentally retarded and normal persons in both the mental and physical domains.

Guidelines for program planning and teaching. The scope of the program for mentally retarded persons should include such activities as swimming, basic movement skills, self-testing, gymnastics and tumbling, trampolining, rhythms and dance, and some of the simple individual and dual games. Team games and others that require extensive rules and strategy should not be included because of the limited intellectual development and low frustration level of the retarded persons.

Since there is so much diversity among mentally retarded persons, specific guidelines would not be meaningful or very helpful. However, there are some general suggestions that might prove beneficial to teachers and/or leaders of programs for mentally retarded persons.*

1. Base the selection of activities on the present level of functioning of the mentally retarded person. Classifications of retarded persons should be used only as a guide for describing the needs, abilities, and characteristics of individuals and the remediation required.

2. Be aware of the extremely slow process of learning and achievement in mentally retarded persons. Constant repetition, drill, and review of skills are needed more often than with nonretarded persons.

3. Consider the principle of progression—from the known to the unknown and from the simple to the complex. When teaching young educable mentally retarded persons, for example, start with a program of activities that stresses basic movement skills, such as running, climbing on stall bars, tumbling, and bouncing on a small trampoline. Once these children learn to control their bodies through basic movement activities, they might be taught simple activities (hopscotch, croquet, ring toss, and the like) that require the use of these basic movement skills.

4. Provide for vigorous physical activity on a daily basis. Since research has shown that the mentally retarded as a group are less developed physically than nonretarded persons, the provision of regular, vigorous physical activity in the physical education program is an important objective.

5. Provide opportunities for group interaction to foster social development and coping skills. Including simple group games and lead-up games to team sports in the program and teaching recreational games that can be played and enjoyed by the family (bowling, bicycling, fishing, sledding, and so on) are ways of fostering the development of social interaction and acceptable social traits. Having retarded youngsters work on group assignments such as setting-up and removing equipment, marking off fields, and planning a

15. Cratty, B. J.: Motor activity and the education of retardates, Philadelphia, 1969, Lea & Febiger.

16. Cratty, B. J.: The perceptual motor attributes of mentally retarded children and youth, monograph, Los Angeles, 1966, Mental Retardation Services, Board of Los Angeles County.

17. Kephart, N. C.: The slow learner in the classroom, Columbus, Ohio, 1971, Charles E. Merrill Publishing Co.

18. Strauss, A. A., and Kephart, N. C.: Psychopathology and education of the brain-injured child, New York, 1955, Grune & Stratton, Inc.

*Adapted from AAHPER: Recreation and physical activity for the mentally retarded, Washington, D.C., 1966, The Association, and Geddes.[11(pp. 33-54)] short story or physical activity for class is another means of developing desirable social behavior.

6. Introduce new or complex activities at the start of the class when students are fresh and alert. For example, do not introduce tumbling and gymnastic skills to the class during the last 15 minutes, after group games have been taught for the first 15 minutes of class.

7. Be firm in the exercise of discipline but also be fair and consistent.

8. Do not remain with one activity too long because of the short attention span of the children; provide for many and varied activities.

9. Make instructions short and simple. Demonstrate often.

10. Remove a disruptive person temporarily from the class situation and deal with him or her in a small group or on an individual basis.

11. If discipline is a constant problem during a particular activity, consider the appropriateness of the skill or activity being taught. The activity possibly requires too much skill, has too many rules, or entails too many verbal instructions.

12. Correlate physical activities with basic classroom activities to reinforce academic concepts, for example, use games such as hopscotch and the bean bag toss to teach word recognition and number concepts. Specifically, arrange the letters of the alphabet in the blocks of a hopscotch drawing. Have the children hop from one box to another, and require them to say the letter on which they hop, spell out words, and so on. When numbers are placed in the blocks, mathematics concepts can be taught. Students may also use bean bags to toss in the boxes that contain either letters or numbers to reinforce alphabet and/or word recognition and number concepts.

13. Do not expect much transfer of skill to be made by the retarded youngster from one activity to another. Be prepared to assist them in making generalizations by emphasizing the common principles of the skills. In teaching the high jump in track and field and the jump for a rebound in basketball, for instance, emphasize the lowering of the body by bending at the knees and the upward thrust of the arms for added momentum.

14. Provide a wide range of stimuli in teaching skills:

   a. Tactile stimuli—The use of touch to relate more effectively the body part to be used in a skill. Touching the triceps muscle when asking the person to perform a push-up is one example of the use of tactile stimulation

   b. Kinesthetic stimuli—Manually guiding the body parts through the desired movement to give the person the feeling of the movement pattern. An example of this principle is the manual turning of a child's head in the water when teaching rhythmic breathing.

   c. Visual stimuli—The use of visual aids such as diagrams, wall posters, demonstrations, films, and the like. The use of film strips in teaching tennis strokes is an example of visual stimuli.

   d. Verbal stimuli—The use of oral instructions in teaching. Keep verbal instructions to a minimum when teaching mentally retarded persons, especially severely retarded persons.

15. Extend free and lavish praise for good performances.

16. For severely and profoundly retarded persons, alternate short periods of activity, work, and rest. Anticipate when these individuals are tired and make changes accordingly.

17. Structure and administer the program whereby all children will experience some success.

Arnheim, Auxter, and Crowe work with mentally retarded children in a variety of settings. They have presented some teaching hints that are appropriate here:

1. Consider individual differences when selecting the activities. It is possible to play many games that account for differences in abilities among class members.

2. Select activities to meet the children's interest level. However, precautions should be taken against participation in one particular activity to the exclusion of others. Be aware of the development of rigid play behaviors.

3. Do not underestimate the abilities of mentally retarded children to perform skilled movements. There is a tendency to set goals too low for these children. This is particularly true for educable mentally retarded children.

4. Develop recreational skills that make it possible for those who are mentally retarded to integrate socially with members of their family and peers, now and in later life.

5. Structure the environment in which the activity takes place so that it challenges the child, yet provides the freedom from fear and physical hurt and gives him/her the satisfaction of some degree of success.

6. The lower grade mentally retarded child must be taught to play. This means that physical education is responsible for creating the play environment, developing basic motor skills that are the tools of play, and, occasionally, initiating the activity.

7. Adapt the activities to the abilities of *each* child. No blanket programs for those who are mentally retarded, as a generic group, should be used.

8. Convey to mentally retarded persons that they are individuals of worth, reinforcing their strengths and minimizing their weaknesses.[3(pp. 360-361)]

Learning disabilities

Individuals with learning problems that affect the development of processes associated with speech, language, reading, writing, and arithmetic are said to have a "specific learning disability" if the problems are caused by one or more of the following conditions: perceptual handicaps, brain injury, minimal brain dysfunction, dyslexia, and developmental aphasia. Specific learning disabilities do not include learning problems that are caused primarily by visual, hearing, or motor handicaps, mental retardation, emotional disturbance, or environmental disadvantage. In essence, an individual with a discrepancy of 50% or more from expected achievement based on his or her intellectual ability is considered to have a specific learning disability.

Some research (Ismail and Gruber[19] and Dillon, Heath, and Biggs[20]) has suggested that programs of motor development and movement stimulation can help to ameliorate, and in some cases prevent, learning problems.

Learning disabled children exhibit many of the same traits as children with other handicaps. However, some characteristics are unique to people with learning disabilities. Gearheart indicates that there are only three characteristics that all learning disabled children have in common: (1) they must have average or above average intelligence, (2) they must have adequate sensory acuity, and (3) they must be achieving considerably less than the composite of their IQ, age, and educational opportunity (health, availability of schooling, and cultural opportunity) would predict.[21]

In addition to the preceding characteristics, many children with learning disabilities also exhibit one or more of the following characteristics: hyperactivity, hypoactivity (not found in many cases), lack of motivation, clumsiness and awkwardness, inattention, belligerence, and unwillingness to relate to peers. Physical educators should be very careful to note any of these characteristics in children while they are in the gymnasium. If the physical educator cannot cope with the condition, he or she should contact the appropriate person in the school.

19. Ismail, A. H., and Gruber, J. J.: Motor aptitude and intellectual performance, Columbus, Ohio, 1967, Charles E. Merrill Publishing Co.
20. Dillon, E. J., Heath, E. J., and Biggs, C. W.: Comprehensive programming for success in learning, Columbus, Ohio, 1970, Charles E. Merrill Publishing Co.
21. Gearheart, B. R.: Learning disabilities: educational strategies, St. Louis, 1973, The C. V. Mosby Co., pp. 9-10.

Causes and consequences. The literature dealing with the causes of learning problems is voluminous. These causes are often said to include factors such as perceptual problems, cerebral dysfunctions, or behavioral disturbances. Bateman further defined the cerebral dysfunctions and other physiological factors as: (1) damage to or dysfunction of certain localized areas of the brain such as angular gyrus, second frontal gyrus, connection between the cortical speech mechanism and the brain stem cetrencephalic system, and the parietal and parietal-occipital areas, (2) hereditary or developmental lag factors such as inherited underdevelopment of directional function, hereditary delayed development of parietal lobes, slow tempo of the neuromuscular maturation, and (3) other factors such as lack of cerebral dominance, minimal brain injury, endocrine disturbance and chemical imbalance, and primary emotional factors.[22]

The consequences of learning disabilities are poor achievement in school, inadequate social development, and poor motor development. These conditions may often cause a child to give up and become a delinquent. In too many cases, children who have learning problems are diagnosed and labeled as mentally retarded and are placed in environments with other mentally handicapped children. To prevent this, special education teachers, physical education teachers of students with learning problems, and others dealing with such children must be careful to make accurate diagnoses and referrals.

Guidelines for program planning. Proper diagnosis is necessary to ascertain the specific learning problem that a person has. (The listing of characteristics indicated that there is a wide range of individual differences in students with learning problems.) Once children are diagnosed, the teacher should be careful to plan the physical education program to meet the needs of those with specific learning problems. (It might be necessary to seek the services of a specialist such as an audiologist, optometrist, psychologist, and the like to make diagnoses.) For example, if a group of children is diagnosed as having perceptual-motor problems, specific difficulties such as poor eye-hand or eye-foot coordination, laterality, or directionality must be identified and provided for.

The following suggestions are offered to help teachers improve programs in which there are students with learning disabilities:*

1. Review carefully the basic principles of learning and adapt them for use with students with specific learning problems. In observing the principle of providing the maximum stimuli in teaching motor skills, for example, the teacher would not use verbal stimulation with persons with aphasia since they do not understand spoken words because of cerebral dysfunction.
2. Plan a wide variety of activities that includes basic movement, rhythms, movement exploration, perceptual-motor activities, games and self-testing activities, aquatics, and so on.
3. Provide a preschool program of movement awareness, if possible. Use activities in which children are required to identify their body parts, move them, and be aware of their position in space. For example, the teacher might start with body awareness by pointing to different parts of his or her body and asking the students to do the same. The teacher would then challenge the children to identify body parts without any visual help from the teacher. Once the children are able to identify their body parts, they can then

---

22. Bateman, B.: Learning disabilities—yesterday, today, and tomorrow. In Frierson, E. C., and Barbe, W. B., editors: Educating children with learning disabilities, New York, 1976, Appleton-Century-Crofts, pp. 13-14.

*Adapted from Geddes[11(pp. 63-65)] and Harvat (Chapter 1).

be challenged to perform certain movements. The following problems might be posed:

"Starting with your left foot, move four steps to the left."

"Throw the ball to Tom with your right hand."

"Walk forward, backward, and sideways on the balance beam while keeping your eyes on a target."

"Hop forward three times with the right foot and three times with the left foot."

4. Keep hyperactive students together in groups and allow them to calm down. Keep them busy with activity, for example, have the children play quiet games such as checkers, old maid, or cribbage. They may also be given self-testing exercises to perform, or they may be assigned to keep score or act as student managers during the class.

5. Keep an uncluttered environment and one that is free from outside noises and distractions.

6. Correlate physical activities with academic work, for example, when working on directionality, have the students identify their body parts as they make certain movements.

7. Create an atmosphere of trust and confidence by being fair but firm and by structuring activities whereby children can succeed.

8. Emphasize an "action" atmosphere by having children act out the activity and describe what is taking place at the same time. Including story plays and drama and games such as charades in which the students are required to act out the story or activity is one means of providing an "action" atmosphere. Another technique is to have students describe to the class an activity or stunt before they perform it, then perform the activity, and finally have the class perform it.

9. Prepare many activities that will relate to language since many children with learning problems have difficulty in this area. Having children write their own descriptions of games, requiring them to explain the rules of a game to the class, and requiring students to write and give an oral report on a current sports event are ways that this suggestion can be implemented.

10. Prepare children for assuming responsibility before giving them wide options for action; it might be necessary to start with command

teaching, for example, and then work toward movement exploration. Students with learning problems need more help in finding solutions to problems than normal children because of the problems they have with language, speech, and other cognitive areas. Therefore, they would probably be overwhelmed by too much freedom in making choices. The teacher can assist in their learning by demonstrating a certain stunt, for example, and then asking students to perform the stunt. If students are able to perform the stunt with relative ease, the teacher might then ask students if they can perform the stunt in any other manner. By gradually giving the students more options to assume responsibility, they will feel more confident and will be less likely to become frustrated.

11. Imitation works well with young children; use it freely. For instance, the teacher might create a certain posture or shape and ask the class to repeat the movement.

12. Have children repeat instructions before they perform the activity to reinforce auditory clues.

13. Prepare a conducive learning atmosphere, paying special attention to room light that avoids shadows and other visual illusions.

14. Seek additional help if children do not respond to the program that is being conducted. It might be necessary for rediagnosis of those children or a change in some aspects of the program.

Multiple handicaps

A person with a physical handicap may become so withdrawn that he or she becomes emotionally disturbed. Likewise, an emotionally handicapped person may develop certain learning problems that will adversely affect academic performance. There are other situations in which one handicap will cause decreased functioning in other developmental areas.

Teachers working with handicapped individuals should realize that some people may have two or more major handicaps simultaneously. For instance, a person might be both blind and deaf, or a person might be mentally retarded and have an orthopedic handicap.

Working with handicapped individuals is a tedious, demanding, and sometimes frustrating job. Obviously, dealing with people who have multiple handicaps is even more difficult. However, the enjoyment and satisfaction gained from helping the handicapped individual make progress, whether there is a single or multiple handicap, should more than outweigh the difficulties.

In dealing with persons with multiple handicaps, the teacher should become as familiar as possible with the handicaps and attempt to help those persons make the best adjustment possible. Emphasis in program planning should be on those aspects of a person's personality and physical self that can be fully developed. The program should be modified to meet the needs of the handicapped person. Hopefully, the program of physical education will enable the person with all kinds of handicaps to develop the necessary physical fitness, motor skill, and general body mechanics to enjoy life to the fullest, in spite of the handicap(s).

Guidelines for program planning and instruction will not be presented for multiple handicapped persons as they were for persons with only one handicap. Such guidelines would be so hypothetical (because of the possible combinations of handicaps) that they would be virtually useless. Teachers of multiple handicapped persons would need to teach those individuals according to their specific handicap. For example, the teacher would need to use different instructional strategies when teaching physically and emotionally handicapped persons than when teaching a person who is visually handicapped and learning disabled. The guidelines for program planning indicated for specific

handicaps, along with the other information presented in this section, are intended to aid in developing programs to meet the needs of persons with more than one handicap.

FACILITIES, EQUIPMENT, AND SUPPLIES

Appropriate and adequate facilities, equipment, and supplies are important to successful programs of physical education for handicapped persons. However, these items must be emphasized in special or adapted physical education programs because facilities and equipment are designed for students in the regular class. Adaptations are also often necessary when handicapped students are mainstreamed into regular programs.

The passage of recent legislation and the results of various legal decisions have prompted school districts to make available the necessary facilities, equipment, and supplies to ensure a quality education for handicapped students. There is some question, however, as to whether handicapped students are in fact being provided with adequate facilities, equipment, and supplies. They are not, according to Stein, a recognized authority on problems of handicapped persons. He believes that "despite federal legislation, mandates in every state, and regulations in some local areas, facilities of all types continue to be built and renovated without consideration of barriers, accessibility, and availability [to the handicapped person]." Stein states that the major problem and cause of these situations and conditions are "attitudonal barriers."[23]

The types of facilities and equipment needed for adapted physical education will

23. American Alliance for Health, Physical Education, and Recreation: Making physical education and recreation facilities accessible to all: planning, designing, adapting, Washington, D.C., 1977, The Alliance, p. i.

vary according to the nature of the program (adapted sports, remedial or corrective exercises, or rest and relaxation), the type of student (mentally retarded, physically handicapped, or some other), and the school level at which the program is conducted. For example, the elementary school program in adapted physical education may be taught in the regular gymnasium, or in less desirable circumstances, in the classroom. In secondary schools and colleges, however, a special room for adapted physical education should be provided.

Arnheim, Auxter, and Crowe[3(p. 451)] have indicated two possible arrangements for providing facilities for the elementary school adapted physical education program. The first arrangement is for the school district to provide special centers, located strategically in the district, for the adapted physical education programs. A specialist in adapted physical education, under the guidance of the medical director for the district, would teach students who would be transported from the various schools in the district. The center would be properly equipped for adapted physical education. The other arrangement is to schedule elementary school children for classes at a nearby secondary school or higher education institution in which facilities and equipment are available. The minimum equipment that is needed for an adapted room in a secondary school or college level facility, according to Arnheim, Auxter, and Crowe, is:

sufficient individual 1-inch thick plastic-covered body mats to accommodate the peak class load, plus five or six more; 2-inch thick mats of sufficient size to cover the floor under hazardous types of equipment such as the horizontal ladder or the horizontal bar; a platform or firm rubber mats to cover the floor where weight-lifting activities will take place; towels for use in the exercise program; a plumb line or posture screen for posture examinations; and miscellaneous, inexpensive pieces of testing equipment such as measuring tapes and skin pencils.[3(p. 456)]

Additional equipment such as ropes, benches, and weights was mentioned as equipment that could be made by personnel in the maintenance department or by the students themselves. The equipment for adapted sports that is needed could be borrowed from the regular physical education program. It was also suggested that special equipment for perceptual-motor training be purchased.

The broadness of the topic and its technical nature precludes a more thorough discussion in this chapter of specific facilities, equipment, and supplies for adapted physical education programs. However, this topic is presented in detail in several books on adapted physical education (sources are listed at the end of the chapter). It is also suggested that persons who are responsible for planning programs of physical education for handicapped individuals peruse catalogues of reputable companies dealing in equipment and supplies.

THE TEACHER OF HANDICAPPED PERSONS

To adequately provide for students with handicaps, all educational institutions should employ only competent personnel. Special education and training are needed by adapted physical education teachers. Personal attributes of these individuals should also be strongly considered before they are hired.

Education and training

The minimum qualification for candidates seeking positions as teachers of adapted physical education in schools should be an undergraduate degree in physical education with a specialization in adapted physical education or leadership in physical education for handicapped persons. This preparation should include experiences that enable students to develop the following competencies:*

1. An understanding of the nature, causes, and consequences of the various handicapping conditions.
2. An understanding of the theory and practice of adapted and corrective physical education.
3. An understanding of the effects of exercise on the physiological functioning in both normal and atypical individuals.
4. An understanding of principles of first aid for both normal students and those with handicapping conditions.
5. An understanding of the care and prevention of athletic injuries.
6. A knowledge of human growth and development.
7. A knowledge of general and abnormal psychology.
8. A knowledge of anatomy, kinesiology and biomechanics, and theories of learning.
9. A knowledge of other professional courses in physical education such as principles, tests and measurements, research methods, and so on.
10. The ability to organize, plan, and conduct a program of physical education to meet the needs of all students. The program must be adapted to meet the special needs of those students with handicapping conditions.

In addition to the above, field work, internship, and/or student teaching should be an integral part of any preparation for a career in adapted physical education. Besides these specialized courses and experiences, the adapted physical education teacher should have an understanding of the hu-

---

*These competencies are listed in accordance with the educational requirements suggested by the staff of the Physical Education and Recreation for the Handicapped Information and Research Utilization Center (IRUC): Professional preparation in adapted physical education, therapeutic recreation, and corrective therapy, Washington, D.C., 1976, The Alliance, p. 34.

manities, social sciences, natural sciences, and fine arts.

Study at a college or university that has a program in physical education and a specialization in adapted physical education is recommended to prepare one for a position as an adapted physical educator. There are no specific certification requirements in most states, and colleges and universities have a great deal of latitude in developing their own curricula in adapted physical education. Because of the variability in curricular offerings of adapted physical education among institutions of higher education and the lack of published curricula for undergraduate programs in this area, no curriculum in adapted physical education is presented. However, the curriculum in corrective therapy (Table 7) that is required by the American Corrective Therapy Association, Inc. is included here. This curriculum is designed to prepare for specialization in corrective therapy and/or adapted physical education. Persons who wish to specialize in corrective therapy and/or adapted physical education should attend an accredited institution that offers a degree in physical education. Following the undergraduate program, the individual can then pursue the corrective therapy program that is presented in Table 7. The curriculum in corrective therapy is very extensive and will probably require an additional year or two beyond the bachelor's degree program. It includes a clinical field experience of 400 hours in a hospital that is approved by the American Corrective Therapy Association, Inc.

Field experiences. The importance of field experiences in adapted physical education cannot be overemphasized. The nature of adapted physical education and the fact that many prospective teachers have had no previous experiences working with atypical students are cogent reasons to stress field work experiences.

Table 7. Curriculum in corrective therapy

Subjects	Semester hours	Quarter hours	Subjects	Semester hours	Quarter hours
Applied sciences	12-18	18-27	Physical and mental habilitation*		
Anatomy*			Tests and measurements*		
Kinesiology*			Evaluation of health and physical education		
Physiology*					
Physiology of exercise*			Research in health and physical education		
Growth and development					
Neuroanatomy*			Skills and applied techniques*		
Neurology*					
Pathology			**Corrective therapy and adapted physical education**	8-14	12-21
Psychology	6-12	9-18			
General psychology*			Physical education for atypical*		
Abnormal psychology*			Organization and administration*		
Physiological psychology*					
Developmental psychology			Corrective therapy		
Mental health			Kinesiotherapy*		
Psychotherapy			Recreation in rehabilitation		
Social psychology			Intertherapy relations		
Health and physical education	16-24	24-36	Evaluation and research applied to corrective and adapted programs*		
Analysis of human movement*					
Health education and problems*					
Principles of health and physical education*					

*Asterisk (*) identifies required courses. Curriculum reprinted by permission of the American Corrective Therapy Association, Inc., Jonesboro, Tenn., 1979.

Note: All candidates for certification in corrective therapy must show evidence of completing a minimum of 400 hours of clinical internship. Such experience must be on referral of a physician, under the supervision of a certified corrective therapist. Candidates must be active members of the American Corrective Therapy Association, Inc., to apply for the certification examination.

The American Association for Health, Physical Education, and Recreation, in cooperation with the Bureau of Education for the Handicapped, United States Department of Health, Education and Welfare, made detailed mention of field experiences in their publication.[24] Specifically, the following recommendations were made:

1. Careful consideration should be given to providing students with maximum exposure to field experiences commensurate with specialized needs.
2. Course work and theory should be integrated and related to practical situations through appropriate observation and participatory experiences.
3. Formal internships or similar arrangements should be structured to provide increasing opportunities for each student to execute and evaluate learning experiences related to his specialization.
4. Field experiences should be available in a variety of situations within a reasonable geographical area. Field experiences will vary depending on the focus of programs, handicapping conditions, and settings in which experiences occur.
5. Supervision of field experiences should be a joint responsibility of faculty and field personnel. Roles of field personnel should be expanded to include participation in developing and modifying programs.
6. Specific sites for field experiences may be judged according to such pertinent characteristics as:
   a. Appropriateness to emphases in programs
   b. Accessibility to college or university
   c. Availability and adequacy of supervision by faculty and field personnel

---

24. American Association for Health, Physical Education, and Recreation and Bureau of Education for the Handicapped, U.S. Department of Health, Education and Welfare: Guidelines for professional preparation programs for personnel involved in physical education and recreation for the handicapped, Washington, D.C., 1973, The Association and U.S. Government Printing Office.

d. Opportunities for interaction and communication with field personnel

Personal qualities. Some of the more important personal qualities needed by adapted physical education teachers are emotional stability, sterling character and personal and professional integrity, agreeable personality, sincere interest in, and respect for, the worth of people with handicaps, good sense of humor, patience, boundless energy and contagious enthusiasm, ability to get along with others, good physical health, and imagination and resourcefulness.

CONCLUDING STATEMENT

The large percentage of handicapped persons of school age receiving inadequate educational services and the demands by parents that their handicapped children receive an adequate education have forced society to recognize the need to improve educational services for handicapped individuals. The recognition of the need for improved educational services for handicapped persons has resulted in legislation, such as P.L. 94-142, P.L. 93-380, and Section 504 of the Rehabilitation Act of 1973. To meet the mandates of this legislation, a program of physical education for handicapped students must be an individualized education program, and it must be conducted in the same facility with nonhandicapped students, unless the handicap is too severe. To meet these requirements, many students are being mainstreamed from special programs into the regular physical education program. When handicapped students are in a regular physical education class with nonhandicapped students, the physical education program for the handicapped students must be adapted to meet their special needs.

To adequately provide for the handicapped students in physical education, there must be special facilities, equipment, and supplies for the adapted program. The physical education faculty must also possess special training in adapted physical education.

DISCUSSION QUESTIONS AND EXERCISES

1. Explain to a parents' and teachers' group the implications of P.L. 94-142 as it relates to physical education.
2. Define the terms *handicapped, disabled,* and *impaired* and discuss the various categories of handicaps.
3. Explain the term *mainstreaming,* the pros and cons of mainstreaming, and the developmental concept of program planning as it relates to mainstreaming.
4. Discuss the various organizational structures for planning educational programs and indicate the ones you think would be most appropriate for persons with specific types of handicaps.
5. Discuss ten guidelines for program planning for physically handicapped persons.
6. Prepare a chart comparing the characteristics of a "normal" person with those of an emotionally disturbed person.
7. As a student teacher, you are assigned a physical education class with four hyperactive fifth grade students. Develop an individualized physical education program for these students, emphasizing plans for behavior control.
8. Discuss the causes and consequences of mental retardation, emphasizing the degree of retardation as it relates to the functioning of the person in society.
9. List and discuss ten guidelines to be used in planning a physical education program for mentally retarded students.
10. As a member of an interdisciplinary team of teachers responsible for the educational program for a class of ten learning disabled children in a sixth grade class, prepare a paper for discussion at an all-school workshop on the topic: "The implications of learning disabilities for teaching physical education."
11. List and discuss the personal and professional qualifications of physical education teachers who teach handicapped children.
12. Discuss the two arrangements that a school district can use to provide adequate facilities for the elementary school adapted physical education program.
13. Prepare a table (according to the following format) that will include information for the various handicaps.

Handicap	Characteristics	Needs	Implications for physical education
Physical handicap			
Emotional disturbance			
Mental retardation			
Learning disability			

14. Discuss some special problems one might expect in teaching persons with multiple handicaps.

SELECTED REFERENCES

American Alliance for Health, Physical Education, and Recreation: Adapted physical education guidelines: theory and practices for 70's and 80's, Washington, D.C., 1976, The Alliance.

American Alliance for Health, Physical Education, and Recreation: Annotated research bibliography in physical education, recreation, and psychomotor function of mentally retarded persons, Washington, D.C., 1975, The Alliance.

American Alliance for Health, Physical Education, and Recreation: Integrating persons with handicapping conditions into regular physical education and recreation programs, Washington, D.C., 1977, The Alliance.

American Alliance for Health, Physical Education, and Recreation: Making physical education and recreation facilities accessible to all: planning, designing, adapting, Washington, D.C., 1977, The Alliance.

American Alliance for Health, Physical Education, and Recreation: Physical education and recreation for impaired, disabled, and handicapped individuals: past, present, future, Washington, D.C., 1975, The Alliance.

American Alliance for Health, Physical Education, and Recreation: Physical education and recreation for individuals with multiple handicapping conditions, Washington, D.C., 1978, The Alliance.

American Alliance for Health, Physical Education, and

Recreation: Professional preparation in adapted physical education, therapeutic recreation and corrective therapy, Washington, D.C., 1976, The Alliance.

American Association for Health, Physical Education, and Recreation and the Bureau of Education for the Handicapped and U.S. Department of Health, Education and Welfare: Guidelines for professional preparation programs for personnel involved in physical education and recreation for the handicapped, Washington, D.C., 1973.

Athletic Institute and AAHPER: Planning facilities for athletics, physical education, and recreation, Washington, D.C., 1974, The Association.

Arnheim, D., Auxter, D., and Crowe, W. C.: Principles and methods of adapted physical education and recreation, ed. 3, St. Louis, 1977, The C. V. Mosby Co.

Arnheim, D., and Sinclair, W. A.: The clumsy child, ed. 2, St. Louis, 1979, The C. V. Mosby Co.

Bucher, C. A.: Administration of physical education and athletic programs, ed. 7, St. Louis, 1979, The C. V. Mosby Co.

Bucher, C. A.: Foundations of physical education, ed. 8, St. Louis, 1979, The C. V. Mosby Co.

Bucher, C. A., and Koenig, C. R.: Methods and materials for secondary school physical education, ed. 5, St. Louis, 1978, The C. V. Mosby Co.

Bucher, C. A., and Thaxton, N. A.: Physical education for children: movement foundations and experiences, New York, 1979, Macmillan Inc.

Cratty, B.: Learning about human behavior through active games, Englewood Cliffs, N.J., 1975, Prentice-Hall, Inc.

Cratty, B.: Remedial motor activity for children, Philadelphia, 1975, Lea & Febiger.

Crowe, W. C., Auxter, D., and Pyfer, J.: Principles and methods of adapted physical education and recreation, ed. 4, St. Louis, 1981, The C. V. Mosby Co.

Fait, H. F.: Special physical education: adapted, corrective, developmental, Philadelphia, 1978, W. B. Saunders Co.

Frierson, E. C., and Barbe, W. B., editors: Educating children with learning disabilities, New York, 1967, Appleton-Century-Crofts.

Gearheart, B. R.: Learning disabilities: Educational strategies, ed. 2, St. Louis, 1977, The C. V. Mosby Co.

Gearheart, B. R., and Weishahn, M. W.: The handicapped student in the regular classroom, ed. 2, St. Louis, 1980, The C. V. Mosby Co.

Geddes, D.: Physical activities for individuals with handicapping conditions, ed. 2, St. Louis, 1978, The C. V. Mosby Co.

Gickling, E., and Theobald, J.: Mainstreaming: affect or effect, Journal of Special Education 3:317-328, 1975.

Harvat, R. W.: Physical education for children with perceptual-motor learning disabilities, Columbus, Ohio, 1971, Charles E. Merrill Publishing Co.

Klappholz, L. A.: Focusing on education for all handicapped children, Physical Education Newsletter 87: 1-8, November 1977.

Moran, J. M., and Kalakian, L. H.: Movement experiences for the mentally retarded or emotionally disturbed child, Minneapolis, 1977, Burgess Publishing Co.

National School Public Relations Association: Educating all the handicapped, Arlington, Va., 1977, NSPRA.

Parish, T. S., Dick, N., and Kappes, B. M.: Stereotypes concerning normal and handicapped children, Journal of Psychology 102:63-70, May 1979.

Stein, J. U.: Sense and nonsense about mainstreaming, Journal of Physical Education and Recreation 47:43, January 1976.

Vodola, T.: Individualized physical education program for the handicapped child, Englewood Cliffs, N.J., 1973, Prentice-Hall, Inc.

Webb, W.: Physical education classes for the emotionally disturbed child, Journal of Health, Physical Education, and Recreation 43:79-81, May 1972.

11 □ Conducting an educationally sound sports program

Courtesy Springfield College, Springfield, Mass.

Contemporary sport has a popular appeal that almost defies explanation. This appeal is revealed by the number of individuals involved in sports both as participants and spectators, the variety of sports, the media coverage of sport programs, and the large sums of money spent on sports. In 1977, it was estimated that approximately 20 million youngsters between 8 and 16 years of age were involved in nonschool sport programs.[1] A 1979 sports participation survey conducted by the National Federation of State High School Associations revealed that some 5.6 million students participated in high school

1. Thomas, J. R., editor: Youth sports guide for coaches and parents, Washington, D.C., 1977, The Manufacturers Life Insurance Company and The National Association for Sport and Physical Education.

Courtesy Springfield College, Springfield, Mass.

athletic programs during the 1978-1979 school year.[2] Although no actual figures could be located, it is common knowledge that sporting events are well attended. An even larger number of individuals watch sports events on television.

According to the 1977 Gallup Poll, nearly half of [the] American adults say they exercise regularly to keep fit. Millions participate in tennis, bicycling, swimming, calisthenics, and other forms of exercise.[3] At the end of 1979, an estimated 55% of American men and women (90 million people) regularly engaged in some form of physical activity.

One of every three adults now spends more than 200 minutes a week exercising, and more than 17 million of them run several times a week.[3(p. 7)]

The recent increase in the number of sports being engaged in by people of all ages also points up the popular appeal of sport. For example, there has been a tremendous increase in the number of participants in such sports as paddle ball, racquetball, road running, tennis, golf, bowling, cross-country skiing, back packing, and so on.

In terms of media coverage of sporting events, the number of hours devoted to them on television (10 to 12 hours almost every Saturday and Sunday), the number of pages covering sports in the newspapers (more space devoted to sports than all the arts combined), and the number of magazines about sports (*Sports Illustrated*, *Sport*, *Runners World*, *Body Building*, *Pro Sports*, and so on)

2. National Federation of State High School Associations: 1979 Sports Participation Survey, Kansas City, Mo., 1979, NFSHSA.

3. President's Council on Physical Fitness and Sports: Nation's improved lifestyle linked to fitness boom, President's Council on Physical Fitness and Sports Newsletter p. 3, December 1979.

Courtesy Lincoln University, Jefferson City, Mo.

Winter Games at Lake Placid, New York, received the maximum television exposure.[4]

Millions of dollars are spent each year by manufacturers to advertise their sports products. Correspondingly, millions of dollars are spent by consumers of sports paraphernalia. In addition to the money spent by manufacturers and consumers, vast sums of money are spent by college and professional organizations for sport programs. The astronomical salaries paid to professional superstars is one illustration of large sums of money being spent on sports. Some professional players, for example, earn $1 million annually.

POTENTIAL VALUES AND POSSIBLE HARM OF SPORTS

Under the proper leadership, sports can be of value to the participants; sports can also cause harm to those who participate in these activities under unfavorable conditions. Some of the potential values of sport are fitness and skill development, social development, and cooperation. Possible harmful effects of sport include excessive pressures, false values, and aggression and violence.

Potential values of sport

Fitness and skill development. Young people can develop several physical fitness components including strength, endurance, flexibility, and agility as a result of participating in competitive athletics. Participation can also promote development of neuromuscular skills. If boys and girls are given opportunities and are encouraged to participate in several sports during their developing years, they will develop skill in a variety of activities. Mohr states that research evidence indicates that athletes are superior to non-

all attest to the popularity of sport. In addition to the regular television coverage of sports events, many additional hours of network time are focused on special sporting events such as the Super Bowl, All Star Basketball Game, and the Olympic Games. During the 1980 Winter Olympics, for example, ABC applied all of its technological resources to ensure that all 51½ hours of the

---

4. ABC ready for Olympics, TV/Radio and Cable Week p. 5, February 10, 1980.

Courtesy Gannett Newspapers, White Plains, N.Y.

Courtesy Springfield College, Springfield, Mass.

athletes in motor ability and motor skill development.[5]

Skill and fitness development do not come automatically, however. Athletes must undergo rigorous conditioning programs to develop the physical fitness necessary to participate in competitive athletics. They must also spend many hours practicing a sport to develop into highly skilled performers.

Social development. Socialization, as defined by Sewell, is ". . . the process by which individuals selectively acquire the skills, knowledges, attitudes, values, and motives current in the groups of which they are or will become members."[6] In this context, organized sports can contribute to social development. When engaged in sport, the athlete must learn to cooperate with members of the team for the common good. Athletes must also compete against each other in the friendly battle of the contest. Good sportsmanship can become an expected part of athletics if the coach sets a good example and instructs the players to exhibit this trait.

Cooperation. Sports activities, according

5. Mohr, D. R.: The contributions of physical activity to skill learning, Research Quarterly **31:**339, May 1960.

6. Sewell, W. H.: Some recent developments in socialization theory and research, Annals of the American Academy of Political and Social Science **249:**163, 1963.

to some educators, are ideal means for developing cooperative traits in young people. Individuals on athletic teams must work together for the common good of the team if they are to succeed. Such working together for a group goal also promotes a feeling of respect for the abilities and limitations of others.

Possible harm of sports

Excessive pressures. Undue emphasis on "winning" in sports at all levels by parents, coaches, and the "home team crowd" produces pressures that are harmful to the players. In many instances, young players starting out in sports do not feel the need to "win at all costs." For example, in a survey on youth football, Thomas[7] reported that 72% of the children indicated that they would rather play regularly on a losing team than sit on the bench of a winning team. On the other hand, Forbis, who studied the behavior of parents at children's hockey games, concluded that parental behavior at games was detrimental to their development. "Winning appeared to be 'an ultimate goal,' and one with the power to influence behavior and thinking."[8] The constant pressures from adults for their children to win may cause some children to develop a negative self-image when they do not win. It may also cause some individuals to cheat or engage in other unethical methods to win. In some cases, the excessive pressures to win may cause some people to give up athletic participation completely.

At later levels of competition, pressures to "win-at-all-costs" result in many undesirable and unethical actions on the part of players, coaches, and others involved with the par-

ticular sports program. The pressure to win at some schools contributes to abuses such as the demonstration of poor sportsmanship by both coaches and players, hatred of opponents, intolerance of losers, cheating, encouragement of athletes to use drugs to improve performance, and so on.

Pressures in college sports cause some coaches to tamper with students' transcripts, use unethical means to recruit "blue chip" high school players, exploit players once they are on campus, and the like. Of the many negative results of the pressures to win at some colleges, tampering with the transcripts of student-athletes to make them eligible or keep them eligible has received increased publicity. At the University of New Mexico, for instance, the former head basketball coach was indicted on mail fraud and racketeering charges in connection with the preparation of junior college transcripts of athletes at the university.[9] According to the *New York Times*, this indictment touched off one of the largest sports scandals in the history of college athletics.

False values. The adulation and attention given to star athletes, and to athletes in general, may cause some of these individuals to place a disproportionately high value on sports. The high school athlete who is sought by the coaches of major colleges might begin to think of sport to the exclusion of studies and personal and social life. In addition, the attention that athletes get from schoolmates and community people could very well make them believe that they are something special because of their athletic prowess. All of this attention could distort a youngster's sense of values regarding the proper place of sport in his or her life.

Aggression and violence. Some observers believe that the violent nature of most popu-

7. Thomas, J. R.: Is winning essential to the success of youth sports contests? Journal of Physical Education and Recreation 49:42-43, March 1978.
8. Forbis, N.: Parents and kids' sport. Cited by Sandy Hotchkiss in Human Behavior 7:11, March 1978.

9. New Mexico ex-coach indicted, New York Times, Section A, p. 27, February 15, 1980.

lar sports actually encourages aggression in players. Furthermore, Eitzen[10] indicates that, in addition to the nature of these sports being to hit an opponent, the sports can encourage excessive violence with little or no penalty. He cites hockey as the prime example of a violent sport and documents the fact that fights between players result in many injuries.

Two theories have been proposed that have directly opposing views regarding the relationship between sports and aggressive behavior. One theory is that aggressive behavior is innate, and that sports provide acceptable outlets for aggression. The other theory postulates that aggression is learned behavior, and sports teach aggressive behavior. Advocates of the latter theory point to the increased violence associated with sports contests as their justification for such a position. They contend that sport tends to heighten a person's aggressive behavior patterns. This point was made by Alderman:

To rationalize that being aggressive is only a means to an end is to ignore the unfortunate result, that violence becomes an end in itself. . . . Sports competition, by its very nature, aggravates and intensifies aggressive tendencies—one's opponents are out there to frustrate one from reaching one's goal; frustration leads to anger, which leads to aggression, which often results in violence, which is sometimes in the form of brutality. Such a syndrome in sport is, unfortunately, too often encouraged and reinforced.[11]

THE QUESTION OF CHARACTER DEVELOPMENT

Although character development is claimed by some educators and coaches as one of the chief virtues of competitive sports,

this assertion has proved to be one of the most difficult to validate. After a critical review of the research dealing with the socialization effects of participation in sport, Stevenson concluded that there is a considerable amount of contradictory evidence.[12] The conclusion of some researchers in studies comparing athletes with nonathletes is that athletes exhibit more socially desirable psychological traits than those individuals who do not participate in sports. They maintain that these desirable personality traits are developed as a result of participation in athletics. On the other hand, a number of researchers have suggested that those athletes with appropriate personality traits remain in athletics. Those persons with undesirable character traits fail to survive in organized sports. Their conclusion is that character development is not nurtured through participation in sport.

Besides doubting that positive character traits are developed through participation in sports, Schafer[13] and Tutko and Burns[14] suggest that participation in competitive sports produces undesirable personality traits. Consider the following comment by Tutko:

. . . we found no empirical support for the tradition that sport builds character. Indeed, there is evidence that athletic competition limits growth in some areas. It seems that the personality of the ideal athlete is not the result of any molding process, but comes out of the ruthless selection process that occurs at all levels of sport.[14(p. 39)]

10. Eitzen, D. S.: Sport and deviance. In Eitzen, D. S., editor: Sport in contemporary society, New York, 1979, St. Martin's Press, p. 75.
11. Alderman, R. B.: Psychological behavior in sport, Philadelphia, 1974, W. B. Saunders Co., p. 245.
12. Stevenson, C. L.: Socialization effects of participation in sport: a critical review of the research, Research Quarterly 46:292, October 1975.
13. Schafer, W. E.: Sport, socialization and the school: toward maturity or enculturation. Paper presented at the Third International Symposium on the Sociology of Sport, Waterloo, Ontario, 1971.
14. Tutko, T., and Burns, W.: Winning is everything and other American myths, New York, 1976, Macmillan Inc.

In more disparaging terms, Schafer has suggested that ". . . sports may be producing conformist, authoritarian, cheerful robots who lack inquisitiveness, autonomy, and the inner direction to accept innovation, contrasting value systems, and alternative lifestyles."[13]

It must always be remembered that negative as well as positive social and psychological outcomes might accrue through participation in sports. Orlick, an advocate of cooperative play and games among children, summarized this idea when he said:

> For every positive psychological or social outcome in sports, there are possible negative outcomes. For example, sports can offer a child group membership or group exclusion, acceptance or rejection, positive feedback or negative feedback, a sense of accomplishment or a sense of failure, evidence of self-worth or a lack of evidence of self-worth. Likewise, sports can develop cooperation and a concern for others, but they can also develop intense rivalry and a complete lack of concern for others.[15]

Positive personality development as well as the realization of the other potential values of sports can be realized, given the proper leadership and athletic environment. Moreover, under these conditions the harmful aspects of sport will be minimized. Physical educators and coaches play key roles in the proper conduct of sport programs. Their role is to provide a philosophy and leadership that will help to ensure that sports make a positive contribution to society.*

This chapter will present information on the characteristics and needs of participants in sport at various levels (that is, children, youth, and adults), the type of sports program that will make the greatest contribution to society, and guidelines for the development of educationally sound sports programs. In addition, the chapter will discuss special topics such as "Girls and women in sport," "Coeducational sports and Title IX," "Sports for handicapped persons," "The role of the coach," and "The governance of sport."

SPORTS FOR CHILDREN (TO 12 YEARS OF AGE)

Sports are conducted in both educational institutions and nonschool agencies and at all educational levels. There are sport programs in public, private, and parochial schools and at the elementary through collegiate levels. Nonschool sports are conducted through such agencies as Young Men's and Young Women's Christian Associations, Little League, Boys Club, and so on. This section will focus on the physical, social, and emotional characteristics of preschool-age and school-age children.

Characteristics*

Growth is a continuous process—from conception to death. However, different body segments develop at different rates during one's lifetime. From birth to 1 year of age, for example, the trunk is the fastest growing segment of the body, accounting for 60% of the total increase in height. From 1 year of age to the onset of puberty, the legs grow the fastest, accounting for 66% of the total increase in height. The arms also show accelerated growth between 1 year of age and puberty.

---

15. Orlick, T. D.: The sports environment: a capacity to enhance—a capacity to destroy. Paper presented at the Canadian Symposium of Psycho-Motor Learning and Sports Psychology, Waterloo, Ontario, 1974, p. 2.
*More detailed information on the coach is presented later in the chapter under the topic, "The role of the coach."

*Information on the characteristics of children, youth, and adults has been summarized from the following sources: Ambron, 1975; Cole and Hall, 1970; Lugo and Hershey, 1974; and Rarick, 1977.

Characteristics of preschool children

Physical characteristics. During the preschool years—from about 2 to 5 years of age—the child makes great progress. The child's physical development is the foundation of this progress. By 3 years of age, the average boy is a little over 3 feet tall and weighs over 30 pounds; by 5 years of age, he has grown to about 44 inches and 43 pounds. Girls tend to be slightly shorter and lighter than boys, although there are individual variations. Boys and girls develop at about the same pace during the preschool years and through childhood until puberty. One of the most significant developmental differences between preschool boys and girls is that boys have more muscle and girls have more fatty tissue.

Muscular development accounts for most of the weight gained during the preschool years by both boys and girls. The large muscles develop more rapidly than the small muscles; therefore, motor abilities proceed from gross motor activity to fine motor activity. The bones of preschool children are not fully developed.

Social and emotional characteristics. Preschool children are ready to increase their social contacts from family to small groups of other children. By 4 years of age, children have a strong desire for friends. They develop a sense of loyalty toward friends but change friends often.

Emotionally, the preschool child seeks approval from adults. Children at this stage in their development do not understand the difference between truth and fiction. Preschool children begin to develop their own identity. They also are able to identify their gender, and they begin to learn the different roles and attributes associated with each gender. One of the most important developments of this period is the establishment of a self-concept. Children's later relationships with others are shaped by their attitudes and expectations of themselves during the preschool years.

Characteristics of school-age children (middle and late childhood)

Physical characteristics. By the time children enter school, their physical growth has slowed down. The rate of growth at this point is not as fast as it is during infancy or adolescence. In boys, the trunk becomes slimmer, the chest broader, and the arms and legs longer and thinner. Girls develop wider hips, slimmer shoulders, and longer arms and legs than boys.

During the early school years, children develop the kind of physique that they are likely to have as adults. They have one of three body types: endomorphic, mesomorphic, and ectomorphic. The endomorph is the round, fat person; the mesomorph is the muscular, broad-shouldered individual; and the ectomorph is the thin, small-boned person. By 11 years of age, most boys have attained approximately 85% of their mature height. Girls, who have already begun their adolescent growth spurt 2 years before boys, will be taller than many boys.

Social and emotional characteristics. During middle childhood, children develop self-awareness. This is a period in which positive socialization experiences and acceptance by peers is important to a child's future development. Children develop close associations with peers whom they consider like themselves. A child's physical development and abilities strongly influence his or her social and emotional development. Research has validated this notion. For instance, Tanner writes:

All the skills, aptitudes, and emotions of the growing child are rooted in or conditioned by his bodily structure. Behind each stage of learning lies the development of essential cell assemblies in the brain; behind each social interaction lies a body image conditioned by the facts of size and early or late sexual maturation. . . . How fast a child grows and what type of body structure he has can exert a crucial influence on the development of his personality. The child's sense of identity is strongly linked to his physical appearance and ability.[16]

As a result of the child's association with family and peers, he or she develops either a positive or a negative self-image. Corresponding personality characteristics range from self-assurance, originality, and industry to fear, anxiety, imitation, and inferiority. Children adopt behavior patterns that will get approval of peers and make them more popular. Boys often become rough and aggressive to demonstrate their manliness. Girls, on the other hand, avoid certain kinds of physical activities that are not considered "feminine."*

Type of sports program that will make the greatest contribution

The type of sports program that will make the greatest contribution to children and society will do the following:

Provide for the necessary conditioning of players. All persons should be well conditioned prior to the start of sports competition. A training program that is consistent with the growth and developmental levels of children should be conducted before actual competition begins. Care should be taken not to overstress the bodies of children. For example, normal activity with a slight overload will cause muscles to get larger and stronger. However, heavy weight training for strength development is questionable because of the possible damage to

the ends of long bones that are not fully developed at this time.

Stress the development of fundamental skills, understanding of rules and strategy, appreciation of the activities, and enhancement of social growth. The major outcomes of a sports program for children should be the improvement in skill, knowledge, attitude and appreciation, and socialization through sport. Once children have been properly conditioned, they can then be helped to develop the necessary skills to achieve some success in various sports. The proper learning atmosphere should also enhance the development of a knowledge of the rules and strategy associated with a particular sport, create a positive attitude toward and appreciation of the sport, and enhance the socialization of the participants.

Keep the competition at the children's level and provide opportunities for all children to participate. The level of sports competition should correspond to the growth and developmental level of the participants. In general, this means that children up through early elementary school age should be allowed to play in situations that have very little structure. These children should be allowed to make up their own rules and play in an informal manner. As a matter of fact, the results of one research study suggest that too many adult-supervised sports activities tend to slow social development. Kleiber, a University of Illinois developmental psychologist, concluded that ". . . when adults are in charge of most of their activities, children are deprived of an opportunity to make decisions and resolve problems."[17]

During later childhood, more structured sports activities may be provided. Competition between children from the same area

---

16. Tanner, J. M.: Growth at adolescence. Cited in Ambron, S. R.: Child development, San Francisco, 1975, Rhinehart Press, p. 307.
*This stereotypical behavior may decrease now that the feminist movement is gaining momentum. In fact, girls are now engaging in activities (Little League baseball, for example) that were once the exclusive domain of boys.

17. Kleiber, D.: Supervised sports: how they slow social development, Human Behavior 8:61, January 1979.

Courtesy Woodlands High School, Hartsdale, N.Y.

or neighborhood (intramural sports) should predominate during this developmental stage (late elementary school years). In some cases, noncompetitive activities should be provided for some children at this age level. For example, Orlick and Botterill[18] indicate that many children prefer participation in more individual and noncompetitive activities such as camping, hiking, climbing, cross-country skiing, sledding, swimming, archery, and horseback riding.

Emphasis in children's sports should be placed on participation! All youngsters should be allowed to participate in the activities. This may require establishing a "no cut" policy, increasing the length of the activity, or increasing the number of activities. The inclusion of noncompetitive activities in the sports program may also serve to in-

crease the number of children who participate in sports.

Besides structuring the activity whereby all children are permitted to participate, opportunities must also be provided so that each youngster can achieve frequent success. Deemphasizing winning and stressing skill development, participation, and fun are possible foundations for each child to experience frequent success in sports activities. Specific strategies for helping children to experience success in sports is to use the positive approach to teaching (giving praise and approval, stressing good points, and the like) instead of the negative approach (belittling, criticizing, ridiculing, withdrawing approval, and the like).

Provide safe equipment and facilities and adequate medical supervision. A safe sports environment is one with adequate facilities and equipment and proper medical supervision. Facilities and equipment may need modifying to suit the developmental level of

18. Orlick, T., and Botterill, C.: What's best for kids? In Eitzen, D. S., editor: Sport in contemporary society, New York, 1979, St. Martin's Press, p. 156.

the children. For example, smaller bats may be used for baseball and lower baskets and smaller balls may be used for basketball. In addition to the modification of equipment and facilities, adequate supervision should be provided so that older youths do not interfer with the games of children.

Proper medical supervision and care are necessary for the conduct of a sound sports program. Children should receive medical examinations before engaging in sports activities. No child should be permitted to participate in sports activities unless he or she is certified as being physically fit by the physician. A physician should be at each game and on call during each practice session.

Provide competent coaches for all sports activities. A knowledgeable, enthusiastic, personable, and caring person should be selected to coach each sport activity. The coach will be largely responsible for implementing the foregoing recommendations. To a great degree, the coach can be the difference between the success or failure of the sports program. For example, a coach who argues with officials, uses profane language, exhibits overly aggressive behavior, and so on, may transmit some of these undesirable character traits to some children because they view him or her as a role model.[19] When children begin to display such behavior, the program will not succeed. On the other hand, a coach who instills exemplary character traits in children by both precept and example will probably ensure the success of the sports program (especially in terms of the socialization of children).

Guidelines for action

Based on the results of research and empirical evidence and the reality of the large number of children engaged in sports programs, the editor and contributors to the *Youth Sports Guide for Coaches and Parents* recommend that sports programs be provided for children. The task of leaders of sports programs is to provide the type of programs that will optimize the values that may accrue through sport. A sound program of sports for children should adhere to the following guidelines:

1. Base the type and intensity of competition on the growth and developmental level of the participants. Two general levels should be established for children: (a) sports competition for preschool and early elementary school children should be individual in nature—competition with oneself; (b) sports for children in late elementary school (grades 4 through 6) should include intramural competition that stresses involvement with classmates and friends in the immediate neighborhood. It does *not* encourage high level competition with championship games, long travel, and trophies.

2. Select coaches who are professionally qualified to hold such positions (either by virtue of their educational training or because of professional experience in sports). It should also be emphasized that coaches who work with children should be teachers and should not be persons who place too much stress on winning. The emphasis at this developmental level should be on the improvement of individual skills and the provision of a fun atmosphere for children.*

3. Select activities appropriate to the age and developmental level of children. Contact sports should be modified or avoided altogether for preteens. For

---

19. Westcott, W. L.: Physical educators and coaches as models of behavior, Journal of Physical Education and Recreation 50:31-32, March 1979.

*Specific information on certification of coaches is presented in the section on "The role of the coach."

example, instead of tackle football, include flag or touch football.

4. Consider activities and contests in which the primary goal is cooperation rather than competition.

5. Arrange the rules so that every person will be allowed to play some part of the game or activity.

6. Do not provide expensive trophies, medals, or other external motivational devices. Emphasize playing the game for the thrill of competition and learning, thus stressing internal motivation.

7. Prohibit the use of the curve ball in baseball and allow children to pitch only three innings per game (one game per week) because of the possible injury to the elbow joint.

8. Provide adequate health protection for the players.

9. Familiarize parents with the goals of the program and their role in helping to achieve program objectives. Establish a policy statement that clearly restricts parents from interfering with the conduct of games and activities. Prohibit parents from coming on the field or court during the game or from yelling instructions to their children.

10. Carefully choose coaches and provide the necessary training programs to qualify them with the competencies to develop children in the cognitive and affective domains, as well as in specific sports skills.

11. Concentrate on skill development in a variety of sports and activities; avoid overspecialization at this early stage of a child's development.

Behavioral guidelines specifically for coaches. The following guidelines are based on research conducted by Smoll and Smith.[20]

---

20. Smoll, F. B., and Smith, R. E.: Behavioral guidelines for youth sport coaches, Journal of Physical Education and Recreation 49:46-47, March 1978.

1. Provide immediate rewards for good performance. Reward children for good effort as well as positive results of performance. A positive statement such as "Good catch" or "Good try" and a pat on the back represent adequate rewards. Expensive, tangible rewards are not necessary.

2. Give encouragement to players immediately after mistakes. Provide corrective instruction when needed to minimize occurrence of the particular mistake in the future. Use positive instructional techniques. ("You will have a better chance to catch the ball if you use two hands instead of one hand.")

3. Do not give corrective instruction in a hostile or threatening manner. Be positive and use an encouraging tone of voice when correcting an athlete who has made a mistake.

4. Do not punish to correct mistakes. For example, do not require a player to run the bases ten times because he or she failed to touch a base after a hit.

5. Maintain order by clearly outlining expectations of all personnel associated with the team. Involve players in the formulation of rules and regulations.

6. Provide instruction as a central focus of coaching. Use demonstrations as a teaching strategy when possible, provided you possess the necessary skill. For example, show the players the correct method of dribbling a soccer ball instead of simply telling them how to dribble.

7. Give instruction in a positive manner. Avoid using sarcasm and ridicule when instructing youngsters.

8. Set a good example for team unity and behavior. Treat all players fairly and do not yell or use abusive lan-

guage when communicating with officials.

9. Teach all players the necessary skills of the sport. Do not spend more time with the highly skilled players.

10. Never stop striving to communicate effectively with your players.

11. Communicate with players at the most opportune time. Wait until the youngster is receptive to your communication. Remember that different individuals are receptive to communication from the coach at different times. For instance, some players respond to immediate corrections while others profit more if the feedback is delayed.

12. Communicate to parents the need to let children have fun while participating in sports. Encourage parents not to place too much emphasis on winning and, most of all, implore parents not to berate their children when they make mistakes in sports. Urge them instead to give positive support and encouragement.

SPORTS FOR YOUTH (13 TO 18 YEARS OF AGE)

With an estimated 20 million youngsters between 8 and 16 years of age participating in agency-sponsored sports and 5.6 million students participating in school sports, a sound program is necessary for these individuals to receive the positive values that sport can provide. This section will provide information and guidelines to help those persons responsible for organizing and conducting sports programs to develop sound programs.

Characteristics of youth

Physical characteristics. The adolescent growth spurt is the most noticeable sign of puberty. There is a tremendous growth increase in both height and weight. The amount and distribution of fat changes, and the proportion of bone and muscle tissue increases. Throughout adolescence, height increases by about 25% and weight increases about 50%.

Although there are general characteristics

Tom Morton.

of growth patterns during the different stages of development, there are wide variations from person to person. It has been reported that a group of 12-year-old boys or girls will customarily include individuals whose body cells are not yet at the maturity level of the average 10 year old, while others will have maturational ages equivalent to 15 chronological years.[1(p. 30)] Boys and girls also differ with regard to the rate at which they achieve maturity. In boys, for example, height and weight increase sharply from 12 to 16 years of age, and in girls, height and weight increase sharply from 10 to 16 years of age. At 15 years of age, most girls have reached their final stature, while most boys do not complete their growth until 17 years of age. The body density of males is greater than females at birth and becomes greater during adolescence. The male skeleton also becomes larger and denser than the female during adolescence.

In terms of body proportions during adolescence, one of the most noticeable changes is in the trunk of the body. The trunk widens at the hips in girls and at the shoulders in boys; the waistline drops in both sexes. Growth of the trunk accounts for about 60% of the increase in height from puberty to adulthood. A layer of fat develops in the hips and legs in both boys and girls. This fat soon disappears in boys but remains with the girls. The increase in growth of the trunk area, along with the previously increased length of the arms and legs, gives the young adolescent an awkward, gangly appearance. The early growth of hands and feet add to the young adolescent's ungainly physique. In fact, the hands, feet, and head are the first body parts to reach their mature size.

The immature skeleton is the most vulnerable part of young athletes engaged in competitive sports. The growing ends of the long bones (epiphyses) in the immature skeleton are particularly vulnerable to continuous heavy pressure, blows, and sudden wrenching. If such stresses are severe enough, they may derange the normal process of bone growth and result in permanent damage.

The appearance of primary and secondary sex characteristics signals the beginning of puberty. A change in the shape of the hips (to become more round and wide) and the development of breasts are noticeable in girls during puberty. Menstruation also begins during this time. In the United States, the average age for the onset of menstruation (menarche) is 13 years of age, with a range of 10 to 17 years of age. In boys, puberty is signaled by the appearance of semen, pubic hair, a lower voice, and growth of the penis and testes. Boys' skin becomes coarser and thicker during puberty, and the pores change. The fatty glands become active and produce the oily secretion that results in acne during adolescence.

Social and emotional characteristics. The adolescent experiences many social and emotional problems. These disruptions are caused by the many changes that are taking place in the adolescent's life; the awkward and gangly appearance, the newly experienced sex drives, exaggerated self-assertiveness, and the strong desire for peer group approval all serve to create social and emotional problems for the adolescent. During this period of development, adolescents vacillate between alertness and irrationalism. They strive for recognition and form close associations with others, at first with members of the same sex and later with members of both sexes.

The development of the self-concept that started during late childhood is a large part of the concerns of the adolescent. The adolescent seeks to determine his or her place in society. Self-concept for adolescents is determined mainly by the way others view them. They have a strong desire to receive admiration and approval from others. The older adolescent takes great pride in personal grooming to gain the needed admiration of peers.

Extreme differences in physical appearance among adolescents can greatly affect their emotional and social development. Youngsters react to differences in physical appearance in various ways, depending on whether these differences are used positively or negatively. For example, a boy or girl who is much larger than his or her classmates might develop a poor self-image and withdraw because of the size difference. On the other hand, if the increased size differential enables the person to excel at sports or some other activity, it could lead to a positive self-concept because of the admiration and approval athletes get from schoolmates.

Type of sports program that will make the greatest contribution

In addition to providing the positive features of sports programs for children, such as proper conditioning for participants, adequate medical supervision, competent coaches, and so on, the type of sports program that will make the greatest contribution to youth and society will do the following:

Base the type and intensity of competition on the growth and developmental level of the participants. Sports programs for youths of junior high school age should consist of intramurals, extramurals, and modified varsity competition. Intramural sports are those that are played among youngsters from the same school or agency in the case of nonschool sports programs. Extramural activities are informal types of games between individuals from different schools or agency-sponsored teams. Types of extramural activities include play days, sports days, and invitational meets. A play day involves competition between youths from several schools or agen-cies, and all the players compete on teams drawn from all the participants. There is no school or agency identity since teams are made up of players from the various schools and agencies. A sports day involves competition between youths from several schools and agencies, in which the school and agency teams retain their identity. Invitational meets involve youngsters from two or more schools or agencies and stress the informal aspects of competition. The emphasis in extramural sports competition is on participation rather than high level competition and winning.

Because of the differences in maturational levels among youth, some will need a more competitive sports program. A modified varsity sports program is recommended for these youngsters. The modified sports program should consist of some of the sports provided for students of senior high school age, but the sports should be modified to suit the needs, interests, and maturational levels of the participants. Examples of modifications include limiting the maximum number of games to be played, limiting travel distance, regulating the number of players (either increasing or reducing as needed), and decreasing the length of games.* The sports program for older adolescents (16 to 18 years of age) should provide opportunities for the highly skilled as well as those youngsters of average skill. To accommodate all persons in this age group, a varsity-level sports program should be provided in addition to the intramural and extramural programs. All these co-curricular activities should be extensions of a broad instructional program of physical education.

---

*New York State Public High School Athletic Association has developed a modified sports program for junior high school students that may be used as a guide in modifying sports programs. See their latest handbook.

Tom Morton

Emphasize the educational values of sports participation. The development of the total person should be the overall objective of all sports programs for youth. Both school-sponsored and agency-sponsored sports programs should stress the development of cognitive and affective outcomes as well as the psychomotor domain in youngsters. For example, participants should be helped to develop good sportsmanship qualities, leadership and followership qualities, a positive attitude toward sport, a knowledge of rules and strategy, and a high level of skill in a variety of sports activities.

In schools, the sports program should be a part of the physical education department. Monies for the sports program should come from the regular educational budget. If fees are charged for admittance to games, they should not be used to subsidize the sports program. Coaches of sports teams should be hired for their abilities as teachers as well as their expertise as coaches.

Guidelines for action

A sound sports program for youth should adhere to the following guidelines:

1. Provide as broad and varied an inter-school athletic program as is possible with the funds allocated for this purpose. Include both team and individual sports and offer selected sports according to the special interests of local residents.

2. Modify the program activities to meet the needs of junior high school students. Because of the transitional stage in the development of adolescents of junior high school age, specific modifications should be made regarding length of season, number of contests, length of playing periods, size of playing areas, and the like.*

3. Equalize competition as much as possible, basing it on the appropriate age, athletic ability, anthropometric measurements, physiological maturity, and emotional stability of participants.*

4. Stress the teaching of skills and participation as opposed to the "win-at-all-costs" philosophy.

5. Do not conduct the interscholastic

---

*The wide discrepancies in maturational growth among boys and girls of the same age create a dangerous situation in contact sports such as football and wrestling. This is one of the greatest complaints of opponents of interschool competition for junior high school youngsters. By equalizing competition and modifying it as suggested by the New York State Public High School Athletic Association, the risks for injury will be minimized.

athletic program as a "feeder" system for the colleges.

6. Require medical examinations for all students before they try out for teams in the interschool sports program. Those students who do not meet prescribed medical standards should not be allowed to participate.

7. Provide for medical supervision (at least one physician) at all interscholastic athletic contests and have a medical doctor on call during practice sessions.

8. Provide adequate insurance coverage for all persons participating in the interschool athletic program.

9. Provide adequate preconditioning and practice sessions prior to the start of each sport season.

10. Abide by the rules and regulations of national, state, and local athletic associations under whose aegis your program is conducted.

11. Provide equal opportunities for female athletes. Make sure Title IX of the Education Amendments Act is not violated.

12. Provide adequate facilities and equipment for members of all teams.

13. Finance all athletic programs with funds provided by the local board of education the same as other educational activities. Deposit all gate receipts from athletic events in the general fund; do not use these funds to finance sports teams.

14. Discourage all-star and/or championships at the conclusion of a sports season. Encourage students to compete for the intrinsic values associated with the activity rather than to determine who's "number one."

15. Discourage expensive awards; simple ribbons and/or medals are sufficient.

16. Develop written statements of philos-

ophy and policies that govern the organization and conduct of the athletic program.

17. Constantly evaluate the program and make changes that are necessary for its improvement. Base change on the results of objective evidence and research rather than community pressure and/or emotional reactions of the various publics.

We would like to emphasize that the senior high school program should be based on the maturational level of boys and girls of that age range (16 to 18 years of age). Although there is less of a maturational disparity among youngsters at this stage than of those at the junior high school level, program modifications are also necessary. The senior high school athletic program should not be a miniature college program; it should be based on the developmental level of students in this age range.

SPORTS FOR ADULTS (18 YEARS OF AGE AND OVER)

The life span of adults represents the longest period of an individual's human development. In 1975, the average life expectancy in the United States was 69 years of age for males and 77 years of age for females. Basing the beginning of adulthood on the legal voting age of 18 (in some states), the average person spends almost two thirds of a lifetime as an adult. The growth and development of people during their adult years is greatly affected by the quantity and quality of physical education and sport activities in which they engage.

Like previous age groups, the sports program for adults should be based on the growth and developmental levels of the participants. For purposes of this discussion, the years of adulthood are divided into three periods: (1) young and early adulthood (18 to 35 years of age), (2) middle adulthood (36 to

Courtesy Springfield College, Springfield, Mass.

64 years of age), and (3) upper adulthood (65 years of age and over). Using these age categories as frames of reference, a general overview of the physical, social, and emotional characteristics is presented. This material is intended to provide a basis for which to determine the types and intensities of activities required for the sports program during adulthood.

Young and early adulthood (18 to 35 years of age)

Physical characteristics. By the time individuals reach young adulthood (certainly by 24 years of age), they will have reached physical maturity. By this stage in life, persons usually have attained their adult height, weight, and general physique or body type. Research has demonstrated that physical abilities improve from adolescence to early adulthood (around 30 years of age).[21] It should be mentioned, however, that persons who fail to keep physically active can decline in physical condition and abilities during early adulthood.

Social and emotional characteristics. Similar to earlier periods in one's lifetime, social and emotional development during young and early adulthood is closely related to and conditioned by physical development. How a person performs in athletics or other physical activities, the kind of physical body that a person has, and the view that a person has of his or her body all play important roles in helping to shape the social and emotional development of that person. For example, the person who is obese and who is very unathletic may develop a poor self-concept, become depressed, and totally isolate himself or herself from others. On the other hand, the person who is athletic, has a positive self-image, and is extremely gregarious may be very socially desirable to friends. These are two extreme examples of the possible relationships between physical development and social and emotional development. There are many more complex interactions between aspects of these developmental areas. Moreover, other areas (cognitive and psychological) of development are also involved.

During young and early adulthood, individuals may graduate from high school, go to college, complete some trade or technical school, or go directly into the world of work. Whatever choice is made, the results of that choice and the subsequent activities pertaining to work or occupation will greatly influence other aspects of a person's life during this period and later. The decision not to attend college, for example, especially if this

action is contrary to family desires and expectations, may have an adverse affect on the emotional development of some people. Some people in this situation might feel inadequate and might feel that they have let their parents down. A person who goes to college, but who is not able to make it scholastically, may react to such an experience in an emotionally negative manner. Others might be able to cope with either of these situations in a positive manner.

Other events during young and early adulthood that may affect social and emotional development are leaving home, getting married, having children, and getting divorced. The critical factor in terms of the effects of these events on emotional and social development seems to be how they are viewed by the persons involved. How others perceive one's situation is also important. In some cases, people are greatly influenced in their own thinking and actions by the way others view them. Do others think they are successful? Are they thought to be socially desirable by others? These and other questions are constantly asked by people during this stage of adulthood. Negative answers to some or all of these questions may cause social and emotional problems for some people.

Middle adulthood (36 to 64 years of age)

Physical characteristics. A decline in human physical abilities usually begins during this period. Strength and muscular flexibility, working of the heart (heart rate, stroke volume, and cardiac output), and body composition change during and by the end of middle adulthood. Strength and flexibility decrease, resting heart rate increases, stroke volume and cardiac output decrease, and fatty tissue increases. These changes, along with decreased physical activity, result in a changed physical appearance. The "middle-

---

21. de Vries, H. A.: Physiology of exercise, Dubuque, Iowa, 1966, William C. Brown Co., Publishers.

age" spread occurs around the midsection. The hair turns gray; the skin becomes less elastic, more taut and wrinkled; and the bones become more brittle. The only biological change that occurs during this period is menopause in women, which typically occurs between 45 and 50 years of age.

Exercise physiologists and others who work with older adults have cited research to suggest that people delay many of the aging processes with regular exercise. Persons in their middle adult years are encouraged to seek the advice of a professional before starting an exercise program, especially if they have been inactive for several years.

Social and emotional characteristics. Some of the negative experiences that have occurred during earlier periods of their lives, plus such possibly traumatic experiences as divorce and the death of a mate, can cause extreme depression—a major emotional problem of adults. Depression may also result from other events that occur during this stage of life, including family problems, being passed over for promotion, and retirement from work. The physiological changes that result from menopause (cessation of menstruation) cause depression in some women.

Some people react to the various events during this period with more serious social and emotional problems. Fear of failure may lead to psychosis (such as schizophrenia) in which the person is unable to function in the real world and lives in a world of fantasy; or it may lead to neurosis in which the person experiences considerable anxiety but is still able to function effectively. In some cases, the person may require professional help and, sometimes, hospitalization.

Upper adulthood (65 years of age and over)

Physical characteristics. Although there are exceptions, by the time a person reaches

65 years of age, physical aging has left its mark. The appearance of the skin is most noticeably changed. It is wrinkled, dry, and inelastic. The cardiovascular system also demonstrates the degenerative effects of the aging process. Blood vessels become lined with fatty plaques, the output of blood from the heart is decreased, and the lining of the blood vessels becomes less elastic (a condition known as arteriosclerosis or "hardening of the arteries"). The tissue of the joints and bones stiffens, and the range of movement is greatly reduced. The older adult also has difficulties with vision, hearing, and respiration.

Social and emotional characteristics. Two events usually occur during older adulthood that add to the social and emotional problems of this period. For the man, retirement (which is legally at age 65) is one of the major "crises" of older adulthood. This change in status from worker and chief provider to a retiree on a much reduced and fixed income often causes severe depression in many men. A major "crisis" in the lives of women during later adulthood is the death of their husband. (It is estimated that women outlive men by about 7 years.) Having to spend these later years without their husbands, many women become depressed and withdrawn and, in some cases, exhibit more severe emotional problems. In some cases, widows are excluded from social gatherings and, therefore, forced into isolation.

The separation of older adults from their family also causes emotional problems. It is estimated that about 5% of the aged population live in institutions, with women making up the majority of this number. Having retired and been placed in an institution, many persons suffer from an extreme loss of self-esteem. They believe that they have been cast aside by loved ones, and their depression becomes more severe. At this point, some withdraw almost totally from social interaction.

The type of sports program that will make the greatest contribution to adults of all ages

The type of sports program that will make the greatest contribution to adults and society will adhere to the following points:

Design the program according to the growth and development of the participant. * The wide range in developmental levels of adults requires that programs be varied, progressive, and sequential. For example, while the program for young adults (18 to 21 years of age) should contain highly competitive athletic games and contests, the program for older adults (51 years of age and over) should be more recreational in nature. The socialization and fun aspects of sports programs for older adults should be emphasized, as contrasted with the skill aspect that would be emphasized more for young adults.

Modify program activities as needed according to the maturational level of the participants. Because of the changing functions and needs of the organism during the various maturational stages of development, program activities and methods of conduct may require modification. In track, for instance, contestants are grouped according to age. Competition could be further equalized by subtracting time in running events for the older competitors. Modification of facilities and equipment may also be required, such as using larger balls, reducing the distances of playing fields or courts, and the like.

A specific example of a modification of a sport activity is provided by Chrisman,[22]

---

*Leonard Larson, in *Curriculum foundations and standards for physical education*, has developed a sequential program of physical activities for people at various periods of the life span. These activities are based on growth and developmental characteristics at each stage of life.

22. Chrisman, D.: Badminton at 65 and older, Journal of Physical Education and Recreation **50**:26-28, October 1979.

who modified badminton competition for women 65 years of age and over by introducing "Trio-Badminton." In this modified game, two players are side-by-side in the front court and follow all the rules of doubles badminton play. One player covers the back court. The only departure from the doubles rules is the allowance of the backcourt player to serve to the opposite backcourt player according to singles play.

Design and conduct the program to achieve outcomes in the cognitive, affective, and psychomotor domains. The sports program for adults should emphasize the development of cognitive learnings, such as knowledge of rules and game strategies associated with playing a variety of sports. It should also emphasize affective learning, such as the development of a positive attitude toward and an appreciation of physical activity, as well as social outcomes such as group membership, cooperation, and sportsmanship. Finally, a sound sports program for adults can achieve worthwhile psychomotor objectives, even for older adults, provided they keep up their interest and participation in physical activity throughout life.[23]

Examples of sports programs for adults. To illustrate the type of sports programs that will make the greatest contribution to adults of various age levels, a college program (Oberlin College) and a program for older adults (Senior Olympics) are discussed. Each of these programs has exemplary features that might be incorporated into other programs. We hasten to add that, no doubt, there are many other sports programs for adults with laudable features; however, only these programs are included because of obvious space limitations.

Athletics at Oberlin College. The sports program at Oberlin College was described

---

23. Kamm, A.: Senior olympics, Journal of Physical Education and Recreation **50**:32, September 1979.

Courtesy Westchester Co., N.Y., Department of Parks, Recreation and Conservation.

Courtesy Westchester Co., N.Y., Department of Parks, Recreation and Conservation.

in a recent issue of the *Journal of Physical Education and Recreation*[24] under the appropriate title "Toward Athletic Reform." The program contains many aspects that are worthy of emulation. The program of athletics at Oberlin is based on a sound philosophy and is supported by clearly stated policies. It is described as an educational program.

STATEMENT OF ATHLETIC PHILOSOPHY AND POLICY. Shults made the following statement about athletics at Oberlin:

This institution views athletics as an educational experience demanding highly qualified physical educators as coaches, and has geared its program toward extending athletic competition to as many students as possible. In order to qualify as an educational experience, this institution accepts striving for physical excellence, encourages grace under pressure, views athletics as a broadening rather than a narrowing experience, promotes the humanistic treatment of athletes and believes in the harmony of mind-body functions. All specific policies serve to implement these principles. . . .[24(p. 18)]

The athletic philosophy promulgated by the physical education department is approved by the general faculty and is part of the entire educational philosophy at the college.

OBJECTIVES AND POLICIES. The broad goals of the athletic program at Oberlin are ". . . mastery of skills, love of sports, a spirit of friendship, good health, and character development."[24(p. 18)] These are laudable goals, indeed. Furthermore, they are said to be the primary objectives at the instructional class activity level, at the recreational intramural level, and in highly competitive intercollegiate sports. It was also stated that the varsity experience is best characterized by the pursuit of excellence.

---

24. Shults, F. D.: Toward athletic reform, Journal of Physical Education and Recreation **50**:18-19, 48, January 1979. By permission of the American Alliance for Health, Physical Education, Recreation, and Dance, Reston, Va.

The following policies have been established to help ensure the achievement of the overall objectives of the athletic program:

1. It is a policy of the department to broaden the base of intercollegiate program to include as many sports as possible. No major-minor or male-female sport distinctions are made, as all sports receive that which is necessary to guarantee a quality educational experience. Concentrating on a few major sports would tend to produce more successful teams; however, from the educational viewpoint of extending athletic opportunities to as many students as possible, major sport emphasis can not be justified.

2. Increased emphasis will be placed on new and unique sports (rugby, lacrosse, ice hockey), and on those sports which can be enjoyed and played in later years (tennis, golf, squash).

3. Squads will not be cut or junior varsity teams eliminated as long as qualified coaches and adequate facilities are available, and there is sufficient student interest and athletic ability to compete on even terms with teams at other colleges. If it is necessary to cut varsity squads and/or eliminate junior varsity teams, it is expected that the intramural and activity class programs will accommodate those athletes not able to participate at the intercollegiate level.

4. Athletes are encouraged to participate in several intercollegiate sports rather than to concentrate on one sport year round. Most coaches fill several coaching assignments, and whenever possible, playing seasons are protected from overlap.

5. Whenever possible contests are scheduled with other educational institutions which are equal in size, have a similar athletic philosophy and offer fair and equal competition.[24(p. 18)]

TEAM EXPERIENCE. Coaches are granted wide latitude in coaching their teams. However, athletes are guaranteed the rights to be treated as mature, intelligent individuals. The following statements support the foregoing assertions:

1. Coaches are granted the right to create their own athletic experience just as other faculty

members are guaranteed academic freedom in the classroom. Democratic team decision-making in such areas as training rules, role and selection of captains, starting line-ups, and game strategy is considered a valid educational experience.

2. No unreasonable demands or special privileges which tend to dehumanize or set athletes apart from their peers will be allowed. Discrimination on the basis of sex or race has no place within the athletic experience. Individual freedom in the areas of personal appearance, political beliefs, and religion is guaranteed.[24(p. 18)]

FACULTY CONTROL. The intercollegiate athletic program is one division in the Department of Physical Education. The other three divisions are the activity program, the intramural program, and the academic major in physical education. The athletic director, who is under the leadership of the department chairperson, supervises intercollegiate athletics.

All head coaches hold faculty rank within the college and are hired according to regular faculty appointment procedures. Assistant coaches may be obtained from outside the faculty or student ranks, but this practice is not encouraged. At any rate, they must be approved by the college faculty council. Coaches are eligible for tenure within the Department of Physical Education, provided they have an academic area of specialty and teach at least one course on a regular basis in the academic major program. Coaches are expected to be teachers just as athletes are expected to be academic students.

ATHLETIC BUDGET. The intercollegiate athletic budget is determined by the same procedure as budgets in other departments of the college. All income and disbursements are handled through the treasurer's office. Except when mandated by conference rules, admission to college athletic contests are free.

ADMISSION POLICY. The applications of athletes are processed by the Admissions Office in the same manner as nonathletes. The first priority in determining admissions of students is the student's academic qualifications. Ability in athletics is regarded as a positive factor in the admissions procedure just as skill in such areas as drama, music, or newspaper work warrants special consideration.

FINANCIAL AID. There are no athletic scholarships. Need is the major criterion for financial aid to students. The college admissions and financial aid offices determine who will be admitted and how much financial aid will be awarded to each student.

RECRUITING. The following guidelines govern recruiting at Oberlin:

1. Recruiting must be informative rather than exploitative in nature, i.e., information explaining the athletic program should be circulated to the general public, and once a student/athlete has expressed an interest he or she will be encouraged to visit the campus. The primary responsibility for locating, encouraging, and accepting student/athletes rests with the Admissions Office, as it does in other departments of the college.

2. Coaches who recruit must do so on their own initiative and will not be compensated with a lightened teaching load or expense account. This institution declares off campus visitations with prospective athletes illegal and only permits coaches to initiate contacts by letter or telephone after the Admissions Office has received an official entrance application.[24(p. 19)]

ATHLETIC COMMITTEE. In addition to the normal General Faculty Athletic Committee, which is composed of six faculty members outside the Department of Physical Education and four student members, there are also the Coaches' Athletic Committee and the Student Athletic Committee. The General Faculty Athletic Committee makes recommendations to the physical education department in matters of athletic policy, approves all schedules, grants permission to participate in special postseason competition, and is consulted when varsity teams are added or dropped from the program. The Coaches' Athletic Committee and the Student Athletic Committee are responsible for matters relating to the rights and conditions of coaches and students, respectively, as they engage in the intercollegiate athletic program.

OTHER FEATURES OF THE ATHLETIC PROGRAM. There is a unique eligibility rule that allows all regular, full-time students to participate either on men's teams, separate but equal women's teams, or coeducational teams that stipulate equal numbers of males and females on the field or court at any one time.

Postseason tournament play is allowed, but not at the expense of the regular schedules of other teams. An Athletes' Bill of Rights is provided to ensure that student-athletes are treated as mature, responsible individuals capable of molding their own destiny. Some of the more interesting aspects of the Bill of Rights are:

1. It is illegal for athletes to be forced to "volunteer" for out of season training or conditioning sessions.
2. All regularly scheduled vacation periods are available to athletes. An athlete may not be dropped from a team for failing to participate in a vacation period contest.
3. Athletes must have official representation on institutional decision-making committees on athletics.
4. Athletes can participate in any on- or off-campus amateur team out of season or during summer vacation periods.
5. Athletes may earn money teaching their sport skill to others.
6. It is illegal for coaches or trainers to administer painkillers or any drug that aims to change the normal functioning of the body or mind.
7. Athletes may not be asked to sacrifice the human rights of opponents by intentionally inflicting injury, cheating, or viewing and treating opponents as enemies rather than a standard by which one can evaluate oneself.

The philosophy and policies relating to intercollegiate athletics at Oberlin College approach the ideal to which all athletic programs should aspire, not in the specifics, but in the intent of the program as related to educational experiences and humane treatment of coaches and students alike.

Senior Olympics. The Illinois Senior Olympics, first conducted in 1977, is an example of a sports program for older adults. This special Olympics was sponsored by the Recreation Department and the Illinois Department On Aging (DOA). The program was conducted for approximately 135 men and women over 54 years of age who competed in 31 different events.[23(pp. 32-33)] Contestants were divided into two competitive age groups for both men and women: 54 to 64 years of age and 65 years of age and over.

The program of events included golf, bike races, horseshoes, trap shoot, table tennis, archery, track and field events, bowling, tennis, racquetball, rope skipping, basketball free throw, swimming, and shuffleboard (which was dropped because of lack of entries). Points were awarded on the basis of 1 for being a participant, 7 for first place, 5 for second place, and 3 for third place. An experienced chairperson was selected to direct each event. Official rules were used for all events.

Publicity for the Senior Olympics included a brochure in which the importance of being in good physical condition was emphasized. It also indicated that prospective contestants should inform their personal physicians of their intent to participate in the Olympics.

Although it was not stated, it is assumed that those individuals who did not receive a medical clearance would not be allowed to participate in the Olympics.

The program began on Friday morning and concluded on Sunday afternoon. The program was opened by a group of high school cross-country runners who brought the torch from Athens, Illinois, a run of about 15 miles. At the conclusion of the competitive events, a short program was held at the Young Men's Christian Association. Awards were presented at a celebration later in the year.

In the 1979 Senior Olympics at Springfield, Illinois, 77-year-old Thomas K. Cureton, the person regarded as the "Father of Physical Fitness in America," won all 11 events that he entered. Some 250 persons participated in the meet, which was directed by Jim Liston, Executive Director of the Illinois Governor's Council on Physical Fitness.

The Senior Olympics is an excellent program for adults. However, an ongoing program of sports should be conducted throughout the year. The sports program for adults could be patterned after the Senior Olympics in terms of the variety of activities for both men and women and the practice of having a person who is knowledgeable in an event to act as chairperson for that event.

Guidelines for action

Recommended standards of action regarding staff, medical and insurance coverage, safety of athletes, and awards have been presented for other levels of sports competition. Many of these guidelines are applicable to some sports programs for adults. Several policies indicated for Oberlin College are also worthwhile to consider as guidelines for sports programs for people during the young and early adulthood periods. In addition to the previously indicated suggestions, a sound program of sports for adults would adhere to the following guidelines:

1. For college and university sports programs, be sensible about the size of the intercollegiate athletic program. Do not insist on having either a big-time athletic program or none at all.

2. Stress the highest ideals of amateurism. Abide by the letter and intent of the rules and regulations of athletic governing bodies under whose jurisdiction the program operates.

3. Organize competition according to the various age categories. Because of the growth and development of individuals at various age levels, participants in a particular age range should compete against each other in sports activities.

4. Apply the recommendations pertaining to coaches, medical supervision, variety of activities offered, and the like that were indicated for colleges and universities to agency-sponsored sports programs for young adults.

5. Provide equal sports programs for women and men.

6. Diversify the sports program by including activities of a passive and semiactive as well as an active nature. For example, include such activities as checkers, cards, archery, and shuffleboard, as well as more active sports such as tennis, track and field activities, and swimming.

GIRLS AND WOMEN IN SPORTS

There has been a gradual change in the attitude of the public in general, as well as professionals in physical education, regarding participation by girls and women in sports. During the advent of men into organized sports, a woman's place was said to be in the home. Women were not even allowed to be spectators at the first Olympic Games in 776 B.C., for example.

Courtesy Springfield College, Springfield, Mass.

When college men began to organize athletic competition in the 1800s, participation by girls and women was frowned on. At this time, however, girls and women were allowed to be spectators, and some were even encouraged to be cheerleaders. The dictates of society still forbade participation by females in competitive sports, however.

By the beginning of the twentieth century, women began to participate in sports at some colleges. In the eastern colleges, this participation was limited mainly to play days and sports days, with an occasional invitational meet with several schools participating. The situation was different in other parts of the United States. For example, a survey in 1909 revealed that nearly half the colleges in the Midwest and West engaged in intercollegiate competition.[25]

The attitude of leaders in the field of women's physical education toward sports for girls and women paralleled the attitude of the general society. The platform statement issued in 1923 by the Women's Division of the National Amateur Athletic Federation indicated the thinking at that time. The stress was on participation in an informal manner and not on high-level competition. The group endorsed participation in athletics by girls and women that:

Promotes competition that stresses enjoyment of sport and development of good sportsmanship and character rather than those types that emphasize the making and breaking of records and the winning of championships for the enjoyment of spectators or for the athletic reputation or commercial advantage of institutions and organizations.[26]

The emphasis was clearly on intramural and informal extramural sports activities for

25. Dudley, G., and Kellor, F. A.: Athletic games in the education of women, New York, 1909, Henry Holt and Co. Cited in Van Dalen, D. B., and Bennett, B.: A world history of physical education, Englewood Cliffs, N. J., 1971, Prentice-Hall, Inc., p. 451.

26. Sefton, A. A.: The Women's Division—National Amateur Athletic Federation, Stanford, 1941, Stanford University Press. Quoted in Lumpkin, A.: Let's set the record straight, Journal of Physical Education and Recreation 48:40, March 1977.

girls and women in 1923. The attitude of leading women physical educators remained that way until the 1960s. Probably the first tangible sign of a change in philosophy by women leaders of physical education toward the participation by girls and women in varsity athletics was in 1967 with the organization of the Commission on Intercollegiate Athletics for Women (CIAW) by the Division for Girls' and Women's Sports (DGWS). The women acted on their changed attitude in 1969 by sponsoring national championships in both gymnastics and track and field. Athletics for girls on the precollegiate level usually followed the lead of the institutions of higher learning.

In some cases, girls and women participated in highly competitive athletics before it was approved by leaders of women's physical education organizations. In Michigan, for instance, the girls' high school team of Marshall won the state basketball championship in 1905 and was greeted by "bonfires, 10,000 Roman candles, crowds, noise, Supt. Garwood, ex-major Porter, and all red-corpuscled Marshallites."[27]

Females in a few black colleges in the South also participated in highly competitive sports during the early 1900s, especially basketball. It was noteworthy, however, that a highly competitive track and field program for girls and women (known as the Tuskegee Relays) was started in 1929 by Tuskegee Institute in Tuskegee, Alabama. Several of the normal schools and colleges in the local area participated in these relays.[28]

Today women are freely participating in almost all phases of American society on an increased basis, including participation in sports and athletics. What is the comparison between males and females relative to participation in competitive sports? The next section is designed to provide information to answer this question.

Present status of girls and women in sports

A 1979 survey by the College and University Administrators Council[29] indicated that the average institution employs more coaches for athletic activities for men than coaches for women for all three divisional levels of the NCAA and AIAW. The greatest disparity was in the Division I institutions (those with the largest enrollments); there were 1320 coaches for men's athletic activities and only 575 coaches for women's athletic activities. There was an average of 13 coaches of sports for men and six coaches of sports for women in each institution in Division I. The average number of sports offered for men and women in each institution did not differ greatly—seven sports per institution for men and five for women. In Division II institutions, the average number of sports offered for men and women was six and five, respectively.

Another revealing conclusion drawn from the survey is that more coaches for women's sports are tenured regular faculty appointments or have split academic and athletic assignments than are coaches of sports for men. However, future trends indicate that new coaches, both men and women, are being hired without regular faculty status. Also, coaches retaining regular academic appointments will be replaced with nonacademic appointees.

27. Van Dalen, D. B., and Bennett, B.: A world history of physical education, Englewood Cliffs, N.J., 1971, Prentice-Hall, Inc., p. 451.
28. Thaxton, N. A.: A documentary analysis of competitive track and field for women at Tuskegee Institute and Tennessee State University, unpublished doctoral dissertation, Springfield College, 1970, Springfield, Massachusetts, pp. 77-79.

29. Richardson, H. D.: Athletics in higher education: some comparisons, Journal of Physical Education and Recreation **50:**56-57, June 1979.

The data for this survey were based on the responses of 65% of 344 institutions of higher education. A random sample was used to select the 344 institutions, all within the geographical divisional structure of the National Collegiate Athletic Association. The NCAA's *Blue Book of College Athletics 1977-1978* was used as a resource in the selection of the institutions.

The situation on the secondary school level is about the same as it is on the college level; males are participating in organized athletic programs in greater numbers than females. Although girls on the secondary school level have made tremendous gains insofar as the total number of participants in interscholastic athletics, they still represent only half the total number of boys who participate in interscholastic athletics.

Figures in the most recent survey by the National Federation of State High School Associations indicate there are more than 1.85 million female participants in athletics on the high school level.[30] The total number of girls participating in high school athletics represents a drop from over two million who participated during the 1977-1978 school year. This decrease in participants resulted from dropping from the figures all Canadian high school participation and all United States junior high school participation previously included in the surveys. However, when compared with only 294,000 female participants in 1970-1971, the 1.85 million female participants for the 1978-1979 figure is impressive.

Girls participated in a total of 29 high school sports. The three most popular sports, in terms of both schools sponsoring teams and number of participants, were basketball, track and field, and volleyball. Over 15,000 schools sponsored basketball teams for girls

with almost 500,000 participants. Field hockey was the tenth most popular sport with 1959 schools sponsoring teams in the sport.

A 1973-1974 survey by the editors of *Women Sports* revealed that budgets for boys' sport activities at the interscholastic level were on the average five times larger than the budgets for girls' sport activities. On the college level, the men received 30 times that received by women, and in some universities, they received 100 times what the women received. At Ohio State, for example, the men's sports program was funded at $2.8 million, while the women's program received only $50,000.[31] Although sports programs for men and women are still not equal in terms of funding, legislation such as Title IX has had a positive impact. Sports programs for males and females on all levels are much more equal in the 1980s.

Present practices indicate that women leaders in physical education and athletics are facing the same problems that beset the men when they were deciding whether to go "big time" in athletics. In an effort to gain parity with athletic programs for men, some practices that have been adopted by men are now being endorsed by women. In 1978, for instance, the AIAW recommended that women coaches be paid to scout high school and junior college athletic prospects.

COEDUCATIONAL SPORTS AND TITLE IX

Coeducational sports should be provided for students in schools and higher education institutions because of the benefits (mainly sociological and cultural) that can accrue from such participation. However, coeducational sports, in most cases, should be limited to the intramural and recreational levels. Highly competitive athletics should not be coeduca-

---

30. National Federation of State High School Associations: 1979 sports participation survey, Kansas City, Mo., 1979, NFSHSA.

31. Coakley, J. J.: Sport in society: issues and controversies, St. Louis, 1978, The C. V. Mosby Co., pp. 255-256.

Courtesy Jackson State University, Jackson, Miss.

tional, as a general rule. In instances when one or two highly skilled females would not otherwise have the opportunity to participate in a particular sport, they must be allowed to participate with males.

The main reason for not advocating coeducational sports participation on the interscholastic and intercollegiate levels is the physiological differences between males and females. It is a fact that the ratio of strength to weight is greater in males than in females. Females would thus be at a decided disadvantage in those sports requiring speed and strength, including all contact sports and some noncontact sports such as track and field and volleyball.

There are other reasons for advocating separate teams for males and females. For instance, if coeducational varsity teams were encouraged, males would comprise most of the teams. Because of the "speed, size, and strength" factors, girls would not be able to

make varsity teams in any great numbers. Consequently, there would be mostly male-dominated teams.

The recent attempt by Ann Myers (a former women's all-American basketball player from UCLA) to make the roster of an NBA basketball team demonstrates the athletic differences between top-level male and female athletes. Myers failed to make the NBA team. The coach said that her weight and overall strength militated against her making the team. He said that she possessed excellent basketball skills. The skills of most of the other basketball hopefuls at that level of play were probably also very high. Thus, size and strength became critical factors. This would not be the case on the intramural and recreational levels. Some females might possess more skill than their male counterparts and thereby make up for the differences in strength and size.

When providing coeducational sports for

the intramural and/or recreational sports programs, the games must be modified to suit both sexes. Several examples of effective coeducational activities were presented in the May 1976 *Journal of Physical Education and Recreation*. Coeducational sports activities were described for basketball, flag football, fencing, water joust, softball, and several other sports. A brief description of three different sports that were conducted on a coeducational basis indicate how three institutions provided coeducational sports for students.

Coeducational basketball at Christiansburg High School

To provide intramural basketball on a coeducational basis, only the following modifications and/or restrictions were required:

1. Teams are comprised of three boys and three girls.
2. The length of the game is two ten-minute halves.
3. Boys are not allowed to shoot from inside the key (free throw circle).
4. Slow break rules are used (that is, when the ball is controlled by the defensive team, everyone must advance. The ball cannot be moved until everyone is down court).
5. Players must alternate passes between boys and girls when the ball is in the forecourt.
6. One set of passes must be completed before a shot can be attempted.
7. Balls are taken out-of-bounds after a foul, unless it was a deliberate or technical foul.

Coeducational flag football at the University of Texas at Austin

The following modifications were made to equalize competition in flag football:

1. Three men and three women comprise a team.
2. Only women are permitted to run the ball from scrimmage. Men can advance the ball only after catching a pass.
3. Men are limited to passing only to women; women may pass to either sex.

Coeducational softball at the University of Tennessee at Knoxville

The following modifications of rules were instituted:

1. A staggered arrangement by playing position and batting order for men and women is required.
2. Two strikes is an out; three balls is a walk.
3. Men are required to bat using their nondominant stance.

The main consideration in establishing coeducational sports programs is to respond to the interests and ability levels of the participants. Because of their level of skill and other reasons, some males and females will not wish to participate in coeducational sports programs, even on an intramural or recreational level. Opportunities should be provided for these individuals to participate on separate teams. When conducting sports on a coeducational basis, appropriate modifications should be made in the rules and conduct of the activities to equalize competition between the sexes.

Influence of Title IX

Whatever gains that have been made in the last decade in improving the status of girls' and women's sports programs have resulted primarily from compliance with the mandates of Title IX and the insistence for equality by the girls and women themselves. Much of the movement toward complying with the regulations of Title IX is a result of pressure exerted by women leaders in the profession of physical education and sport.

Title IX of the Education Amendments of 1972 was enacted by Congress in June, 1972. The legislation specifically states that "no person in the United States shall, on the

Courtesy Springfield College, Springfield, Mass.

basis of sex, be excluded from participation in, be denied the benefits of, or be subjected to discrimination under any education program or activity receiving Federal financial assistance." The legislation refers directly to physical education and athletic programs. The final Title IX regulation was issued by the Department of Health, Education and Welfare in 1975.

In a fact sheet dated December 4, 1979, the Department of Health, Education and Welfare sought to clarify the proposed policy "Title IX and Intercollegiate Athletics," which was issued in 1978.[32] The policy interpretation of Title IX of the Education Amendments of 1972 was published in the Federal Registrar on December 11, 1979. The policy is designed to clarify what the regulation requires and proposes to determine whether a school's athletic program is in compliance with Title IX by assessing three factors of the athletic program:

1. *Financial assistance*—scholarships and grants-in-aid provided on the basis of athletic ability.
—The Title IX regulation requires that:
Colleges and universities provide reasonable opportunities for male and female students to receive scholarships and grants-in-aid in proportion to the number of male and female participating athletes.
—The policy explains that:
Schools must distribute all athletic assistance on a substantially proportional basis to the number of participating male and female athletes. (Example: Total scholarship fund = $100,000 in a school with seventy male and thirty female athletes. Male athletes are entitled to $70,000. Female athletes are entitled to $30,000.) Unequal spending for either the men's or the women's program may be justified by sex-neutral factors, such as a higher number of male athletes recruited from out-of-state.

2. *Athletic benefits and opportunities*—equipment and supplies, travel, compensation of coaches, facilities, housing, publicity, and other aspects of a program.
—The Title IX regulation specifies the factors that HEW should assess in determining whether a school is providing equal athletic opportunity. This "equal opportunity" regulation applies to all aspects of athletic programs, such as equipment and supplies, scheduling of games and practices, compensation of coaches, housing and dining services, publicity, travel and per diem costs, opportunities for coaching, locker rooms and other facilities, medical and training services, and other relevant factors.
—The policy explains that schools must provide "equivalent" treatment, services, and benefits in those areas. HEW will assess each of those factors by comparing:
  • Availability
  • Kind of benefits
  • Quality

32. HEW Fact Sheet: Title IX and Intercollegiate Athletics Policy, Washington, D.C., December 4, 1979, U.S. Department of Health, Education and Welfare, p. 1.

• Kind of opportunities

3. *Accommodation of student interests and abilities*—the third section of the policy sets out how schools can meet the requirement of the regulation to "effectively accommodate the interests and abilities of both sexes."

—The Title IX regulation requires that schools effectively:

Accommodate the interests and abilities of students of both sexes in the selection of sports and levels of competition.

—The policy explains how to accommodate interests and abilities through:

• Selection of sports

1. When there is a team for only one sex, and the excluded sex is interested in the sport, the university may be required to:

—Permit the excluded sex to try out for the team if it is not a contact sport; or

—Sponsor a separate team for the previously excluded sex if there is a reasonable expectation of intercollegiate competition for that team.

2. Teams do not have to be integrated.

3. The same sports do not have to be offered to men and to women.

• Levels of competition

Equal competitive opportunity means:

1. The number of men and women participating in intercollegiate athletics is in proportion to their overall enrollment; or

2. The school has taken steps to insure that the sex underrepresented in athletic programs is offered new opportunities consistent with the interests and abilities of that sex; or

3. The present program accommodates the interests and abilities of the underrepresented sex.

and

4. Men and women athletes, in proportion to their participation in athletic programs, compete at the same levels; or

5. The school has a history and practice of upgrading the levels at which teams of the underrepresented sex compete.

—Schools are not required to develop or upgrade an intercollegiate team if there is no reasonable expectation that competition will be available for that team.

• Measuring of interests and abilities

The recipient must:

1. Take into account the increasing levels of women's interests and abilities;

2. Use methods of determining interests and ability that do not disadvantage the underrepresented sex;

3. Use methods of determining ability that take into account team performance records; and

4. Use methods that are responsive to the expressed interests of students capable of intercollegiate competition who belong to the underrepresented sex.

Guidelines for action

Some women might think it is presumptuous of us to offer guidelines for the administration and conduct of girls' and women's athletic programs when the men's programs have experienced so many problems. It is precisely because of the experiences that men have encountered with the overemphasis on winning, excessive commercialization, unethical recruiting practices, and the like, that we might be able to offer worthwhile caveats to administrators of athletic programs for girls and women.

The basic recommendation is to comply with the regulations of Title IX. We would also implore the females not to copy programs that have been developed by so-called big time athletic "factories" for men. As a matter of fact, women leaders in athletics and physical education have established principles and policies that are sound and that should be put into practice. Although the specific means of carrying out the philosophy and principles espoused by leaders in the profession might differ from institution to institution, the basic tenets of an educational philosophy of athletics should be achieved.

As a general frame of reference, the philosophy and standards set forth by the Division for Girls' and Women's Sports in 1973 are worthy goals for athletics for girls and women.

Elementary schools (grades 1-6)

We believe that intramural sports experiences in appropriately modified sports activities should supplement the instructional program for girls in grades 4, 5, and 6, and that in most cases these experiences will be sufficiently stimulating and competitive for the highly skilled girls. We believe extramural sports activities, if included in the upper elementary grades, should be limited to occasional play days (sports groups or teams composed of representatives from several schools or units), sports days, and individual events.[33]

Secondary schools (grades 7-12)

We believe that in secondary schools a program of intramural and extramural participation should be arranged to augment a sound and comprehensive instructional program in physical education for all girls. Extramural programs should be organized to supplement broad instructional and intramural programs, provided sufficient time, facilities, and personnel are available for these additional programs.[33]

College and universities

We believe that college and university instructional programs should go beyond those activities usually included in the high school program. There should be opportunities to explore and develop skills in a variety of activities, with emphasis on individual sports. It is desirable that opportunities for extramural experiences beyond the intramural program be accessible to the highly skilled young women who wish these opportunities.[33]

Some guidelines are presented to help those school personnel who are faced with the task of starting a program of athletics for girls and women or providing coeducational sports. They are consistent with the latest, current information related to medical, psychological, sociological, and educational aspects of sports for girls and women. They reflect a philosophy of athletics as an educational experience for the highly skilled as well as the less skilled student.

1. Conduct athletic programs in accordance with regulations promulgated by athletic governing bodies; that is, the National Federation of State High School Associations, National Association for Girls and Women in Sports, and the Association for Intercollegiate Athletics for Women. However, seek to change those regulations and resolutions that are contrary to the best interests of student-athletes. For example, the provision of the AIAW providing women coaches with subsidies for recruiting should have adequate safe guards attached. The dangers of excessive emphasis on recruiting should be watched very closely.

2. As a general rule, when size, strength, or other special conditions place girls and women at a disadvantage in some sports (football and wrestling, for example), provide separate teams for males and females. In special cases when a highly skilled girl or woman wishes to participate in a sport that is offered for males only, allow her to try out for that sport.

3. Maintain an educational emphasis in the athletic program. Keep schedules to a point that students will not be away from school and classes for long periods.

4. When coeducational teams are provided, modify the rules to equalize competition.

5. Provide qualified coaches for all girls' and women's sports. Allow qualified

33. American Association for Health, Physical Education, and Recreation, Division for Girls' and Women's Sports: Philosophy and standards for girls' and women's sports, Washington, D.C., 1973. By permission of the American Alliance for Health, Physical Education, Recreation, and Dance, Reston, Va.

men to coach sports for girls and women, with the ultimate aim toward having the best qualified person coaching athletic teams.

6. Base the athletic program on the needs, interests, and capacities of the students. Do not develop and conduct the program to foster the recognition of the institution or the coach.

7. Encourage and facilitate research on the effects of athletics on girls and women and disseminate these findings to the various publics.

SPORTS FOR HANDICAPPED PERSONS

Persons with handicaps can receive the same benefits from a program of competitive sports as nonhandicapped persons. The following reasons for including adapted sports activities in the physical education program were listed by Arnheim, Auxter, and Crowe:

1. There are many students assigned to an adapted physical education class who are unable to correct an existing condition, but who also are unable to participate in regular physical education. A program of adapted sports would be ideal for such students [because it would give them some form of physical activity].

2. Students in the adapted physical education program need activities that have carry-over value. They may continue exercise programs in the future, but they also need training in carry-over types of sports and games that will be useful to them in later life.

3. Adapted sports activities may have a therapeutic value if they are carefully structured for the student.

4. Adapted sports and games should help the handicapped individual learn to handle his or her body under a variety of circumstances.

5. There are recreational values in games and sports activities for the student who is facing the dual problem of overcoming some type of handicap; some of his or her special needs can best be met through recreational kinds of activities.

6. A certain amount of emotional release takes

place in play activities and this is important to the student with a disability.

7. The adapted sports program, whether it is given every other day or several weeks out of the semester, tends to relieve the boredom of a straight exercise program. No matter how carefully a special exercise program is planned and organized, it is difficult to maintain a high level of interest if students participate in this kind of activity on a daily basis for one or more semesters.[34]

History and present practices

It is estimated that there are approximately 50 million handicapped persons (between six and nine million handicapped school-age children) in the United States. The percentage of this number who are participating in sports activities of an organized nature is not known. As a result of various legislation and court decisions, however, it is assumed that more handicapped individuals are participating in physical education and athletic programs than ever before. However, this number is small when compared with the total number of people participating in organized sports. Furthermore, attempts should be made to provide each handicapped person with an experience in sports activities.

Orr believes that the reluctance of school personnel to provide sports opportunities for handicapped persons results from myth, superstition, and sports control. In elaborating on the myth surrounding the handicapped athlete, he writes:

The imposed myth is that the handicapped person participating in sports is inferior and different from the so-called "normal" athlete. The reality is that while the handicapped person usually does not have equal marks in performance of a quantitative nature, the qualitative performance may equal or surpass any other athlete. The effect of

34. Arnheim, D. D., Auxter, D., and Crowe, W. C.: Principles and methods of adapted physical education, ed. 3, St. Louis, 1977, The C. V. Mosby Co., pp. 170-171.

the myth has been to obstruct opportunity for the handicapped as time, energy, and funds have been funneled in other directions.[35]

Federal legislation, specifically P.L. 94-142 and Section 504 of P.L. 93-112, has undoubtedly played a great part in improving the educational opportunities of the handicapped. However, the Joseph P. Kennedy Jr. Foundation probably has focused more attention on sports for handicapped persons than any other single organization or legislation. The Kennedy Foundation can also be credited with promoting and causing others to provide significant services to handicapped persons through its many programs and activities.

The most visible activity promoted by the Kennedy Foundation is the Special Olympics, which was organized in 1968. It was designed to provide mentally retarded youths, 8 years of age and over, with opportunities to participate in a variety of sports and games on local, state, regional, national, and international levels.

In 1979 the International Summer Special Olympic Games were held at the State University at Brockport, August 8-12. There were 3500 competitors from the United States and 30 other countries.

The basic objectives of the Special Olympics are to:

1. Encourage development of comprehensive physical education and recreation programs for mentally retarded in schools, day care centers, and residential facilities in every community.
2. Prepare the retarded for sports competition—particularly where no opportunities and programs now exist.
3. Supplement existing activities and programs in schools, communities, day care centers, and residential facilities.

4. Provide training for volunteer coaches to enable them to work with youngsters in physical fitness, recreation, and sports activities.[36]

Thousands of people volunteer to coach mentally retarded youngsters in Special Olympic events such as track and field, swimming, gymnastics, floor hockey, and volleyball. The volunteers include professional athletes in many sports.

A Special Winter Olympics was started in 1975 for mentally retarded children and young adults. These Games are sponsored by New York Special Olympics, Inc., which is affiliated with the International Special Olympics.

Nearly 300 retarded and handicapped children and young adults gathered at a Catskill Mountain ski resort in Woodridge, New Jersey, to participate in the Fourth Annual Winter Games. Events included tobogganing, snowshoeing, downhill and cross-country skiing, and figure and speed skating.

Wheelchair sports are another specialized series of athletic events designed for handicapped individuals. Wheelchair sports were initiated in Veterans' Administration Hospitals all over the United States as part of the medical treatment for disabled veterans returning home after World War II. The stated purpose of wheelchair sports is to ". . . permit those with permanent physical disabilities to compete vigorously and safely under rules that are kept as close to normal rules as possible."[37]

Wheelchair basektball was the first sport in the Wheelchair Games. Presently, track and field events, archery, dartchery, lawn bowling, table tennis, snooker, weightlifting,

35. Orr, R. E.: Sport, myth, and the handicapped athlete, Journal of Physical Education and Recreation **50:**33, March 1979.

36. Stein, J. U., and Klappholz, L. A.: Special Olympics instructional manual, Washington, D.C., 1977, AAHPER and the Kennedy Foundation, pp. 1-2.

37. American Association for Health, Physical Education and Recreation: Competitive sports for the handicapped, Journal of Health, Physical Education and Recreation **41:**92, November-December, 1970.

and swimming are also included in the Wheelchair Games.

The first National Wheelchair Games in the United States were held at Adelphi College in 1957. A total of 371 athletes competed at the twenty-third National Wheelchair Games at St. John's University, Queens, New York, in 1979.

Competitors are grouped at the Wheelchair Games according to various disability classes: quadriplegic, paraplegic, and amputee. The various classes are also broken down into levels, based on degree of disability. For example, Class IA includes incomplete quadriplegics who have involvement of both hands, weakness of triceps, weakness throughout the trunk and lower extremities, and loss of voluntary control. The most severely disabled compete in this class. The next classification (IB) includes those incomplete quadriplegics who have some upper extremity involvement, but less than IA, with other disabilities similar to those of IA. There are three additional classifications.

Sports opportunities are also available for handicapped persons in the special schools for the handicapped as well as the regular schools where handicapped students are mainstreamed. In some cases, handicapped students in special schools are permitted to compete against athletes in regular schools. For instance, the Texas University Interscholastic League (UIL) has rules that allow mentally retarded students to participate in all levels of interscholastic athletic competition. Provided they meet certain requirements, special students are allowed to compete in athletic contests when they participate in Texas Education Agency–approved secondary school programs.[38]

Another illustration of handicapped stu-

dents being allowed to participate in competitive athletics with regular students is the case of Ken Jones. Ken is a 14-year-old, educable, mentally retarded student at Lincoln State School (Lincoln, Illinois) who, competing against students in area public schools in Lincoln, was undefeated in the high jump during the 1971 regular season. In the state finals, Ken placed fifth with a leap of 5'5".[38(p. 24)]

THE ROLE OF THE COACH

According to a select committee of professionals in health, physical education, and recreation, "sports influence the life, development, philosophy, personality and character of participants. One of the most important factors influencing participants and assisting them to achieve desired educational goals is the coach. . . ."[39]

To fulfill their duties and responsibilities properly, coaches must exhibit desirable personal qualities, such as the following:

1. *Interest in coaching.* For a coach to be effective, he or she must be interested in coaching. Research studies have demonstrated and practical situations have supported the conclusion that people who are interested in a profession or vocation spend more time and energy trying to be successful than those who show less interest. An interest in coaching will provide an impetus for getting the necessary competencies to be an effective coach.

2. *Pleasing personality.* Since a major part of the job of coaching involves motivating people, the coach should have an agreeable personality. A coach should be enthusiastic, friendly, cooperative, and cheerful to successfully work with people. In other words,

38. American Association for Health, Physical Education and Recreation: The best of challenge, vol. II, Washington, D.C. 1974, The Association, p. 21.

39. American Association for Health, Physical Education and Recreation: Professional preparation in physical education and coaching, Washington, D.C., 1974, The Association, p. 32.

a coach must be a "likeable" person. This does not mean that coaches should not be forceful in supporting their convictions. Quite the contrary. However, a person interested in coaching must be able to be agreeable even when disagreeing.

3. *Good health.* A person interested in coaching must be in a good state of health—mental, emotional, and physical health. A coach should be able to physically endure the many hours needed for the job. To be successful in working with different kinds of people, a coach must be of sound mental health and possess the emotional stability to withstand the stresses of the coaching profession. A coach who is in a state of total good health will provide an adequate role model for players.

4. *Sense of humor.* A good sense of humor will enable a coach to endure many of the pressures associated with the job. The ability to relieve a tense moment with a joke, laugh at the humorous remarks of another person, and enjoy the lighter moments of life are admirable traits for anyone. They are an asset to coaches.

5. *Ability to get along with people.* A coach must be able to work well with other people. The coach must deal with colleagues, administrators, parents, and players. If a coach is to be successful, he or she must develop those personal qualities that will foster a smooth working relationship with others.

In addition to these personal qualities, coaches must have professional preparation to fulfill their duties and responsibilities properly and effectively. Some states have special certification requirements for coaches. However, these requirements vary from state to state. Realizing that such disparities exist, standards for coaching certification were suggested by the AAHPER through the Division of Men's Athletics' Task Force on certification of high school

coaches. The Task Force centered their standards around the following five areas:

1. Medical aspects of athletic coaching
2. Sociological and psychological aspects of coaching
3. Theory and techniques of coaching
4. Kinesiological foundations of coaching
5. Physiological foundations of coaching

Concepts and experiences for acquiring the competencies are suggested for each of the areas. The standards are considered minimal essentials for coaching certification and are not intended to be applicable for teacher certification in physical education. However, students who are majoring in physical education and who have completed courses in the theoretical areas listed above may apply them toward certification requirements if they plan to coach.

A person should be an effective and successful coach if he or she possesses the personal qualities identified here and the professional competencies identified by the AAHPER Task Force on certification of high school coaches. The success will be measured by the degree to which coaches help young people to develop in a total manner—physically, mentally, socially, and emotionally—and not by the number of wins and losses.

GOVERNANCE OF SPORTS

Several organizations and committees are designed to govern the conduct of organized sport and athletics in the United States. A brief overview will be presented of the major national governing organizations for school sports (National Federation of State High School Associations [Athletic] and the National Association for Girls and Women in Sport), intercollegiate sports (National Collegiate Athletic Association and Association for Intercollegiate Athletics for Women), and nonschool amateur sports (Amateur Athletic Union of the United States). Many other organizations exist for the governance of sport, for example, the National Association of Intercollegiate Athletics (for athletics at small colleges), and the National Junior College Athletic Association. There are also organizations for the governance of specific sports, such as the United States Track and Field Federation, Little League Baseball Incorporated, Pop Warner Junior League Football, and the Amateur Fencers League of America. For information about organizations governing sport that are not included here, consult the Encyclopedia of Associations (1979 edition), Gale Research Company, Detroit, Michigan. In addition to the national organizations that govern sport and athletic programs and governing bodies for specific sports, there are also state and local athletic organizations.

Governance of school sports

National Federation of State High School Associations (Athletic) (NFSHSA). The National Federation of State High School Associations is the major national governing body for school sports for both boys and girls. From its beginning in 1920 as the Midwest Federation of State High School Athletic Associations with five states as members, the Federation has grown to an association of 50 state high school athletic associations in the United States and nine Canadian affiliates.

The primary purposes of the National Federation are to coordinate the athletic activities of the various state high school athletic associations and to regulate, supervise, and protect athletic activities on an interstate basis. To these ends the Federation sponsors experimentation and testing programs for sports equipment, annually publishes rules and officials' training material for a number of sports, and maintains a national press service and official sports film service.

The address of the NFSHSA is 11724

Plaza Circle, Box 20626, Kansas City, Missouri 64195 (Telephone: 816-464-5400).

National Association for Girls and Women in Sport (NAGWS). The National Association for Girls and Women in Sport is one of the seven associations of the American Alliance for Health, Physical Education, Recreation, and Dance and is concerned with the governance of sports for girls and women.

The specific functions of the National Association for Girls and Women in Sport are:

1. To formulate and publicize guiding principles and standards for the administrator, leader, official, and player.
2. To publish and interpret rules governing sports for girls and women.
3. To provide the means for training, evaluating, and rating officials.
4. To disseminate information on the conduct of girls' and women's sports.
5. To stimulate, evaluate, and disseminate research in the field of girls' and women's sports.
6. To cooperate with allied groups interested in girls' and women's sports in order to formulate policies and rules that affect the conduct of women's sports.
7. To provide opportunities for the development of leadership among girls and women for the conduct of their sports programs.[40]

For more information, contact the national office of the American Alliance for Health, Physical Education, Recreation, and Dance, located at 1900 Association Drive, Reston, Va. 22091 (Telephone: 703-476-3400).

Governance of intercollegiate sports

Association for Intercollegiate Athletics for Women (AIAW). The Association for Intercollegiate Athletics for Women, established in 1971 as a structure of the National Association for Girls and Women in Sport, presently is an autonomous organization with its

40. National Association for Girls and Women in Sport: NAGWS softball guide, 1976-1978, Washington, D.C., 1976, American Alliance for Health, Physical Education, and Recreation, p. 5.

own charter and bylaws. It established its own legal identity on June 1, 1979. The purpose for establishing the organization was to provide governance and leadership for women's intercollegiate athletics. There was a total of 1007 member schools in the AIAW for the 1978-1979 academic year.[41]

The functions and activities of the AIAW are many and varied. For example, the organization sponsors national championships in many sports; fosters programs that will encourage excellence in performance of participants in women's intercollegiate athletics; sponsors conferences, institutes, and meetings designed to meet the needs of individuals in member schools; stimulates the continual evaluation of standards and policies for participants and programs; and cooperates with other professional groups of similar interests for the ultimate development of sports programs and opportunities for women. The expressed purpose of all the activities and work of the AIAW is "to foster broad programs of women's intercollegiate athletics which are consistent with the educational aims and objectives of the member schools and in accordance with the philosophy and standards of the NAGWS."[41]

Membership is open to any institution if:

The institution is an accredited college or university of higher education in the United States or its territories;

The institution provides an intercollegiate athletic program for women in one or more sports;

The institution is willing to abide by the policies and regulations of the organization;

The institution is a member of the appropriate regional organization.

Additionally, associate, affiliate, junior/community college allied or subscription memberships are available.[41(p. 3)]

41. Association for Intercollegiate Athletics for Women: AIAW handbook, 1979-1980, Washington, D.C., 1979, American Alliance for Health, Physical Education, Recreation, and Dance, p. 11.

Courtesy Lincoln University, Jefferson City, Mo.

National Collegiate Athletic Association (NCAA). The National Collegiate Athletic Association (NCAA) is the chief governing organization for college athletics in the United States. The day-to-day business of the NCAA is conducted by an executive secretary and a staff of assistants. The administration of the NCAA is under the direction of the Council, composed of the president, secretary-treasurer, eight vice-presidents, one from each of the eight districts, and eight members-at-large. In addition to the office in Shawnee Mission, Kansas, where the executive director and his staff work, the NCAA has a ten-person Service Bureau in New York City. An Executive Committee is elected by the Council to transact business and to carry out the affairs of the association.

The purposes of the NCAA are many and varied. According to its constitution, these services are:

1. To uphold the principle of institutional control of and responsibility for all collegiate sports in

conformity with the Constitution and By-laws of the Association.

2. To stimulate and improve programs, to promote and develop educational leadership, physical fitness, sports participation as recreational pursuit, and athletic excellence through competitive intramural and intercollegiate programs.

3. To encourage the adoption for its constituent members of strict eligibility rules to comply with satisfactory standards of scholarship, amateur standing, and good sportsmanship.

4. To formulate, copyright, and publish rules of play for the government of collegiate sports.

5. To preserve collegiate records.

6. To supervise the conduct of regional and national collegiate athletic contests under the auspices of the association and establish rules of eligibility therefore.

7. To cooperate with other amateur athletic organizations in the promotion and conduct of national and international athletic contests.

8. To study any phases of competitive athletics and establish standards therefor, to the end that colleges and universities of the United States may maintain their athletic activities on a high plane.

9. To legislate through by-laws or resolutions of a convention any subjects of general concern to the members in the administration of intercollegiate athletics.[42]

Membership in the NCAA requires that an institution be accredited and compete in a minimum of four sports each year on an intercollegiate level. At least one sport must be competed in during the normal three major sport seasons.

The services provided by the NCAA are as extensive as its stated purposes for existence. These services include publication of official guides in various sports, provision of a film library, establishment of an eligibility code for athletes and provisions for the enforce-

ent of this code, provisions for national meets and tournaments in 12 sports with appropriate eligibility rules for competition, provision of financial and other assistance to groups interested in the promotion and encouragement of intercollegiate and intramural athletics, and provision of administrative services for universities and colleges of the United States on matters of international athletics.

Amateur Athletic Union of the United States (AAU). Founded in 1888, the Amateur Athletic Union of the United States is probably the oldest, as well as the largest single organization designed to regulate and promote the conduct of amateur athletics. Certainly it is the most influential organization governing amateur sports in the world. The AAU is a federation of athletic clubs, national and district associations, educational institutions, and amateur athletic organizations.

Many persons associate the AAU only with track and field events. However, it is concerned with many more sports and activities, including basketball, baton twirling, bobsledding, boxing, diving, gymnastics, handball, judo, karate, luge, power lifting, swimming, synchronized swimming, water polo, weightlifting, and wrestling. In addition to governing the multiplicity of sports and activities, the AAU is vitally concerned with ensuring that the amateur status of athletes is maintained at all times when participating in amateur sports. To this end, the leaders of the AAU have developed and promulgated a precise set of guidelines describing amateurism.

Some of the other activities of the AAU include registering athletes to identify and control the amateur status of participants in sports events, sponsoring national championships in many sports, raising funds for American athletes in international competition and the Olympic Games, conducting tryouts for the selection of Olympic competitors, and sponsoring Junior Olympic competition. The

42. Steitz, E. S., editor: Administration of athletics in colleges and universities, Washington, D.C., 1971, National Association of College Directors of Athletics and Division of Men's Athletics, AAHPER, pp. 332-333.

AAU has established a number of committees for the various sports and activities (examples: Age Group Diving, Track and Field, Youth Activities, Swimming, and so on) to help with the monumental task of performing the myriad duties associated with governing such a large number of sports and activities. An executive director directs and coordinates all activities of the AAU.

The address of the AAU is 3400 West 86th Street, Indianapolis, Indiana 46268 (Telephone: 317-297-2900). Ollan C. Cassell is the executive director.

DISCUSSION QUESTIONS AND EXERCISES

1. Discuss the reasons for the popular appeal of sport.
2. Assume that you are in a debate on the topic of sport in America. Assume further that you are to debate for the affirmative side of the topic: "Resolved: that there are many positive values of sport."
3. Discuss the problems of excessive pressures, false values, and violence in sports.
4. Discuss the pros and cons of character development through sport.
5. Survey a coach and a physical education teacher to get their thinking on sports for children. Compare their views with the information presented in this chapter. Indicate your reaction to all viewpoints.
6. Discuss the type of sports program that will make the greatest contribution to children.
7. Without consulting the text, list and discuss ten guidelines for youth sports.
8. Discuss five guidelines that are applicable to sport programs on all levels.
9. List and discuss the social and emotional characteristics of adolescents, young adults, and older adults.
10. Present your reactions to the sports program at Oberlin College. Indicate the positive and negative points, if any, of the program.
11. Do you think that older adults should compete in competitive events such as those in the Senior Olympics? Support your views with sound evidence.
12. What has been the influence of Title IX on the growth of girls and women in sports?

Give an historical overview of both topics.
13. Interpret to your students the new guidelines for Title IX.
14. Produce a set of guidelines for coeducational basketball and volleyball.
15. Discuss the role of the coach in sport programs for children, college students, and adults.
16. What are your views on sports for handicapped persons?
17. List and discuss the personal and professional qualities that are desired in a coach.
18. Discuss the important role that the various governance bodies play in the conduct of sports programs.

SELECTED REFERENCES

Ambron, S. R.: Child development, San Francisco, 1975, Rhinehart Press.

American Alliance for Health, Physical Education, and Recreation: Equality in sports for women, Washington, D.C., 1977, The Alliance.

American Alliance for Health, Physical Education, and Recreation: Programs that work—Title IX, Washington, D.C., 1978, The Alliance.

American Association for Health, Physical Education, and Recreation: Professional preparation in physical education and coaching, Washington, D.C., 1974, The Association.

American Association for Health, Physical Education, and Recreation: Women's athletics: coping with controversy, Washington, D.C., 1974, The Association.

Arnheim, D. D., Auxter, D., and Crowe, W. C.: Principles and methods of adapted physical education and recreation, ed. 3, St. Louis, 1977, The C. V. Mosby Co.

Bucher, C. A.: Administration of physical education and athletic programs, ed. 7, St. Louis, 1979, The C. V. Mosby Co.

Bucher, C. A.: After the game is over, The Physical Educator **30:**171-175, December 1973.

Bucher, C. A.: Athletic competition and the developmental growth pattern, The Physical Educator, **28:** 3-4, March 1971.

Bucher, C. A.: Foundations of physical education, ed. 8, St. Louis, 1979, The C. V. Mosby Co.

Bucher, C. A., and Dupree, R.: Athletics in schools and colleges, New York, 1965, The Center for Applied Research in Education, Inc.

Burke, E., and Kleiber, D.: Psychological and physical implications of highly competitive sports for children, The Physical Educator **33:**63-69, May 1976.

Cobb, R. A., and Lepley, P. M., editors: Contemporary philosophies of physical education and athletics, Columbus, Ohio, 1973, Charles E. Merrill Publishing Co.

Cole, L., and Hall, I. N.: Psychology of adolescence, New York, 1970, Holt, Rinehart & Winston.

Competitive sports for the handicapped, Journal of Health, Physical Education, and Recreation **41**:91-96, November-December, 1970.

Crowe, W. C., Auxter, D., and Pyfer, J.: Principles and methods of adapted physical education and recreation, ed. 4, St. Louis, 1981, The C. V. Mosby Co.

Dellastatious, J. W., and Cooper, W.: The physiological aspects of competitive sports for young athletes, The Physical Educator **27**:3-5, March 1970.

Dowell, L. J.: Environmental factors of childhood competitive athletics, The Physical Educator **28**:17-21, March 1971.

Durso, J.: The sports factory: an investigation into college sports, New York, 1975, Quadrangle/The New York Times Book Co.

Eitzen, D. S.: Athletics in the status system of male adolescents: a replication of Coleman's *The Adolescent Society*, Adolescence **10**:266-275, Summer 1975.

Eitzen, D. S.: Sport in contemporary society, New York, 1979, St. Martin's Press.

Encyclopedia of associations, Booktower, Detroit, Mich., 1979, Gale Research Co.

Flath, A.: A history of relations between the NCAA and the AAU, 1905-1963, Champaign, Ill., 1964, Stipes Publishing Co.

Gerson, R.: Redesigning athletic competition for children, Motor Skills: Theory into Practice **2**:3-14, Fall 1977.

Gould, D. and Martens, R.: Attitudes of volunteer coaches toward significant youth sport issues, Research Quarterly **50**:369-380, October 1979.

Hotchkiss, S.: Parents and kids' sports, Human Behavior **7**:35, March 1978.

Howe, H., II: On sports, Educational Record **58**:218-219, Spring 1977.

Hult, J.: Equal programs or carbon copies, Journal of Physical Education and Recreation **47**:24-25, May 1976.

Lopiano, D. A.: A fact-finding model for conducting a Title IX self-evaluation study in athletic programs, Journal of Physical Education and Recreation **47**:26-30, May 1976.

Lugo, J. O., and Hershey, G. L.: Human development, New York, 1974, Macmillan Inc.

Lumpkin, A.: Let's set the record straight, Journal of Physical Education and Recreation **48**:40, 42, 44, March 1977.

Magill, R., Ash, M., and Smoll, F.: Children in sport: a contemporary anthology, Champaign, Ill., 1978, Human Kinetics Publishers.

Martens, R.: Joy and sadness in children's sports, Champaign, Ill., 1978, Human Kinetics Publishers.

The National Association for Physical Education of College Women and The National College Physical Education Association for Men: Perspectives for sport, Quest Monograph 29, Winter Issue, 1973 (entire issue devoted to sport).

The National Association for Physical Education of College Women and The National College Physical Education Association for Men: Sport in America, Quest Monograph 27, Winter Issue, 1977 (entire issue devoted to sport).

Orr, R. E.: Sport, myth, and the handicapped athlete, Journal of Physical Education and Recreation **50**:33-34, March 1979.

Rarick, G. L., editor: Physical activity; human growth and development, New York, 1977, Academic Press, Inc.

Richardson, H. D.: Athletics in higher education: some comparisons, Journal of Physical Education and Recreation **50**:56-57, June 1979.

Seefeldt, V., coordinator: Youth sports, Journal of Physical Education and Recreation **49**:38-51, March 1978.

Shaffer, T. E.: Athletics for elementary-school youth: a medical viewpoint, Motor Skills: Theory into Practice **3**:97-99, June 1964.

Shults, F. D.: Toward athletic reform, Journal of Physical Education and Recreation **50**:18-19, 48, January 1979.

Smoll, F. B., and Smith, R. E.: Behavioral guidelines for youth sport coaches, Journal of Physical Education and Recreation **49**:46-47, March 1978.

Smoll, F. B., and Smith, R. E., editors: Psychological perspectives in youth sports, Washington, D.C., 1978, Hemisphere Publishing Corp.

Steitz, E. S., editor: Administration of athletics in colleges and universities, Washington, D.C., 1971, National Association of College Directors of Athletics and Division of Men's Athletics, AAHPER.

Stevenson, C. L.: Socialization effects of participation in sport: a critical review of the research, Research Quarterly **46**:287-301, October 1975.

Thaxton, N. A.: A documentary analysis of competitive track and field for women at Tuskegee Institute and Tennessee State University, unpublished doctoral dissertation, Springfield College, Springfield, Massachusetts, 1970.

Tutko, T., and Burns, W.: Winning is everything and other American myths, New York, 1976, Macmillan Inc.

Wilkerson, M., and Dodder, R. A.: What does sport do for people? Journal of Physical Education and Recreation **50**:50-51, February 1979.

Index